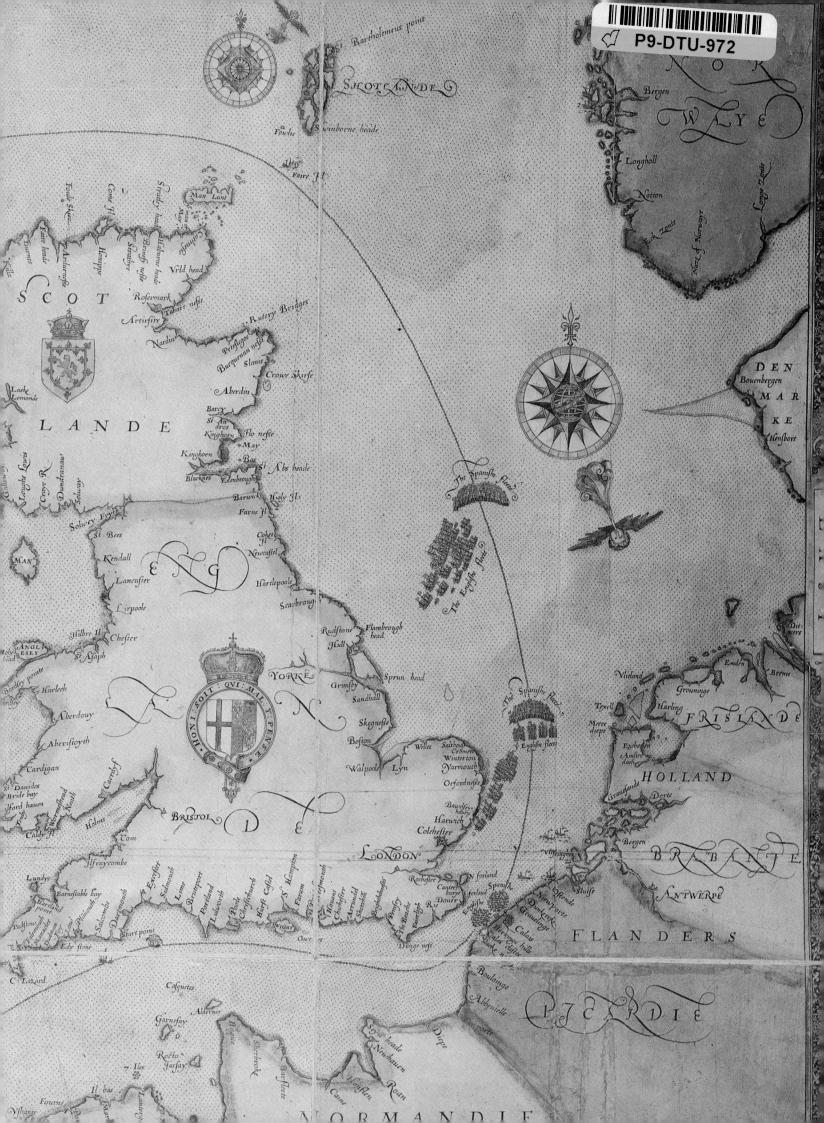

The Illustrated History of Britain

endpapers *An Elizabethan map of Britain*
above *London Bridge and the Tower of London
in the fifteenth century*
overleaf *The Battle of Copenhagen, 1801.*

CRESCENT BOOKS
NEW YORK

The Illustrated History of Britain

A. L. Rowse

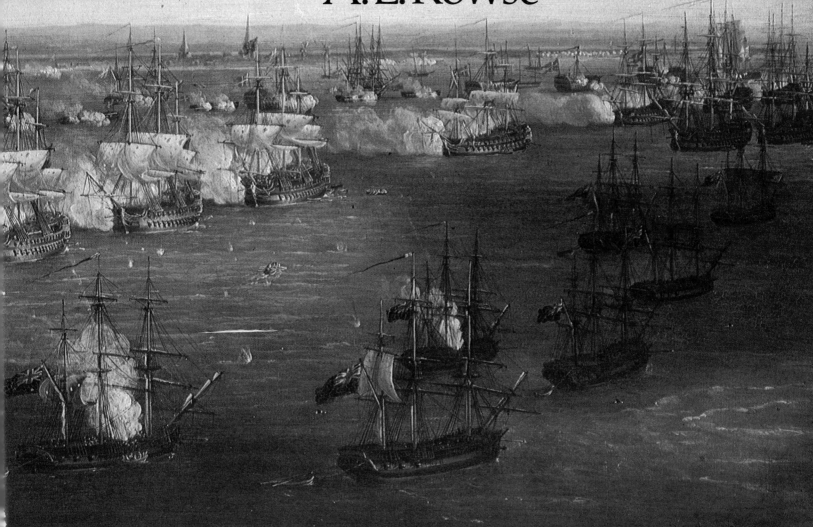

Contents

First English edition published by
Artus Books Ltd, 1979
Copyright © MCMLXXIX by
A. L. Rowse
Library of Congress Catalog Card
Number 79–88139
All rights reserved.
This edition is published by Crescent
Books a division of Crown Publishers,
Inc., by arrangement with Weidenfeld
(Publishers) Limited
a b c d e f g h
CRESCENT 1979 PRINTING
Printed in Italy
Designed by Allison Waterhouse

Chapter 1

Island Peoples

THE STORY OF BRITAIN IS THAT OF THE island which has influenced the outside world more than any other island in history. This unique good fortune has been owing to a combination of favouring factors. The fact of being an island has given her much more security than most (like Venice for centuries); while Britain was readily accessible from the Continent, that usually enabled her to impose her own control upon the influences coming thence, giving the country time to work out her own solutions. The island was propitious to settlement, fertile and ultimately found to be rich in mineral resources. The peoples that infiltrated it gradually made a successful and creative mixture. Strategically placed at the shorter crossings from North-West Europe to the New World, sea communications, especially with the development of North America, made her fortune.

As an Edwardian poet, William Watson, wrote, with some complacency, looking back over Britain's past:

> *Time, and the ocean, and some fostering star,*
> *In high cabal, have made us what we are.*

Even the climate has played its part, for, temperate as it is, it has not been so severe as to impede human effort, while rendering work necessary to survive; as Charles II said, there is hardly a day when it is not possible to spend some time out of doors.

The physical configuration has helped enormously: most parts of it are easily accessible from the sea or by navigable rivers. Very important all through its history has been the division between the Highland and Lowland Zones. Draw a line from Newcastle in the North-East to Exeter in the South-West: most of what lies to north and west, including Scotland, Wales and Ireland, belongs to the Highland Zone; all south and east is Lowland Zone. These two Zones are very different in character, and the contrast carries on from prehistoric times to today. During most of our history, from early times till the nineteenth century, the Highland Zone was more conservative and backward, less open to external, progressive influences than the South and East. We can see this line of division operating again and again: to some extent (with exceptions) at the Reformation in the sixteenth century; again with the Civil War in the seventeenth. During the Industrial Revolution, the contrast took another shape with the North taking the lead for once; but contrast remained. Even in the twentieth century the electoral map has continued to show it, the Highland Zone tending to be Labour's stronghold, the South-East the Conservatives'.

OPPOSITE *One of the many splendid remains of Roman art in Britain; this detail from a floor mosaic uncovered in Cirencester, Gloucestershire (Corinium in Roman times), shows the head of the figure representing Autumn.* TOP *A bronze candle-holder in the shape of a stag, dating from the 2nd to 4th century AD, found at Bath.*

ABOVE *A statue of Julius Caesar in Rome; he was the first Roman to send forces over to Britain, in 55 and 54 BC, but the true conquest of Britain was undertaken by the emperor Claudius in AD 43.*

With the increase of archaeological knowledge in our time, we have come to think of prehistory as the first chapter in history. And indeed the British Isles are extraordinarily rich in prehistoric remains. Stonehenge and Avebury are the most remarkable prehistoric monuments in Europe. But that is not now our theme.

We begin here at the moment the island peoples, particularly the Britons, come into the light of day, recorded history, with Julius Caesar. He made a reconnaissance raid across the Channel at the shortest crossing in 55 BC. The Roman historian Suetonius tells us that Caesar was after pearls from the oyster-fisheries, which were numerous and rich. It is more likely that he came for strategic reasons, for the Britons were sending help to their Celtic kin in Gaul, which Caesar had conquered; and also for a further instalment of glory.

He found none: his cavalry transports never made a landing. The Britons harassed the legionaries from their antique war-chariots; a high tide damaged Caesar's shipping at his beach-head. The best thing he could do was to withdraw. Next year he came with more powerful forces and crossed the Thames to storm the fortress-camp of Cassivellaunus, the predominant king in the South-East. This did not end the matter. The Britons kept up a harassing guerrilla warfare; meanwhile, storms damaged the transports at the beach-head once more, and Caesar withdrew.

Though Caesar wrote up his attempts as triumphs, the truth was expressed by Shakespeare in *Cymbeline* (his name for Cunobelinus, who ruled over most of the South-East of Britain.)

> *A kind of conquest*
> *Caesar made here, but made not here his brag*
> *Of 'Came, and saw, and overcame': with shame*
> *(The first that ever touched him) he was carried*
> *From off our coast, twice beaten. And his shipping*
> *(Poor ignorant baubles) on our terrible seas,*
> *Like egg-shells moved upon their surges, cracked*
> *As easily 'gainst our rocks.*

It was not until a century later that Rome seriously planned and decided on the conquest of Britain. In the interval trade and cross-Channel contacts increased, and Roman influence extended itself in the South-East. Cunobelinus ruled successfully from his capital at Colchester, issuing coins which followed Roman patterns. On his death, with the British kingdoms disunited and some of them ready to collaborate with Rome, invasion in force followed. Cymbeline's son, Caratacus (Welsh Caradog), was decisively beaten at the line of the Medway. He fled to South Wales for help in his resistance movement, and ultimately to the North (Yorkshire territory), whose queen, Cartimandua, handed him over to the Romans; he was taken to Rome, where he lived on in honourable captivity.

We see that the Britons had no objection to women rulers in their devotion to Boadicea (Boudicca), heroine of the resistance in the first phase of the conquest. Actually, her tribe, the Iceni – of roughly Suffolk and the Fens – were allies of

Rome, but were appallingly treated by a rapacious proconsul: excessive taxation was exacted, Boadicea flogged and her daughters raped. The queen took an almighty revenge upon the Romans, burning London and Verulamium (St Albans), massacring and killing, before her ultimate defeat, when she took poison rather than submit. She is one of the first historic figures to come down to us in the folklore of the nation, which is a people's memory – to be celebrated more than a thousand years later in Cowper's famous ode, with its prophecy of an empire greater than Rome's:

> *Regions Caesar never knew*
> *Thy posterity shall sway,*
> *Where his eagles never flew,*
> *None invincible as they.*

The most memorable figure in the Roman conquest of Britain was the Roman general Agricola, who had the good fortune to have his biography written by the greatest of Roman historians, Tacitus. Agricola spent years in Britain, and had indeed fought through Boadicea's resistance movement, when he was made governor in AD 78. An ambitious man, a planner of long-ranging views, he planned the conquest of the whole island and meant to go on to tackle

ABOVE *In AD 122 the emperor Hadrian came to Britain and began the construction of a wall to defend its northern frontier. Over seventy miles long, Hadrian's Wall marked the northernmost boundary of the Roman Empire.*

Ireland. He led an army up the east coast to penetrate into the Highlands and overthrow the Caledonians at Mons Graupius (presumably in the Grampians). A change of policy in Rome prevented him from completing the subjugation of the British Isles; he retired, a disappointed man, with one of the great grievances of history – and no-one can say what the consequences might have been if he had imposed Roman civilization on Ireland.

As it was, civilization contracted behind the great fortress-frontier-barrier, Hadrian's Wall, from the Tyne to the Solway, the longest and most imposing of any such monuments the Romans erected in Europe. On the whole the conquest of the southern half of the island, once undertaken in earnest, proceeded rapidly enough, though it was a complex affair. Some fortress-camps had to be taken by direct assault, like Maiden Castle outside Dorchester, where piles of pebbles from Chesil Beach and skeletons with arrow-heads in the neck have been found, telling their own story. Some tribesmen were restless, like the Silures of South Wales; but most submitted,

The Emperor Hadrian, the second reigning emperor who crossed the Channel to Britain.

9

or were ruled indirectly through their own petty kings. Such a one was Cogidubnus of what is now West Sussex, the foundations of whose splendid palace at Fishbourne near Chichester have been laid bare in our time. Here were hypocausts (central heating), mosaic pavements, colonnades, courts and fountains – the advantages of Mediterranean civilization. The pattern of the conquest was urban; all over the country we find relics of it in towns with *chester* (from *castrum*, camp) in their names, like Dorchester with its amphitheatre (as again at Caerleon-upon-Usk), Winchester, Gloucester, or Chester itself.

The Romans tapped the mineral resources of the country, from the coal of Tyneside, lead in the Pennines, copper in Anglesey, to the iron of the Weald and the tin of Cornwall. They erected their buildings in stone, like the splendid remains

OPPOSITE ABOVE *Baths were an important part of Roman life, and at Bath (or Aquae Sulis), after discovering mineral springs, the Romans established a small town centring on the baths, as well as a temple and houses for guests, officials and visitors.*

OPPOSITE BELOW *The process of bathing was often a complex one; the bather was first anointed with oil and sometimes followed this with exercise, after which the body was scraped of its accumulation of oil and sweat by means of a strigil, shown here; he then proceeded to hot and cold baths.*

LEFT *Housesteads was one of the major forts along Hadrian's Wall, and it has been extensively excavated. The drainage system was quite sophisticated; here we see the remains of the latrines.*

BELOW *Among the most important legacies of the Romans in Britain were the roads they built, mostly with slave labour. This one is Wade's Causeway, along the Wall.*

of Bath or the Mithraic temple and baths under the pavement of the City of London. They had the art of making bricks – and we see these durable materials built into later Saxon churches, or the bricks from Verulamium in the walls of St Albans cathedral. They drained and irrigated some of the Fens, increasing corn production, while such villas as Chedworth in the Cotswolds testify to their sheep breeding and cultivation of a woollen industry.

Most of all, they left their legacy in the road system which knitted the country together, such roads as we still follow, in Watling Street from Dover to Chester (A5), or the Fosse Way from Exeter to Lincoln (A46). Mostly these roads pivoted upon London, and increased its importance, which was commercial, not governmental, though it was dominated by a huge statue of the Emperor Hadrian, who had taken a

personal interest in Britain's affairs. In the nineteenth century the railways still largely followed these early routes. The stone foundations of the roads were laid by slave labour – there always have been slaves in most human societies, and Britons were no exceptions.

Urban life, which set the standards of Mediterranean civilization, did not really catch on in the very different conditions of rural and forested Britain, and, with the sapping of the Roman Empire's strength from the centre, the vitality of the more distant provinces ebbed. Already by AD 300 evidences of decline appeared in the urban life of Britain. A century later Rome was confronted by the irresistible pressures upon the frontiers of its Empire caused by the migrations of peoples, lunging westward from seismic population movements in western Asia. Even before the fall of

In about 296 AD the future emperor Constantius Chlorus was sent to Britain to settle a rebellion by the Roman commander there and strengthen the defences against the northern Picts. He is shown on this medal arriving in London (Londinium).

the Western Empire, attacks on Britain from Germanic rovers had necessitated the organization of the defence of the south-eastern coasts under 'the Count of the Saxon Shore'; we still have remains of forts against these marauders, as at Richborough. The enemy was already within the gate, in the numbers of Roman legionaries in Britain who had been recruited from other areas, including the Rhine. They would have known the prospects within the island. With the withdrawal of Roman forces the Britons were left to defend themselves; appeals for help against attack were sent to Rome in 414 and finally in 446 – but in vain.

The whole Continent was in a swirl of movements of peoples; Britain was under attack not only from across the Channel but from Picts and Scots in the North, and from the Irish in the West. In the South-West people were already migrating across Channel to form a lesser Britain in Brittany. Perhaps more important than the withdrawal of Roman legions – for the Britons showed that they could put up a defence – was the collapse of any central, co-ordinating government. The historian Gildas, himself a Briton, refers to their *civitates* or communities, which indicates that when unity had broken down – the genius of Rome – Britain lapsed into its tribal divisions and petty kingdoms again, squabbling and fighting with each other. One of these kings, Vortigern, called in Saxons from Germany to his aid in Kent, and never got them out again. This time, under their leader Hengist, they had come to settle, to fight for possession of the land. Consolidating their beach-head, others followed, in two prolonged waves or migrations, separated by an interval of a generation or so from about AD 500 to about 540.

A WORSE CONSEQUENCE of the Roman withdrawal, from the historian's point of view, is the closing down of records as to what happened, the scantiness of any written evidence; these were, truly enough, the Dark Ages. Various things stand out,

however, like rocks, among the swirling waters. The Britons fought back, and, by the victory of Mons Badonicus, held up the conquest of their land for some forty years. Even when the Angles, Saxons and Jutes resumed their progress, their conquest never reached the full extent of Roman Britain: the impulse spent itself before it reached the nearest frontiers.

In these centuries of fluid movement, from *c.* 400 to *c.* 600, the age was not wholly dark, and the native Celtic civilization of the island experienced a revival of its own idiom, away from Rome, as witnessed in its arts. A direct legacy from Rome continued in the form of Christianity, which had reached the island in the second century, and recruited its most noted martyr in St Alban, of Verulamium. It may not be altogether fanciful to see something of a British idiosyncrasy in the character of the philosophic layman Pelagius (or Morgan), who left Britain for Rome in 380. He upheld the idea of the essential goodness of human nature, as against the Latin St Augustine's insistence upon the doctrine of original sin and the necessity of divine grace. Pelagius entertained a less gloomy, a perhaps too optimistic, view: that men could improve themselves morally by their own efforts.

The course of human history – certainly in their time (and in ours) – justified the gloomier view, and Pelagius was condemned as heretical. However, it was to put down Pelagian dissenters that St Germanus, bishop of Auxerre in France, paid two visits to Britain in 414 and 447; so some contacts with the continent were kept, in this dark time, which coincided with an extraordinary outburst of missionary activity among the Celtic peoples, both northern and southern. About 400 St Ninian embarked on converting the Picts, of what is now Scotland, from his base in Galloway. In 432 Patrick, a southern Briton, was consecrated bishop for the purpose of spreading the Gospel in Ireland, where he worked for thirty years. In South Wales St Iltud established a missionary centre at Llantwit, the ultimate fruits of which perhaps we may see in the numerous missioners of the 'Age of the Saints', who went across to preach and work in Cornwall and Brittany.

For turn the map of Europe about and you see that these Celtic lands along the western coastline, separated by narrow seas, in that age when communications by sea were easier than by land, formed one cultural western world. The Germanic peoples coming in on the South-East formed, of course, quite another. However, as Collingwood, the historian of Roman Britain, says:

In the Highland Zone this general dislodgement of the people did not happen. When early English history emerges into the light of day, that Zone is still everywhere inhabited by British peoples, preserving their sub-Roman heritage at least to this extent, that they are everywhere Christian and everywhere keep some faint tincture of Latinity, setting up tombstones after the Roman model to their dead.

Everywhere in the Celtic areas we find these inscribed monoliths and gravestones.

OPPOSITE *This beautifully decorated bronze shield once belonged to an ancient Briton, and was found in the river Thames near Battersea.*

AFTER THIS PAUSE in the early sixth century, which is associated in Celtic memory with the figure of King Arthur, and the legends woven around him, the onward march of the Germanic invaders was resumed. The Angles, or English, had come from the more northerly area of Jutland; Saxons and Jutes from the Rhine delta of the Netherlands – the area at which Britain is most exposed to the Continent and to which she has always been strategically sensitive through the ages. The Jutes, in close contact with the Franks, exhibited some cultural affinities of a superior order. Though these peoples had some differences, they had much more in common and belonged to the same grouping of Germanic peoples. They were closer to each other than were the two main Celtic groups: the northern, consisting of Scots, Manx, Irish; the southern of Welsh, Cornish, Bretons. That gave the invaders greater unity and striking power. When they resumed their westward march, they separated Wales from the Celtic South-West by the battle of Dyrham in 577; by their victory at Chester in 613 they cut Wales off from contact with the Celtic kingdom of Strathclyde. The Highland Zone, the Celtic world, was permanently fragmented; henceforth the Lowland Zone of Britain was dominated by the English, and became England.

The ebbing of Rome's strength had meant a decline in civilization, and this went further with the continued fighting between the older inhabitants and the newcomers, and with each other within these peoples, the scuffling of 'kites and crows' in Gibbon's phrase. The drainage system of the Fens went out of use, land became waterlogged, towns were deserted, some of the Romans sites even forgotten, as at Silchester near Reading – to be re-discovered a millennium later, their coloured mosaics sleeping through the centuries under English fields. Plague weakened the Britons' resistance, areas became depopulated, there was room for new settlements. The newcomers were forest folk, who built in wood, not stone, and tended to shun urban sites for the country, where they cleared and settled.

The Jutes settled in Kent and the Isle of Wight; other settlements we can follow in their names: South Saxons in Sussex, East in Essex, West in Wessex. The Angles settled in East Anglia, the Midlands and Northumbria, the land beyond the Humber right up to Edinburgh, which was founded by the Northumbrian king Edwin. Presumably it was the much larger area occupied by the Angles that gave the name England eventually to the whole country. Northumbria enjoyed a brief early primacy, never to be forgotten, for this area produced the greatest scholar in the Europe of the Dark Ages in the Venerable Bede (died 735), a beacon of knowledge shining out

OPPOSITE In 669 St Chad established the episcopal see of the Mercians at Lichfield in Staffordshire. This page from the Lichfield Gospels (or St Chad's Gospels) of about 720 AD shows the exceptional beauty of their illuminations.

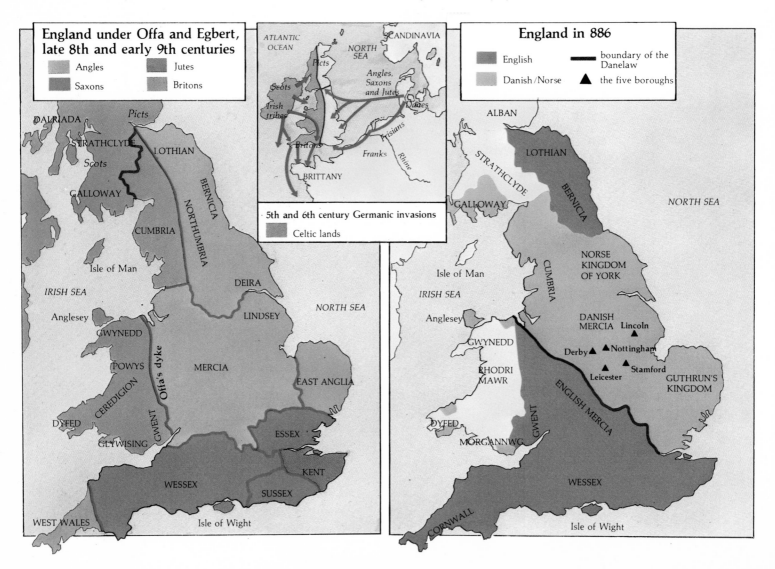

over those grey waters of the North Sea. Among his works one is immortal, his *History of the English People*, which tells us much about their origins and record.

Then the middle kingdom of Mercia had its day with a great king, Offa (reigned 757–96), whose name we still remember in Offa's Dyke, the long boundary earthwork dividing Mercia from Wales, the largest public work of the whole Anglo-Saxon period. London came into the Mercian area; it is owing to this that wherever English is spoken – whether at Oxford, Edinburgh or Dublin; New York, Los Angeles or Johannesburg; Delhi, Singapore or Canberra – we are all speaking varieties of Mercian.

This is rather odd, because the dominant Old English of Anglo-Saxon literature (which was the richest literature of all

which developed the capacity not only to conquer but to fuse and integrate peoples, led to its leadership. Exeter came to have Saxons and Celts living peacefully side by side, with Celtic saints as patrons of churches alongside Saxon dedications. Perhaps significantly, the name of the head of the West Saxon royal house, Cerdic – from whom our present sovereign remotely descends – is not English, but Welsh, Ceredig.

When the English arrived in Britain they were pagans, worshipping the gods whose names appear in our weekdays, Tuesday, Wednesday, Thursday, Friday: Tiw, Wodin, Thor, Frig. From about AD 600 a two-pronged campaign was launched to convert them to Christianity and bring them within the pale of Roman civilization through the Church. In 597 a Roman mission arrived in Kent under St Augustine, who

among the early German peoples) – the language of the *Anglo-Saxon Chronicle* (a unique document of the Dark Ages), of *Beowulf* and the fine poetry of the *Exeter Book*, the speech of Wessex, is represented subsequently only by the dialect of Somerset and Dorset and the poetry in it of William Barnes. It is rather hard that this expressive speech was used for comic effect on the Shakespearean stage, to laugh at provincial rustics.

This is the more curious in that Wessex ultimately achieved supremacy over the other English kingdoms for centuries up to the Norman Conquest and went furthest in achieving what unity there was before that shattering event. This supremacy was initiated by Egbert (died 839), the grandfather of Alfred (849–99), the greatest of all Anglo-Saxons, whose memory is alive with us today. Egbert pushed west, to subdue the West Welsh of Devon and Cornwall; the good fortune of Wessex,

A 7th-century Anglo-Saxon royal burial ground discovered in this century at Sutton Hoo in Suffolk has revealed priceless treasures, many of them of possible Viking origin, including this gold and garnet purse.

was given a welcome by the local king, Ethelbert, and used the old Roman church of St Martin at Canterbury, which has therefore that historic continuity. Rome's genius had always been for organization and order; this now was carried forward by the Church. Missions were sent to other kingdoms, such as that of Paulinus, who converted king Edwin of Northumbria, and established his see at York. Gradually dioceses took shape, kings and then their peoples were brought within the fold.

Celtic Christianity took a hand from the North, inspired from Ireland, whence St Columba had come to found the missionary centre upon the island of Iona in 563. St Aidan

ABOVE *The crucifixion, carved on an ivory plaque of 10th-century Anglo-Saxon workmanship.*

THE LATER NINTH AND TENTH CENTURIES were filled by the restless predatory attacks all round Northern Europe from the peoples of Scandinavia. Already before Egbert's death, from 865, the Danes had begun their attacks upon the Anglo-Saxon coasts which went on for decades. The old English had to face a catastrophe similar to that which they themselves had wrought upon Celtic Britain. Magnificent seamen as these Vikings were, the destruction which they wreaked everywhere they could reach from the sea was tremendous. They next took to horseback, riding in armies across the land, plundering its riches, carrying off booty – especially the treasures from the churches and monasteries.

From looted Lindisfarne the relics of St Cuthbert were carried to Durham for better safety. One tell-tale detail: from a valley in Cornwall, there was discovered in the eighteenth century the Trewhiddle Hoard (now in the British Museum). It contained the earliest piece of Anglo-Saxon church-plate, a silver chalice filled with coins, a priest's silver scourge, and other valuable items. The coins came to an end about 875, at the height of Danish attacks on Wessex; the priest had hidden the wealth of his church in an old tin-work: he never came back to fetch it.

This was in the reign of Alfred, who thoroughly deserved the title of Great, for it was owing to him that more than half

BELOW *King Alfred saved England from being overrun by the Danes and made this treaty confirming them to the Danelaw. Here is a detail from a Latin text of it.*

joined in the work in Northumbria; and later St Cuthbert presided over the community on the island of Lindisfarne, which produced a superb work of art in the Gospels written and illuminated there, a creative fusion – like the splendid sculpted crosses – of Celt and Anglo-Saxon. Irish missionaries penetrated as far south as Lichfield in Mercia. It became necessary to co-ordinate the two traditions, Roman and Celtic: at Whitby in 664 Rome, with its stricter discipline, prevailed over Celtic looseness and individualism. The structure of the Church could now be built up more firmly, as it was under the primacy of Canterbury by a learned Greek, Theodore of Tarsus, who made it also a centre of learning.

In Wessex – tribute to the maturing of its civilization – grew up one of the greatest of all Englishmen, St Boniface (680–735). He devoted his life to making Christians of the English kith and kin on the Continent, the Frisians, then the Germans along the Rhine, and even some of the inhabitants of Hesse and Thuringia. He is the prime apostle of Germany, where he organized the Church under the aegis of Rome. In this stupendous work Boniface engaged the energies of numbers of his countrymen who felt the call to christianize their folk in their old homes: men such as Willibrord, the apostle of Utrecht, or Willibald, founder of the see of Eichstädt. In his last attempt to convert the Frisians, Boniface and all his companions were martyred; his relics were taken to his foundation at Fulda, whence the encyclicals of the Church in Germany still issue forth.

of England was saved from the Danes. At one time, during the worst of his prolonged struggle of 871–8, it looked as if they would win. He was driven to take refuge in the marshy fastnesses of Athelney (whence the folklore about his burning the cakes). From there he built up the forces of Wessex, the *fyrd*; when he emerged again, his people – in the touching phrase of the *Anglo-Saxon Chronicle* – were 'fain of him', i.e. adored him. He led them to ultimate victory – the preservation of Wessex – though he judiciously accepted Danish settlement in the area to the north and east of Watling Street, the Danelaw.

Meanwhile, he initiated fortified *burhs* (like Oxford), pushing the suzerainty of Wessex into the Midlands. He built a fleet, and organized the county levies so that Wessex was better able to withstand the next wave of Danish onslaughts. During an interval of peace he set himself to recover something of the ground lost in culture and civilization from all the warfare and depredation. He summoned Welsh Asser (who wrote his biography) from St David's to teach him and his Court to read and write; he learned Latin himself to

OPPOSITE *The design on this Viking tombstone, found in St Paul's churchyard, testifies to the fierce nature of the 10th-century Norse invaders.*

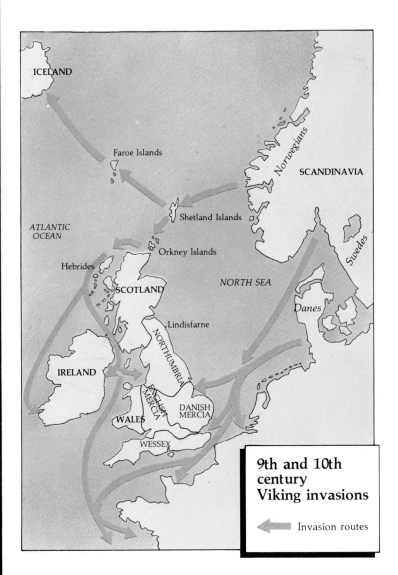

ICELAND

Faroe Islands

Norwegians

SCANDINAVIA

ATLANTIC OCEAN

Shetland Islands

Swedes

Orkney Islands

Hebrides

NORTH SEA

SCOTLAND

Danes

Lindisfarne

NORTHUMBRIA

IRELAND

ENGLISH MERCIA

WALES

DANISH MERCIA

WESSEX

9th and 10th century Viking invasions

Invasion routes

translate and circulate devotional and educational works. To us the most interesting are the Notes he himself added to a work describing the early voyages of Othere up the coasts of Scandinavia and into the White Sea. In Alfred's phrase (touching, when one thinks of his lifetime of effort to save his country and his people) – 'I know nothing worse of a man than that he should not know' – he comes across to us, after a thousand years, as a living spirit, first and best of Englishmen.

By the time of his death, 899 – born at Wantage, he was buried at Winchester – another wave of invasion, this time of the Norsemen, from Scandinavia, swept all round the coasts of the North-West, Scotland, the Hebrides and Ireland. These people have left their settlements and names in these areas, particularly in Cumbria.

Cornwall. Edgar was crowned at Bath in 973, probably to solemnize his overlordship of all the English. The coronation rite of today goes back to that date and is in essence the same. Even our folklore remembers him as being rowed on the Dee at Chester by eight tributary princes.

In the latter half of the tenth century, from 954, the Danes redoubled their attacks against the unfortunate Ethelred (the 'Unready', or 'Redeless'), who tried in vain to buy them off with heavy payments of Danegold – precursor in a way of modern taxation. It was a beginning of the end of old Anglo-Saxon England; for the blows re-doubled until a powerful Danish king, Canute, annexed it to his Scandinavian empire. The country was so smashed up by his family's raids that the *Witan*, or royal Council, accepted him as king in England, where he reigned from 1017 to 1035. We see how much

We can best sum up the positive contribution of these peoples – as against their barbaric destructiveness – by saying that they were wonderful seamen, and as such contributed ultimately to the maritime achievements of the nation. They had little difficulty in settling side by side with the English to colonize in the North and East – where one can watch their place names ending in -by, -wick, and -thorpe, side by side with English -ing, -ham, and -ton – for, after all, they were cousins, out of the same Germanic world. They were, also, free-spirited peoples, independent and breezy (as one still remarks in Yorkshire). Much more freedom existed in their areas than in the old South-West, where slavery and serfdom continued. Perhaps this freedom was a contribution ultimately worth having, to set off against the cultural damage they did, and the effect they had in the decline of Anglo-Saxon England from its earlier promise and achievement.

There were ups as well as downs in later Anglo-Saxon England, recovery as well as decline. Alfred's grandson, Athelstan (died 940), expanded Wessex by annexing

personality counted when we note that neither of his two sons reigned for long, and that the old Wessex line was reinstated in the person of Edward the Confessor, who ruled from 1043 to 1066.

He too has come down to us as a strong character. His reputation for saintliness – based partly on his refusal or inability, to consummate his marriage – has tended to ignore the fact that he was rather a good politician to have survived. Unfortunately for the English, his celibacy left the succession wide open. The dominant figure in his reign was the Danish Earl Godwin, who had murdered Edward's elder brother. Edward had had to take to wife Godwin's daughter, Edith, as saintly as the king, since she was no less celibate. Edward's lasting work was the founding of Westminster Abbey, a sanctuary which proved a magnet for the monarchy, hitherto based upon Winchester where its treasury was, and it was at Westminster that the kings were henceforth interred.

It is hardly surprising that Edward's sympathies were Norman, for his mother came from the ducal house of

Normandy, where he himself had grown up in the years of his exile. As and when he could he promoted Normans to bishoprics and offices in England; cross-Channel contacts increased, with a growing infiltration of Normans. Godwin's power was inherited by his son Harold, who proved his ability by a successful campaign against the Welsh. It was Victorian sentimentality that canonized this half-Dane as 'the last of the Saxons.'

Harold certainly had hard luck – and luck seems to be an essential constituent of historic greatness. Wrecked on the coast of Normandy, he was made to swear a holy oath to support Duke William's claim to succeed Edward as king, of whom he was a remote cousin. On Edward's death, his nephew, Edward the Atheling (i.e. the eldest son), was too young for the crisis brewing, with threats from the North Sea and from Normandy, where a powerful invasion force was being mounted. The *Witan* chose Harold as king. All that summer of 1066 he kept watch on the south coast, with forces ready against William. In September he had to march them

north against the invasion of the Viking Hardrada and his own brother Tostig, whom he defeated in two battles. This left the south coast open, and William's army landed unapposed.

Harold made a rapid march south to Hastings, where the issue – the future of England – was decided on 14 October 1066. For there was a great slaughter, in which Harold, his brothers and closest adherents were killed, and William the Norman emerged victor. He had no support in the country, but there was no longer any effective opposition. He received the submission of London and of the *Witan*, and was crowned king in the Confessor's Westminster Abbey on Christmas Day 1066.

Chapter 2

Growth of the Nation

However much historians may dispute it, the Norman Conquest revolutionized the old England of the Anglo-Saxons. All societies need a shake-up from time to time, and England certainly got it. It was achieved by a small military aristocracy of some 5000 armoured knights fighting on horseback: this was the new technique of combat which enabled the Normans to prevail and found kingdoms as far afield as Sicily, Cyprus and Jerusalem, as well as England and Scotland, and to push into Wales and Ireland.

The Normans were the makers of medieval England, and no less of the new Scottish kingdom; they imprinted their mark everywhere, on everything. We can see it today in the castles they built – not least in the Tower of London which the Conqueror erected to guard the Thames and overawe the city, or Rochester Castle, to defend the Medway. Castles, raised up on a *motte* or mound, were one way of holding the countryside around; a network of these covered the land. Alongside – as at Rochester or Durham – a splendid cathedral often arose by the castle: eye-witness to their reform of the Church.

The great man who inspired and headed all this was William the Bastard (1027–87), son of a tanner's daughter and Duke Robert II of Northmen (Norsemen) stock. So, in a sense, the Norman Conquest was the last successful invasion of the Northmen – but these were inspired by their contact with France. William's guardian had been Count Alan of Brittany, and one wing of his army was Breton – a revenge upon the English for having originally dispossessed the Bretons of their land. The Breton counts gained the earldom of Richmond in Yorkshire.

William I was a big, burly man, strong in every sense of the word, of iron will, stern aspect, balding in front but of regal dignity. In a sense a self-made man, he owed his good fortune and his place in history to his own qualities. For, strict with others, he was also strict with himself, upright, regular in his life, and religious. Wise and far-seeing, he was naturally a hard man, or he would never have survived, let alone ruled others, in such rough and rude times.

He shared out the conquered land among his leading followers, making them responsible for order in their areas. At the apex of his system, a kind of pyramid, stood the king; all these fortunate grantees owed fealty (allegiance), duty and service to him. The essence of the system was a hierarchy of lordship from top to bottom, based on land with its various

OPPOSITE *Durham Cathedral is one of the greatest masterpieces of English Norman architecture. Its construction was begun in 1093 by William of St Carileph, the first Norman bishop, to house the shrine of St Cuthbert.*
LEFT *After the conquest of 1066, William I shared out England among his chief followers; here, attended by his knights, he presents his nephew Alan with a grant of land.*
TOP *Domesday Book.*

23

tenures and services. This is essentially what is meant by feudalism: fief or fee means land-holding in return for service.

William had meant to run the country in co-operation with the Anglo-Saxons, but this did not work out – there was a gulf between them, in language for a start. The lands of the Anglo-Saxon governing class were largely expropriated, and their place taken by the foreigners. The worst act of severity was William's ruthless laying waste of the North, and this ended resistance. All directive power throughout the country was henceforth in alien hands; the governing language, up to about 1400, was French. This was a shattering experience for the English – brought home the more by the vast extension of 'forest' and forest law (one thinks of it in the New Forest even today) for the private hunting of the Norman kings and their Court. We may wonder whether the Celtic sub-populations cared much about the change of masters: they remained silent, while the Anglo-Saxon Chronicle, continuing for a time, expressed its resentment.

We must not underrate Anglo-Saxon achievements in the arts, or the influence of their religious missions in civilizing Scandinavia, for example. Some aspects of Anglo-Saxon administration were even ahead of the Norman; even so, Norman force braced it up. At the end of William's reign the nation-wide survey of the country's resources in land ownership, wealth, cattle, woodland, minerals, population, resulted in *Domesday Book* (1086). This unique survey is the outstanding monument to effective administration in medieval Europe. A Russian historian has paid tribute to Britain's exceptional administrative history as hardly less remarkable than its more widely boosted constitutional history – its parliamentary institutions have been taken for model all over the world.

Governmentally, England enjoyed throughout most of its history the advantage of smallness of size. In larger European countries powerful feudal lords could do much as they liked with their people. In England a strong monarchy meant that, wherever the king's writ ran, there was something of the 'king's peace', i.e. protection for his subjects. In the counties the sheriffs were the important officials, responsible to the central government; while a network of local courts for hundred, township and manor, kept society together and organized it locally. Towns grew as trade grew – effective government enabled the country to develop its resources. Gradually there evolved responsibility in local government, with the justices of the peace, the leading figures in the localities, to oversee justice and maintain order, holding their quarter-sessions. This system was locked together by sending the royal judges on circuit through the country to decide major matters and offences at assizes. These institutions continue today, their working essentially the same over the centuries.

The king was advised by his Council, consisting of the chief magnates of the realm. As they were usually occupied in ruling in their own districts, there gradually grew up a bureaucracy of clerks – writing men, often churchmen – around the king. As medieval kings had to be perpetually on the move, an embryo civil service became fixed at Westminster – especially

after the Treasury was moved thither from Anglo-Saxon Winchester. London itself gained a large measure of independence with responsibility as its trade and financial power continued to grow, especially after 1215, when it gained the right to elect its own mayor annually. Already by the Middle Ages it was one of the largest cities in Europe, the only one to combine being a great seaport with being a capital. This was reflected in old St Paul's, among the largest cathedrals in Europe, with many splendid monastic buildings and more than a hundred parish churches to vary the skyline.

The seat of the primate of the Church, the archbishop of Canterbury, was just across the Thames from Westminster at

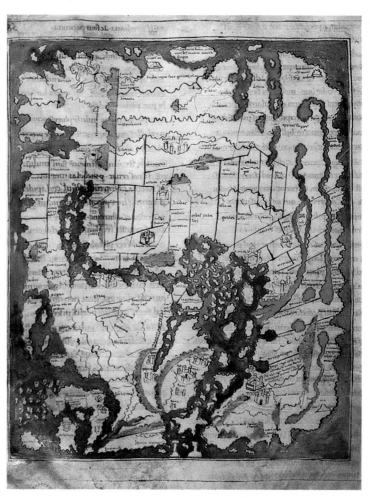

An 11th-century map of the world, showing Britain in the bottom left-hand corner. Ireland was then still called 'Hibernia'.

Lambeth. The Conqueror stood for reform of the Church no less than of government. He displaced the irregular Stigand as archbishop by an Italian, Lanfranc, a remarkable spiritual leader, reformer and scholar. Still more so was his successor, another Italian, Anselm, who was also an original philosophic thinker. One sees how England was wrenched away from its former Germanic-Scandinavian orbit, into the mainstream of European civilization.

The Conqueror's successor, William Rufus (reigned 1087–1100), had a bad press from clerical historians, for he was as free in his morals as in his thinking: he was a tough masculine homosexual, who laughed at superstition. Yet he was able: he recovered Cumbria from the Scots, and thus the frontiers remained up to James VI of Scotland's accession to the English throne in 1603. The expansive energy of the Normans was as active in the British Isles as it was in Southern Europe, which they also colonized. They pushed into South Wales – where a Norman-Welsh marriage produced a writer of genius in Gerald of Wales. Another product of Norman-Celtic fusion was Geoffrey of Monmouth, whose *History of the Kings of Britain* spread the Arthurian legends into the literatures and arts of Europe.

With increasing integration and communication, things came together, making for creative fusion. David I of Scotland took a wife of the old English royal house; so did the Conqueror's able son, Henry I, who reigned from 1100 to 1135. The Scottish monarchy moved away from its Celtic moorings, and became Normanized, especially with the Norman Stuarts (i.e. Stewards), who held the English earldom of Huntingdon. From Pembrokeshire the Norman 'Strongbow' led his following to an easy conquest – with their advanced military technique – of antiquated Ireland. Some fusion followed, whence the great Norman-Irish feudal families of Butler, Fitzgerald, Burke, etc. Strongbow had the sense to surrender formal suzerainty in Ireland to his feudal superior, Henry II.

Henry II (reigned 1154–89), great-grandson of the Conqueror, succeeded to the throne after a period of anarchy under King Stephen. Both claimed the throne through females. Stephen, easy-going and kindly, was unable to keep order in the jungle and for some years anarchy prevailed. We see again how much personality counts in history, sometimes decisively. Anarchy was ended by Henry, an able and energetic ruler, reformer and lawgiver. His full title was King of England, Duke of Normandy and Aquitaine, Count of Anjou. By inheritance from his father he added Anjou and Maine to Normandy, and by marriage all Aquitaine and Gascony, so that the Angevin Empire (of the house of Anjou) included more of France than the French king possessed. This involved the English monarchy more than ever in the affairs of Europe, especially since one of Henry's fighting sons, Richard Coeur-de-Lion (the Lionheart) took a leading part in the Third Crusade, becoming a legendary figure in Europe.

Henry was enmeshed in Church affairs by his historic quarrel with Thomas Becket, his former Chancellor, whom he made – against Becket's will – archbishop of Canterbury. Henry's reasonable desire to reform the Church courts was opposed by the archbishop, who had an uncompromising personality and undoubted charisma. After years of embittered conflict, Becket was murdered in his own cathedral by four of Henry's knights. The event created an enormous sensation all over Europe, the one event in our history Europeans knew best. For Becket was later canonized as St Thomas of Canterbury, where his shrine, and the offerings made at it, glorified the cathedral. Best known of all English saints, his highly dramatic story was taken into European art, in fresco and stained-glass, and has not ceased to inspire in literature, both French and English, even today.

Henry's youngest son, King John (reigned 1199–1216), has a dual importance in history. He lost his family's possessions

The murder of Archbishop Thomas Becket in Canterbury Cathedral on 29 December 1170. (From a medieval manuscript).

in France – which confirmed his nickname 'Jean sans Terre', John Lackland. His reign was one long crisis: there were conflicts with the Church and with his barons, which led ultimately to the showdown at Runnymede and his acceptance of Magna Carta (1215). The importance of this was that it was a coherent statement of rights and objectives, which could be interpreted and applied nationally. Some of its clauses still echo in English ears at home and overseas: 'To none will we sell, or deny, or delay right or justice.' 'No free man shall be arrested or imprisoned or dispossessed save by the lawful judgment of his peers or by the law of the land.' Magna Carta came to be regarded as a charter of English liberties. Its subsequent history was even more important – it was later re-interpreted by the Parliamentarians of the seventeenth century as a statement (anachronistically) of their case. It suggested in embryo the text for the American Revolution in the eighteenth century: 'No taxation without representation.'

The century leading to Magna Carta witnessed the coming together and integration of an English nation. Its consciousness as such was reinforced by the loss of Normandy: the magnates had now to choose between Normandy and

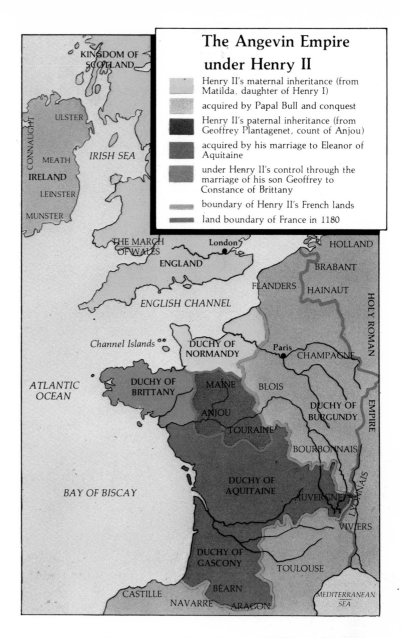

The Angevin Empire under Henry II

Henry II's maternal inheritance (from Matilda, daughter of Henry I)

acquired by Papal Bull and conquest

Henry II's paternal inheritance (from Geoffrey Plantagenet, count of Anjou)

acquired by his marriage to Eleanor of Aquitaine

under Henry II's control through the marriage of his son Geoffrey to Constance of Brittany

boundary of Henry II's French lands

land boundary of France in 1180

OPPOSITE *A page from a manuscript showing* top left *Henry* II, top right *Richard* I, bottom left *King John*, bottom right *Henry* III. *Between Henry* II *and Richard* I *is Henry, the Young King.*

ABOVE *Magna Carta, the 'great charter' of English liberties, signed by King John at Runnymeade on 15 June 1215.*

England. The prime social movement of the twelfth century was the internal colonization of the land. In this the monastic orders helped, especially the Cistercians, who chose remote places such as the Yorkshire dales or the Welsh hills to cultivate the soil and breed their flocks upon the wolds. The woollen industry grew, England producing the finest wool for the cloth-manufacturing cities of the Netherlands and Italy.

The thirteenth century saw a flowering of this civilization – of which we have visual evidence in such a cathedral as Salisbury, or the Angel Choir in Lincoln cathedral, and such sculpture in stone and alabaster as survived Reformation and Civil War. The contribution of the friars of the Franciscan and Dominican orders gave an impulse to philosophic thought as well as to popular piety. This was specially notable at Oxford, which took shape as a university (Cambridge not long after) early in the century. Here the leading intellects were

Franciscans, Roger Bacon, Duns Scotus, William of Ockham. For the century *c.* 1300 to 1400 Oxford was a chief intellectual centre of Europe, on a par with Paris, with which there was much interchange.

The sense of nationhood was much strengthened by the development of Parliament as a talking place – which is what the word means – for the whole nation. The significant step in its formation was the summoning of representatives from the counties, 'knights of the shire', and of the chief towns in them, 'burgesses', for their assent to the raising of money for the government on a national scale. This developed naturally as the prerogative of the Commons, since they represented the 'communities' from all over the country. Other countries assembled their estates, but the status of the Commons – arrived at by 1300 – gave a peculiarly effective form to representative institutions in England. It has proved the most lasting as well as the most flexible of all such, and has had a wider career overseas as a model for young growing nations.

On the basis of increasing economic and political development a strong king, Edward I (reigned 1272–1307), was able to resume the expansion natural to all efficient organisms. He conquered North Wales, and planted the noble

estre mis en la main de souurier iusques a ce quil soit
repare. Lequel colier aussi ne pourra estre enrichy de
pierres ou daultres choses reserue les ymage qui pourra
estre garny au plaisir du cheualier. Et aussi ne pourra
estre ledit colier vendu engaigie dyme ne aliene pour
necessite ou cause quelconque que ce soit

Alexander Rex
Scotore

le wellin
princeps
wallie

castles we still see – Caernarvon, Conway, Harlech – to contain the Welsh within bounds. He went on to extend the English administrative and judicial system, organizing North Wales into counties. He tried to appeal to Welsh sentiment by constituting his son and heir, Edward of Caernarvon, Prince of Wales – a title to continue in the son and heir of the reigning monarch.

Edward I made strenuous efforts to enforce a suzerainty over Scotland, leading several campaigns into the heart of the country. But the subjugation of Scotland and the unification of Britain proved beyond English resources, or capabilities. The incapable Edward II was defeated at Bannockburn (1314): this proved, like Hastings, one of the decisive battles of history – it settled the future for a long time to come. Not until the Act of Union of 1707, during Queen Anne's reign, were the two countries integrated into one, Great Britain, expressed in one Parliament with complete reciprocity of citizenship and trade.

Up to the middle of the fourteenth century society was in a promising way; wealth and population were expanding together. One can see something of its blithe spirit, its expansive humours, in the sculpture of the time still, on capitals and bosses in churches, and in their gargoyles. Then an appalling blow was struck in the Black Death, a series of bubonic plagues which ravaged all Europe. England was smitten heavily in 1349, and again in 1361–2 and 1369. After that, plague was endemic, with bad outbreaks every ten years

– notably the severe plague, at its worst in London in 1665 – until the extermination of the old black rat that carried the fleas which carried the bacillus. In some parts of the country one-third of the population perished – one can read the evidences today in church lists of parish priests who had to be replaced.

The social consequences were hardly less striking. When labour became scarce, competition for their services enabled the peasantry to demand more. This speeded up a process already in existence, by which the old fixed system of services in kind became transformed more and more into money values, and the institution of rents and wages. The upward trend of wages resulted in something new: labour legislation was introduced in Parliament to attempt to control them. Tremors ran through the whole social system, disturbed by these seismic movements and exacerbated by the taxation necessary for Edward III's long war in France. The glad days of the early medieval England, with the smile upon them – 'Merry England' of ballad and song – were over.

Taxation sparked off the alarming Peasants' Revolt of 1381. The poll-tax – taxing every poll (or head) – was a new and effective idea; suddenly, in 1381, the peasantry understandably revolted, on a large scale in the eastern counties, concentrating upon London. Abroad, similar movements had been aroused by the devastation caused by the wars of the military, knightly class, whose occupation was war. In England the movement was largely agrarian, with popular resentment directed particularly against tax-gatherers, treasurers and lawyers. In London an unpopular archbishop was murdered; John of Gaunt's palace of the Savoy was burned down, with all its treasures of tapestries, books and illuminated manuscripts. In this crisis the young Richard II – who was to come to a tragic end in Pontefract Castle – appeared in a bright light, bravely confronting the rebels.

OPPOSITE *Edward I presides over his Parliament. On his right is Alexander III, King of the Scots, and on his left Llewellyn, Prince of Wales. In the centre of the picture are people seated on the original woolsacks.*
ABOVE *Conway Castle, Wales, built in 1284 by Edward I to help to enforce control over Wales.*

They had been inspired by the egalitarian ideas of a preacher, John Ball:

> *When Adam delved and Eve span,*
> *Who was then the gentleman?*

The crisis was soon over, but the rising had one good result: no more was heard of poll-tax, until the twentieth century.

The upshot of all this was that the social structure of rural England came to look much as it was right up to the last century: namely that of gentry, larger and smaller, farmers, and peasantry dependent on wages. However, it was a free society, unlike most abroad.

A FRENCH-SPEAKING MILITARY ARISTOCRACY dominated much of Europe, as France set its cultural standards. Living evidences of it remain for us in Froissart's *Chronicle*, and in the Order of the Garter which Edward III created, with its motto *Honi soit qui mal y pense* (evil to him who evil thinks) and its home in St George's Chapel at Windsor Castle.

So it is not surprising that Edward III (reigned 1327–77), a pure Frenchman, should press his claim to the French throne; and it was a politic calculation to engage the surplus energy of a fighting class and release their aggressions abroad, rather than at home.

Edward III's war began promisingly. He had the financial resources of the prosperous wool trade to rely on, and the new military tactics of combining skilled archers with ordinary infantry. These were first tried out in the naval battle of Sluys (1340) – a variant of land-fighting, with ships grappling – in which the king himself led his fleet to total victory. Sluys has the importance in history of being the first in the long line of victories at sea, by which the small island power won her exceptional position in the world. Famous victories on land were won by Edward's son, the Black Prince (so named because of the black armour he wore), at Crécy (1346) and Poitiers (1356). These events entered into the country's patriotic saga and into the memories of the people: the consciousness of a nation now maturing as English. No less important, they bore witness to the greater efficiency of a flexible society of free men, against the much larger masses of a static feudal society, as in France.

The war dragged on and on, with truces and diversions from Aquitaine into Spain. This was the beginning of what is known as the Hundred Years' War, though it was by no means continuous – an intermission occupied most of the reigns of Richard II and Henry IV. Most of the Black Prince's life, however, was spent campaigning in France; regarded as a *preux chevalier* (a valiant knight), he was in fact a harsh ruler and ruthless pillager of enemy territory. He came back to languish of disease contracted in his strenuous life of campaigning, and the hopes placed upon him were destroyed by his early death. One still sees him upon his splendid tomb at Canterbury, his celebrated armour and habiliments of war

The 100 Years War was sparked off by the claims of Edward III and his successors to the crown of France (he was French on his mother's side and Duke of Gascony). At the battle of Crécy in 1346, shown here, his son, the Black Prince, won a resounding victory over the French.

about him. The old king Edward III dragged out his life without dignity: senile, he was under the thumb of his mistress, Alice Perrers.

The boy Richard II (reigned 1377–99), came to the throne under no favourable auspices, and his critical reign represents something of a watershed. So long as the king's senior uncle, John of Gaunt, head of the Lancastrian line, lived, he kept peace among Edward III's too numerous family and was a restraining influence upon Richard. Problems of all kinds came boiling up – personal and governmental, financial and political, religious and intellectual – with which Richard was ill-equipped to cope. He was no tough fighting man, as a medieval king needed to be; he was neurotic, an aesthete, given to favourites whom he spoiled, a man who could not be trusted – and that was fatal in a sovereign.

Since he was in favour of peace with France, there was the less outlet for the martial instincts of barons and knights, and a source of income was cut off in the absence of plunder and ransoms – for war had become a trade (as to some extent it has always been). Richard's chief rival, Gaunt's son Henry of Bolingbroke, went off to campaign with the Teutonic Knights against heathen Prussia – this was regarded as a kind of crusade. Richard's conflicts with his barons reached a crisis over and over again: he was incapable of firm and constant government. But neither were they. In 1388 the Lords Appellant, a powerful combination, defeated and humiliated him; by the Merciless Parliament, as it was named, that followed, his friends and supporters were condemned and put to death with little sense of justice. Nine years later Richard had his personal revenge upon his opponents, with equal vindictiveness, improper in a king.

Meanwhile he had paid two visits to Ireland, where Anglo-

LEFT *Scenes of the Peasants' Revolt, 1381. After days of rioting the peasants, led by Wat Tyler, invited Richard II to a conference at Smithfield, London; when Tyler drew his sword he was cut down by the Lord Mayor of London, William Walworth (left). Richard, only fourteen at the time, then managed to placate the mob by promising them their rights (right).*

OPPOSITE BELOW *Richard II hands over the crown and sceptre at his abdication in the Tower; his place was taken by Henry of Bolingbroke (Lancaster) who became Henry IV.*

Norman rule had received a heavy blow from the invasion and devastations of the Scot, Edward Bruce. Large areas slipped back to the antiquated pre-medieval ways of Gaelic pastoral life. With his temporary triumph over the baronial opposition in 1397 Richard took to the personal, irresponsible courses of a tyrant, which could not last, and were fatal to him. To the opposition of the governing class, of which he was the natural head, was added that of the Church, in the person of Archbishop Arundel. When John of Gaunt died, with his heir Bolingbroke in exile, Richard confiscated his vast Lancastrian inheritance for the Crown. This unwise act reinforced the sense of insecurity throughout the governing class. Richard went off to Ireland, to lose his heir, the Earl of March, who was killed in a skirmish – he was next in line of Edward III's descendants, but in the female line. Next in the succession was Bolingbroke, and in the male line. At this juncture he returned, while Richard was still in Ireland, to claim his rights.

Bolingbroke intended to claim no more than his dukedom; the course of events forced him to claim the kingdom. For, at the next turn in the wheel of fortune, Richard would have had him by the neck – as he had already had his uncle, the duke of Gloucester, murdered at Calais. When Richard got back from Ireland support for him melted away like snow, and everyone turned to the alternative. Henry of Lancaster (Bolingbroke)

was called to the throne as Henry IV by the will of the country, as it was expressed by its representative institutions, Parliament and Church. Such was the revolution of 1399, from which these consequences flowed.

Henry IV made a far abler king than Richard, but his reign (1399–1413) was one long crises. Or perhaps we may say that the crisis continued from Richard's reign.

These decades before and around 1400 formed a watershed in several ways. Take the crucial question of language. English came up again to the surface, and to the fore. French was still the first language at Richard's court, as it was with the king himself; with the Lancastrians it became English. In Chaucer England produced a writer of European stature – he was well acquainted with both France and Italy and with their literatures. A Shakespearean writer in the warmth of his humanity and his variety, there is historic propriety in the fact that his chief masterpiece, *Canterbury Tales*, should celebrate the touring pilgrimage to the shrine of St Thomas. Hardly less a work of genius is Langland's *Piers Plowman*, a touching monument to the old alliterative English verse, as also to the spiritual depths of medieval piety; nor is it inferior to Chaucer in its more egalitarian style of humanity. John Gower was almost as popular a Court poet as Chaucer, and even more prolific.

The fact was that this disturbed time had something of a Renaissance about it. Richard had been a patron of the arts; Chaucer was a courtier, married to the sister of John of Gaunt's mistress, and later wife, mother of all the Beauforts. Masterpieces of painting, sculpture, and architecture were produced during this period – like the portrait of Richard that still stands in Westminster Abbey, or the bronze effigies of Edward III and Richard there. The Abbey itself, entirely French in conception, had been the work of another aesthete-king, Henry III. But Richard's reign saw the development of an entirely English style of architecture, the Perpendicular, and the creation of such masterpieces as the choir at Gloucester Cathedral, Westminster Hall, or the halls of Eltham, Penshurst, or Dartington.

After all, works of art outlive the transitory events of politics and the workaday world.

Movements in the world of the mind also had their reverberation in the country and across Europe. They came especially from Oxford, where John Wyclif (d.1384) went on from theological and philosophical speculation to call in question the dogmas which were the foundation of the Church's authority, challenging the claims of the papacy along with the utility of monasticism, pilgrimages, invocation of Saints. His attack on the vast wealth of the Church and its

TOP LEFT *A 14th-century tavern scene, from a treatise on the Seven Deadly Sins.*
TOP RIGHT *The frontispiece of Chaucer's* Troilus and Criseyde *from a manuscript of about 1400, showing the poet narrating his works. Courtier, diplomat, civil servant and poet, Chaucer, the 'Father of English Poetry', was the first of England's great poets.*
ABOVE *Men at work in the 14th century:*
left *a blacksmith's shop*
right *stonemasons. Note the trowel, set square, hammer and level.*

accumulation of property naturally attracted the support of laymen and, for a time, Gaunt's patronage. Thus was this firebrand of an Oxford don saved from burning. But the revolutionary implications of his teachings had to be suppressed in the interests of social order.

A regular campaign against Wyclif's following at Oxford was mounted. The Lancastrians represented something of an orthodox reaction. Oxford was never much favoured by them; they directed their patronage towards Cambridge, which moved up in consequence, and Oxford lost something of its unquestioned medieval ascendancy. Wyclif's movement was driven underground, to continue its activity with the Lollards (the name given to his followers) right up to the eve of the Reformation, for which it helped to prepare the ground. They circulated their translations of the Bible into English, some of them emanating from such scholars as the Cornish Trevisa. He had already had a leading part in changing the teaching in grammar schools, which had previously been in French, to English. Others of Wyclif's Oxford followers went to Bohemia, to take a leading part in John Hus's reform movement there. An earlier Oxford philosopher, William of Ockham, of great logical acuity ('Ockham's razor'), had already gone abroad to become the chief intellectual exponent of the secular claims of the Holy Roman (actually German) Empire to supremacy, against the claims of the Roman papacy. One sees the signs and portents, the shape of things to come: they point to Luther and the German Reformation, an end to the unity of the medieval world of thought.

HENRY IV (reigned 1399–1413) was always insecure on his throne; upon a first attempt to replace Richard, the latter was made away with a Pontefract, no-one knows how. The general insecurity, along with the oppressions the Welsh endured from Border lords, offered a grand opportunity for Welsh resistance; it found an inspiring leader in Owen Glendower, who made the resistance national. He may have been descended from the old line of princes of North Wales, and he had the support of the Tudors of Anglesey – one sees the meeting of past with future.

The Welsh resistance joined up with the Percy family in the North, who had had a large share in placing Henry on the throne but now moved jealously into opposition. Marching swiftly, Henry defeated the joint forces at Shrewsbury (1403), where the celebrated Henry Percy, 'Hotspur', was killed. His father, Northumberland, continued the struggle in the North, while Glendower rallied even South Wales to his cause and won diplomatic recognition from France, which dispatched a force to his aid but achieved nothing effective. The struggle lasted for years and gradually English resources wore down the Welsh, Harlech castle being at last starved out in 1409. Glendower disappeared into the hills, never betrayed by his people, and no one knows where he died. He is an unforgettable figure in the Welsh memory; Shakespeare has expressed in poetry the charisma that surrounded him.

The prolonged strain upon Henry – and perhaps remorse for his crime against Richard (for Henry was a medieval, with a religious conscience) – wore him out before his time. If the French had been in a condition to intervene they might have overthrown him at one or other of the crises that would have overwhelmed him but for his energy. But they were themselves paralysed by the struggle between the two parties of Burgundy and Orléans. This schism within France gave young Henry V a grand opportunity of renewing claims against France and, in alliance with Burgundy, of invading.

Henry V (reigned 1413–22) had been brought up in war and politics, and, before his father died, had tried to take his place. Such is life's irony that he was fonder of the dead Richard, who had been kind to him as a boy, than he was of his own stern, sad father. When Henry IV died, in the Jerusalem chamber of Westminster Abbey, his son spent the night alone with an anchorite and underwent a religious conversion. He emerged a dedicated king, grave and upright, devoted to justice and reform in Church and state. Henceforth, he was personally chaste; lithe and athletic, as a youth he could outrun a greyhound. Immensely ambitious, he meant to achieve the French throne, and go on from that to 're-edify the walls of Jerusalem', as he said on his early death-bed. For, of course, his astonishing achievement exhausted him.

His father had been right, after all, and all the soil of his achievement was to go with him into the grave. With England secure behind him, the young king invaded France and, with a small army, inflicted disaster upon vastly superior forces at Agincourt (1415). This victory on French territory has entered, almost more than any other, certainly in the Middle Ages, into our folk-memory. In my schooldays we still sang the old solemn tune of the fifteenth century, 'Our King went forth to Normandy'. Shakespeare has expressed it best for us in his play *Henry V*:

> *This day is called the feast of Crispian:*
> *He that outlives this day and comes safe home*
> *Will stand a tip-toe when this day is named ...*
> *He that shall live this day and see old age*
> *Will yearly on the vigil feast his neighbours,*
> *And say, 'Tomorrow is Saint Crispian.'*
> *Then will he strip his sleeve and show his scars,*
> *And say, 'These wounds I had on Crispin's day.'*

In the last war this was the speech that a young Yorkshire captain spoke to his men, as his landing-craft approached the Normandy coast, this time for the liberation of France, in 1944. He did not return home to keep the vigil.

In the next few years Henry subdued all Normandy, and re-organized it as his base: he was as able an administrator and diplomat as he was brilliant in the field. Relying on the alliance with Burgundy he made the Treaty of Troyes (1420), by which he was accepted by the French king as heir to France, and married his daughter. He took her to England to be crowned; then, returning to complete the conquest of all France north of the Loire, he contracted a disabling disease – perhaps dysentery – of which he died in the royal castle of Vincennes, aged thirty-five.

The Treaty of Troyes held good – or, perhaps we may say, held bad. For, thought it was maintained for the next three

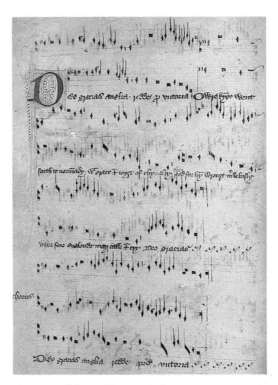

A song written to celebrate Henry V's famous victory at the Battle of Agincourt in 1415.

A later version of a portrait of Henry v *in Chichester Cathedral, Sussex.*

decades, it really depended upon Burgundy adhering to the English alliance. Once the French recovered unity, it was unthinkable that a country three times the size of England, with perhaps four times the population, could have been held permanently. And if Henry had lived to become king of France, England would have taken second place. As it was, his marriage turned out fatally: his little son, Henry VI – actually crowned king of France in Paris – inherited the mental debility of the Valois house, and this ultimately ruined him as king in England.

A leading authority on the period regarded Henry v as 'all in all, the ablest king to have sat on the English throne'. This seems excessive, when one considers William the Conqueror, for example, whose achievement was lasting. Henry's, astonishing as it was, was of short duration and incurred endless trouble, until the English were driven out of France. Then currents returned to their normal channels, and all was as if Henry had never been. Such is the irony of history.

THE CONSEQUENCES IN ENGLAND, were, however, grave. In medieval times, to have a minor on the throne was asking for trouble – as had been seen in the case of Richard II. In France, Henry v's able brother, John of Bedford, ruled as regent, and married Burgundy's sister to keep the alliance together. When she died, it fell apart. Meanwhile, the French cause recovered strength under the inspiration of Joan of Arc; from her repulse of the English from the siege of Orléans, the tide began to roll back, and the end could have been envisaged by the prescient.

Foremost of these was the boy King's great-uncle, Cardinal Beaufort, who led the party wanting peace with France. He was vehemently opposed by Humphrey, Duke of Gloucester, who appealed to patriotic sentiment and was always therefore

popular. The conflict swayed to and fro, while ground was lost in France and nothing could stop the decline. A fatal marriage was made for the young king, with Margaret of Anjou, the French king's niece. It would have been better for him if he had never married but remained celibate, like the churchman he was more suited to be. Not wholly incompetent mentally – he was not badly educated – he was quite incompetent at ruling. When the queen presented him with a son, to his surprise, during one of his complete breakdowns, this opened the question of the succession. She and her party were determined to fight for the boy's rights, against the Duke of York, whose claims went to Richard II's heir, the Earl of March.

It was this struggle for the throne that became known, later, as the Wars of the Roses – the White Rose of York against the Red Rose of Lancaster. Peace-loving Henry VI (reigned 1422–61 and 1470–1), distracted by it all, entered into a compromise by which York should rule as regent, and then he and his family succeed to the throne. This would have been better for all concerned, but neither Margaret nor her party would accept it. The sympathies of the country at large, and especially the Church, were with the Lancastrian royal house. Even poor Henry VI knew his rights, and said that his family had occupied the throne for three generations, by the will of Parliament representing the country at large. London, however, was more concerned for good government, which Henry could not provide, so the city tended to back the Yorkists. They had another strong base of support in York and on the Welsh Border, while the nobility and gentry divided in accordance with their family affiliations and local feuds. Thus, in the West Country, the Lancastrian Courtenays fought the Yorkist Bonvilles; in Cornwall, Lancastrian Edgcumbes fought Yorkist Bodrugans. The enormous territorial spread of the Neville family, in the North and Midlands, helped to decide the issue.

One must not think of these contests for power – and what went with it, lands and riches – as continuous; they came to a head at several decisive junctures. Once again we see the crucial importance of personality: the issue would never have been raised if Henry VI had been able to govern. Even so, the royal house might not have been overthrown but for the decisive fact that young Edward of York proved to have great military ability. And so he won the throne, to become Edward IV, and made an able king (he reigned from 1461 to 1470, and from 1471 to 1483).

He lost the throne temporarily through offending his grandest supporter, Richard Neville (Warwick the Kingmaker), and because of the treachery of his own brother, Clarence. Henry VI was brought out of the Tower and reinstated for a time. Edward IV returned, to defeat and kill the Kingmaker at Barnet (1471), and raced across country to finish off the Lancastrian cause at Tewkesbury, where the young Prince of Wales was killed. Now that the son was dead, it made sense to make an end of Henry VI, who died in the Tower on the night when Edward's youngest brother, Richard of Gloucester, was there (21 May 1471). Henry was not yet fifty. Next day his corpse was exposed in St Paul's, where the

After the Yorkist victory at Northampton in 1460, Edward of York, later to become Edward IV, kneels to the defeated Henry VI.

body bled, telling its own tale.

Edward IV settled down to an enjoyable and popular period of rule for another twelve years. The Yorkists could have gone on indefinitely, if it had not been for their murderousness and the tendency to feuding within the family. Edward was one of the handsomest men in Europe, an enthusiastic womanizer (no impediment to popularity – he scattered his favours right and left), with a tendency to fat. His next brother, Clarence – 'false, fleeting, perjured Clarence' – hardly less handsome, was envious of his brother. By joining Warwick the Kingmaker, he won the hand of the elder co-heiress to his vast Neville estates. Now the youngest brother, Richard, who had none of his elder brothers' physical advantages, was bent on winning Anne, the younger co-heiress of the inheritance. The brothers quarrelled bitterly over this, for Clarence wanted the lot. In 1478 he too came to an end in the Tower. Thus there were only two brothers left of York's large brood of sons.

In April 1483 Edward died unexpectedly, not quite forty, leaving two boys: the elder, twelve and a half, the younger not yet eleven. The elder was immediately recognized as Edward V, and summoned from Wales – though his personal following and escort were overthrown on the way by his uncle Gloucester, as protector during the minority of the young king. A sharp contest for control of his person had been won by his uncle Richard, against the Woodvilles, the queen mother's unpopular family. She took to sanctuary in Westminster Abbey with her younger son. Pressure was applied to surrender him, and Richard got both boys into his possession at the Tower.

His *coup d'état* was announced by the summary execution of Edward IV's bosom-friend, Lord Hastings, when Richard found that he would not go along with him in usurping the throne. In circumstances of crisis – for renewal of war with

France was threatened – there was a case for his taking the throne: no-one wanted the repetition of a boy king's minority, as with Henry VI. Richard cleared the way at breakneck speed, bringing his armed following from the North to overawe resistance; resistance in the Council was overcome – Archbishop Rotherham and Bishop Morton were confined in Welsh castles, Lord Stanley kept at arm's length in Lancashire. Edward IV's marriage was declared null and, for good measure, himself illegitimate – to the discredit of their mother, the Duchess of York. The Duke of Buckingham, promised a vast appanage, went along with this, and arranged Richard's coronation at high speed on 6 July 1483, a fortnight after his nephew's should have taken place.

At the end of June young Edward V's uncle, Rivers, his half-brother, Lord Richard Grey, and his Chamberlain, old Sir Thomas Vaughan, were all beheaded at Pontefract. At the coronation Queen Anne's train was borne by the Lady Margaret Beaufort, heiress-general of John of Gaunt and all the rights of the House of Lancaster. Her son, Henry Tudor, to whom she transmitted them, had been spirited abroad on

Portrait of Richard III, the last Yorkist king, by an unknown artist.

Edward IV's return - but was not safe in Brittany, where Richard was after him with tempting offers for his surrender.

Young Edward V and his brother in the Tower were never seen alive again after August 1483. Richard was then on progress, and at Warwick, whence the order for their murder went forth. The country in general did not know what had happened to them; for that autumn there were risings in every county town in the southern counties demanding their release. The Duke of Buckingham, however, must have learned what had happened to them; for he now changed sides and came out against Richard – in the name of Henry Tudor, the unknown Lancastrian claimant hovering off the coast. These movements, spontaneous and unco-ordinated, were defeated in detail: Richard was fain to have Buckingham (who had intended to stab him if admitted to his presence) beheaded at Salisbury, and his own brother-in-law at Exeter. At New Year 1484 the prolocutor of the French Estates – Generally specifically charged Richard with making away with his nephews. If only he could have produced them ... the only answer to his gathering enemies.

The fact was that he had turned the country's stomach. In all the horrors of the Wars of the Roses, one did not kill women or children. Richard had perpetrated the unforgivable crime; henceforth there was no peace, or peace of mind, for him. Nothing prospered. In September 1483 – a month after the two princes had been smothered in the Tower – Richard created his son and heir, another Edward, Prince of Wales. In April 1484 the boy died; Richard was left childless. A year later, on 16 March 1485, his wife died.

It was rumoured that Richard would seek a dispensation to marry his niece Elizabeth who, now that her brothers were dead, was heiress of the house of York. Everybody at the time recognized this, for Henry Tudor abroad – now not only the Lancastrian claimant but the candidate of all the Yorkists whom Richard had turned against him – had pledged himself to marry the Yorkist heiress when he came to the throne.

Henry's second attempt was much better planned. He had the help of 2000 French mercenaries, and he invaded via Wales, where he had patriotic feeling in his favour. Richard was furious at learning that the Lancastrian claimant whom he despised – the country had hardly ever seen him – had penetrated to the heart of his kingdom before he was aware of it. The fact was that the country ruled by a 'homicide' – the exact term awarded him by Parliament after Bosworth – was honeycombed by disaffection and treason against him, and supported Henry.

The issue was decided in a couple of hours at Bosworth on 22 August 1485, for Richard's army would not fight for him. Throughout the weeks before the battle various leading personalities and groups had been coming over to Henry, but he had only some 5000 to the king's 10,000. On the morning of the battle the Stanley forces – Henry's mother was married to Lord Stanley – took up a decisive position between the two

Richard III and his queen, Anne Neville.

armies. When Richard threatened to execute Stanley's son and heir, whom he had detained as a hostage, unless Stanley joined him, the king found that he could not get his order carried out. When battle was joined, he saw that the whole northern half of his army stood on their arms and would not engage for him. Only his cronies fought desperately for him, such as 'Jack of Norfolk', whom he had made a duke for his support. The issue was soon decided, and Richard's circlet picked up and placed on Henry's head; the King's naked body was borne off the field to Leicester, receiving maltreatment as it went. The body of an anointed king would never have been so treated if he had not been what he was – a murderer. In Elizabeth I's reign – she was grand-daughter of the victor of Bosworth – Jack of Norfolk's great-grandson, Lord Henry Howard, wrote a book which mentions the private family tradition as to Richard's 'heinous crime'.

Henry was free to marry Elizabeth of York and begin anew. The admirable medieval historian, Hamilton Thompson, used to have a joke about the *Leicester Evening Herald* coming out with the headline: 'Battle of Bosworth: End of the Middle Ages!'

OPPOSITE *A knight rides through the courtyard of the Tower of London to the royal lodgings to present himself to the King. He is accompanied by heralds, trumpeters and his squire carrying his sword and spurs. Illustration from a late 15th-century manuscript.*

Chapter 3

Reformation and Expansion

ENRY VII (THE NAME HENRY WAS ALWAYS pronounced Harry) turned out to be just the right man the country needed at the time: he reigned from 1485 to 1509. With him personally the monarchy returned to respectability: he lived happily and monogamously with his Yorkist wife, and as little as possible was said about the horrors that besmirched her family. Henry's able and pious mother, the Lady Margaret – foundress of St John's and Christ's Colleges at Cambridge – undoubtedly regarded herself as the true heiress to the throne and signed herself, rather improperly, 'Margaret R'.

Henry told Polydore Vergil, his historian, that the first half of his life had been passed either in confinement or in exile. He was more Welsh and French than English, and probably spoke with a foreign accent, as indeed his reading was mostly in French. He was remarkably well informed about foreign affairs. Unlike the Yorkists, who were extrovert and overconfident, Henry was secretive, far-seeing and wise – and so never popular. He managed everything for himself, especially the country's finances, which he well knew to be the foundation of its well-being. He built up and built up (saving money, a symptom of early insecurity, grew upon him); his life's work was the basis of the overall success of the Tudor monarchy. His alliance with Spain through the marriage of his son Prince Arthur did not work out as he hoped; on the other hand, marrying his daughter Margaret to James IV of Scotland led ultimately to the union of the two kingdoms as Great

OPPOSITE *A view of fifteenth-century London with the White Tower and shipping.*
ABOVE *A medal struck to commemorate the marriage of Henry VII to Elizabeth of York.*
BELOW *The effigy of King Henry VII in Westminster Abbey, on the tomb designed by Torrigiano in 1511–18.*

Britain. The present occupant of the throne owes it to this marriage.

For some years Henry had to face Yorkist attempts at a come-back, but the country was with him and recognized its need for peace and strong government after all the chops and changes. It is notable, for example, that Henry summoned no less than six Parliaments in the first twelve years of his reign. The year 1497 was critical, with two rebellions starting from Cornwall. The Cornish objected to being taxed for war preparations on the remote Scottish frontier; they managed to march an army the length of southern England before being defeated by the king in person at Blackheath. That didn't teach the unquiet spirits of the Lizard district, where the sanctuary of St Keverne collected many felons. They came out again in support of Perkin Warbeck, the Yorkist impostor backed by Edward IV's widowed sister in the Netherlands, with nothing better to do. Clement by nature and policy, Henry took it out of the Cornish in cash – no further trouble from that quarter for half a century.

A business man, rather than a fighting fool, Henry promoted the country's trading interests with the Netherlands; though he over-trumped his hand when ill

BELOW *Cardinal Wolsey, founder of Christ Church, Oxford, was Henry VIII's chief minister for fourteen years, and reached a position of unrivalled eminence before his fall in 1529.*

weather drove their Habsburg rulers in upon the Dorset coast and Henry inflicted a too-advantageous commercial treaty upon them, which they went back upon. In rivalry with Spanish support of Christopher Columbus, who was making his voyages of exploration at that time, Henry backed John Cabot's voyages to North America, in 1496–7, actually claiming priority so far as the discovery of the mainland was concerned. But there were no ancient civilizations or precious metals to predate upon, such as the Spaniards found in Central and South America to make the fortunes of Spain. It was ultimately the rich fisheries of Newfoundland and New England that were the key to the future for old England.

Henry VIII (reigned 1509–47) was a very different kind of man from his father: he took after his Yorkist grandfather, Edward IV. Like him he was a big, burly fellow who turned to fat (unlike the slim, spare Lancastrians); an outgoing extrovert, he was an out-of-doors sportsman, who took women as they came; he was well educated, musical and able.

his minister, Cardinal Wolsey, who had difficulty in restraining the young king in this field and sometimes had to give way against his better judgment. Wolsey started from the poorest origins – his father was an unrespectable butcher of Ipswich – to rise through the Church to a dazzling but dangerous pinnacle of eminence, to walk with emperors and kings. This answered to his over-weening ambition, for he had administrative drive, and aimed at justice for all and prudent measures of reform – such as closing down a number of small monasteries, to found educational institutions, Christ Church at Oxford and his school at Ipswich. A churchman, he was inspired by the idea of the *Magnificat*, putting down the mighty from their seats and doing what he could for the poor.

For the first part of Henry's reign Wolsey, fifteen years his senior, largely governed the country. But he became too much involved in the complexities of European politics, and was ultimately brought down by the worse dilemma raised by Henry's over-riding personal problem. He *had* to produce a male heir to the throne; after years of marriage to Catherine of Aragon, there was only a sickly girl, Mary, to succeed. This

LEFT *Henry VIII embarks for France – a stained-glass window in the Maison Dieu, Dover.*
BELOW *Portrait of Henry VIII by the court painter Hans Holbein, who executed many portraits of the king and his family.*

Royally secretive, like Edward IV he was capricious and cruel, a thoroughly masculine egoist. This did not prevent him from being popular, as his more admirable father never was. A towering personality and of masterful will, it is likely that the country might not have held together through the quasi-revolution of the Reformation but for his firm grip – let alone impose so comparatively successful a solution as it ultimately turned out to be.

Henry VII left a large treasure behind him. It did not take his son long to spend it, and for the rest of his reign he had financial problems. Anxious to win renown as a warrior, he was always ready to go cavorting in France. Actually, England's wealth tempted him to try and cut a figure against his rival, Francis I of France, and to play the diplomatic game of holding the balance between him and the Holy Roman emperor Charles V. This strained the resources of the small country to no good purpose.

Henry was aided in this ambition by the immense ability of

was dangerous, as everybody realized, with the Wars of the Roses over the succession only a generation behind. Most people appreciated Henry's problem; but how to resolve it? This divided people. Wolsey could not solve it, for his religious authority depended on the papacy, and the pope, after 1527 and the sack of Rome, was under the thumb of the emperor Charles v, Catherine's nephew.

Meanwhile Henry, who had fallen in love with one of Catherine's ladies, Anne Boleyn, convinced himself that his marriage to his deceased brother's widow was contrary to the Scriptures; and, when Anne proved pregnant, he married her, hoping that this was at last the so much desired son and heir. The child was a girl, Elizabeth, to his chagrin (history was to show that he had done better than he knew).

We need not go into Henry's various matrimonial

Figures from the Tudor court.

misadventures and his monstrous execution of both Anne Boleyn and Catherine Howard. The clue to it all was political: Henry's necessity to have a male heir. In the end he finished up with a royal family of three children, each of whom succeeded to the throne and reigned as follows: Edward vi, 1547–53; Mary i, 1553–8; Elizabeth i, 1558–1603.

Various crises came together with the dramatic fall of the cardinal. Henry's personal problem, both as man and king, was linked with the authority of the Church, and more – its rôle and place in society. Though a conservative in religion – he believed in Catholicism without the pope – Henry found an archbishop who would go along with him in Thomas Cranmer, a Cambridge scholar (far more of a gentleman than the cardinal), who took a leading part in reshaping the Church

Thomas Cranmer, Archbishop of Canterbury, who was later burnt at the stake at Oxford under the Catholic rule of Mary Tudor.

of England, as it ultimately emerged from the furnace of the Reformation. The Church urgently needed reform, as the whole circle of Catholic reformers, led by Erasmus, Dean Colet and Thomas More had recognized. With the spread of the European Reformation the crisis became international; England was caught up both in it and the prolonged duel between the Empire and France.

As happens in human affairs, i.e. history, solutions to urgent problems could never be ideal ones, and they worked out, in the usual human way, in all the lurid murk of faction and conflict, bloodshed and martyrdom on both sides. It was heart–breaking, like all revolutions, for those involved in it, and produced sad disappointments and surprises for those who had hoped for so much from the glad days of Henry's earlier years. He himself emerged a harder man, more brutal and capricious. And yet, after the black decades from 1530 to 1558, what took shape was not so far from the spirit of Erasmus, the moderate humanist reformer who inspired Elizabethan education and religion.

The first impulse of the humanist Renaissance may be seen, broadly, as Oxford-based and Catholic; the second, with a new generation and the movement of the time, as Cambridge-based and Protestant. At Oxford John Colet had set in motion the critical study of the New Testament text. The humanist movement meant moving away from medieval theorizing, a return to classical standards, the recovery of Greek with new vistas of knowledge, and – with the questioning of the medieval cosmos – an emergence from the cocoon of faith into

the strife of man's confrontation with his own nature. Here was the essence of the Renaissance experience – the growth of man's self-awareness: it was expressed by such artists and writers as Leonardo and Michelangelo, Montaigne and Shakespeare.

We can see the effects of the explosion in the splintering, the schisms and martyrdoms. William Tyndale left Oxford for Cambridge and abroad, whence he issued his epoch-making translation of the Bible into English, an inspiration to dynamic Protestantism. Thomas More, who had written the classic work of the earlier humanism in his *Utopia*, relapsed into medievalism in answer to its challenge. More had succeeded Wolsey as the first layman to be lord chancellor and had gone some way with Henry in the first steps in his new deal; when he saw the full implications of the break with Rome he went into opposition – the most eminent Englishman of the day. Everybody tried to save him from himself, but the king, by whom More had been much favoured, regarded it as a personal betrayal. In having him executed, he gave Catholicism a martyr; he struck out equally against Protestant dissidents. It was a necessity to enforce uniformity to prevent society from splitting apart; but in the struggle, Henry turned savage.

He had found a minister to help him to steer through the revolution in Church and state – Wolsey's agent, Thomas Cromwell – and they were careful to make their drastic changes at every step along with Parliament. The Reformation Parliament continued during the whole period 1529–36, so that the revolution was carried through by the will of the majority of the country, i.e. its politically-conscious governing class, notably of the progressive South and East, of

TOP *The Base Court and Gateway at Hampton Court, begun by Cardinal Wolsey, and continued by Henry* VIII, *who built the Great Hall.*
ABOVE *A modern statue of Sit Thomas More in Chelsea, London, where he lived.*

45

the towns, led by London, against the backward North. From the northern counties came the Pilgrimage of Grace, a rebellion inspired by the whole new course (1536–7) – 'Yea and that the beastliest in the whole realm,' declared Henry, referring to Yorkshire, and took personal control in the emergency. By a mixture of deception and force, he suppressed the pilgrimage and exacted savage retribution against the conservative aristocrats and churchmen who connived at it. Not a town-cat mewed at the noble and tonsured heads that rolled.

The Church had already been outmanoeuvred and subjected; independence from Rome was completed by the Act of Supremacy, which made the English Church the national one by law as it had effectively been in practice. Henry took over its headship, with Cromwell as vicar-general to put through what – from their economic and social consequences – were revolutionary moves: the Dissolution of the Monasteries and the nationalization of their properties. This affected something like one-sixth of the land over the whole country. Reform, if not the ending, of monasticism was overdue. In place of monasteries, with some thousands of unproductive monks and nuns, there came into being hundreds of country-houses and estates – many for successful professional people, rising from the middle class through

LEFT *The ruins of Fountains Abbey in Yorkshire, one of the many which were destroyed at the Dissolution of the Monasteries under Henry* VIII.
OPPOSITE BELOW *Thomas Cromwell, who organized a survey of the monasteries and was the main purveyor of the Dissolution.*
BELOW *An artist's impression of what Fountains Abbey looked like before the Dissolution.*

commerce or the law, or for younger sons of gentle families – with an immense increase in productivity, initiative and social dynamism. One sees the evidences in every county: monastic buildings transformed into secular houses, schools, put to productive uses. Some became cathedrals, colleges or parish churches, as many of the pensioned monks, accepting the new deal, remained on to staff them. Altogether, it led to an enormous reinforcement of the gentry and middle classes in English society, which they came to dominate, with tremendous consequences for the future, at home and in expansion abroad.

The diminishing of the over-large clerical element, the effective secularizing of society, the greater productivity of the land, the release of initiatives, meant an energetic upward movement which led to the dynamism and achievements of the Elizabethan age in every sphere – once the Reformation experience, with its sharp turns, reactions and changes of course, was digested. As always in revolutions there were regrettable losses. The chief of these were artistic and cultural – the 'bare, ruined choirs' Shakespeare noticed everywhere he went, the destroyed churches and smashed sculpture, the monuments and ripped-up brasses 'slave to mortal rage'. No less shocking was the dispersal and destruction of so many monastic libraries.

On the other hand, we must offset against this the concurrent change of taste with the growing impact of the Renaissance: the advanced taste of the Court was turning away from the Gothic towards the classical. Henry, himself a cultivated composer, was a patron of the arts. He gave the painter Holbein the opportunity to depict his Court as no medieval Court had ever been painted. Henry was a builder of splendid palaces: Hampton Court, Whitehall, St James's, above all the fantasy of Nonsuch. He was personally interested in shipbuilding, naval engineering and fortification. Some of the wealth (and lead) of the monasteries went into the complete fortification of the southern and eastern coasts with castles, forts and gun-posts one can still see today. He built a powerful navy. Altogether he made the island power immensely stronger than ever before, and hammered England into something like a modern state.

Wales he re-organized, and virtually annexed. The Tudors were popular in Wales, whence they came; the Welsh were proud of them, and a powerful following grouped itself round them at Court, notably Cecils and Herberts. Cromwell himself was really a Welsh Williams. From his administrative genius came the Statute of Wales (1536), organizing the small country into counties, each with one member in Parliament and with the English system of local justice. A Council of

47

Wales and the Marches supervised this from Shrewsbury and Ludlow. Wales experienced not only better order and government but a flowering of talent in many fields, both within Wales and in the wider spheres now opened to her. The Welsh were very much to the fore in the total Elizabethan achievement.

In Ireland Henry VII had asserted legislative supremacy with the famous Poynings' Law (1494), but in practice he and Henry VIII, for the first part of the latter's reign, were content to rule indirectly through the native feudatories, particularly the Kildare Fitzgeralds, who were dominant in the neighbourhood of Dublin and its English Pale. With the modernizing of the English state, this was not to endure. Advantage was taken of the rivalry between Kildare and Ormonde (who was connected with the Boleyns) to imprison Kildare in the Tower, where he died. The Reformation was formally imposed upon Ireland and accepted without much difficulty by Irish ecclesiastics and the Dublin Parliament. Lay lords had no objection to swallowing Church property; monasteries – much poorer and smaller than those in England – everywhere fell into ruin. The recovery of Ireland for Catholicism was effectively the work of the Counter-Reformation later in the century.

Ludlow Castle. Ludlow was a main centre of administration for Wales under the Tudors: the Council of the Marches held its court here.

In Scotland Henry VIII was decidedly checked and this infuriated him. His aim was the sensible one of unifying the two kingdoms, through the marriage of his boy Edward to his infant great-niece, Mary Stuart. This would have saved a great deal of trouble, but the Scots were not ready for this desirable consummation, nor were they willing to adopt the English model of the Reformation. This left the way open for a more drastic and destructive Reformation of their own later. Nor would James V meet his formidable uncle at York to discuss these matters – wisely, considering it is usually thought that Henry had a hand in the assassination of his leading opponent, Cardinal Beaton, at St Andrews.

Henry had been involved in his last war with France by the Emperor Charles V, who thereupon left him in the lurch, to grapple alone with a country of three times England's size and resources. The upshot showed what power Henry had generated through the Dissolution of the Monasteries and his naval and military programme. The Auld Alliance always precipitated a Scottish invasion in the North on behalf of France, as it did this time. Henry marched an army into

Scotland, to burn Leith and Edinburgh, but died without achieving his aim. He left the continuation of his policy to his son's uncle, Somerset, whose renewed hammering of the Scots persuaded them to send their infant queen Mary to France, and marry her to the heir there. This postponed the sensible solution, after many dramas, to 1603, when a Scots king succeeded to the English throne.

EDWARD VI's ACCESSION as a boy of nine showed that Henry VIII had indeed been belated in getting rid of Catherine of Aragon, and at once the disadvantages of a royal minority were seen. For all Henry's Catholic prejudices, his acute political sense led him to leave his son in the tutelage of Protestant advisers, under the boy's uncle, Somerset, and thus to keep in touch with the strong current the Reformation had released. Henry's last push in this direction was acted upon in the dissolution of chantries all over the country. This provided further amounts of land for secularization, but in smaller pieces, which smaller people could buy. Yet another social element was invested in the Reformation dynamic and the urge to put religion to more productive uses than praying for the dead.

Unfortunately the chantry foundations were often interwoven with education at an elementary level. Government attempts to disentangle the two elements were not always successful, and the education of the poor suffered. To offset this, expansion of grammar-school education for the growing middle classes was begun – witness many Edward VI Schools – which gathered momentum right up to the disastrous Civil War.

With a mere boy on the throne, the greedy oligarchy around him proceeded to a hand-out of titles, offices, wealth and land among themselves, to the detriment of the general interest. For it was the Crown that was identified with the interests of the nation as a whole, and the resources of the Crown were diminished by the governing class helping itself. As Queen Mary told her councillors, when she succeeded her brother on the throne: 'My father made the more part of you out of almost nothing.'

In religious usage and doctrine the Reformation impulse pushed a stage further, and this cracked the unity which the strong hand of Henry VIII had enforced. A First Prayer Book in English took the place of the Latin Mass in 1549; this produced a rebellion in Devon and Cornwall, while Norfolk was convulsed by Ket's Rebellion, largely directed against enclosures. Similar movements affected the southern Midlands. All this coincided with a growing European inflation which disturbed economic operations and the relations within society. The first half of the century was a prosperous time for the cloth trade: exports grew, commerce in general – especially with the Netherlands – expanded. In 1550–1 the market collapsed, with widespread unemployment among craftsmen, while peasants were thrown off the land, especially through the enclosures for sheep which were created in the Midlands.

These were years of much misery, dislocation and disarray. In retrospect we see new beginnings in the voyages of

Edward VI *as a child, portrait by Holbein.*

exploration, prospecting for trade southward to the Guinea coast and Brazil, northward into the White Sea to make the first oceanic contact with Russia and open up trade with her.

Edward VI died at only sixteen, but not until he had already exhibited a masterful Tudor will in attempting to change the succession to his indubitably Protestant and legitimate cousin, Lady Jane Grey. But the country insisted on the due succession of Henry VIII's children; a reaction took place in favour of his elder daughter Mary, and she came in with a deal of good will.

Unfortunately she was a reactionary who wanted to put the clock back to where it had ceased to be. More Spanish than English, she had little political sense but was a fanatical Catholic; with no idea of compromise she brought back the pope, with her cousin Cardinal Pole as legate – whose Yorkist family her father had all but obliterated – to receive the submission of the country and undo the work of the Reformation. As if this were not unpopular enough she married her Spanish cousin, Philip II; this produced a dangerous rebellion which almost overthrew her. She proceeded on her blind course, hoping against hope for a Catholic heir, while intelligent people looked to her half-sister Elizabeth – whose life she threatened – waiting in the wings.

Meanwhile the burnings at the stake were set on foot, from Henry's Archbishop Cranmer downwards, to include nearly three hundred ordinary folk, mostly from the lower classes. This turned the country's stomach against Mary; by the end she could hardly maintain her rule in London. To please Philip, England was dragged into his war with France, in which the last Continental outpost, Calais, was lost. Everything had failed with her – except, paradoxically, in Ireland, where the English Pale around Dublin was extended, and plantation undertaken in Leix and Offaly, which became 'King's County' and 'Queen's County', i.e. Philip's and Mary's.

We may regard Mary's reign, 1553–8, as a brief and tragic hiatus – the death of young Edward VI had not been expected. If he had lived, the Reformation would have proceeded on its course normally, if not without local reactions. Mary's politically extreme course, with its unprecedented burnings, turned the country against Catholicism and ensured the resumption of the Protestant dynamic at her death – in fact it made it inevitable and irresistible. All the people who were

ABOVE *Little Moreton Hall in Cheshire, a 'black and white' moated building of the Tudor period, with a typical knot garden.*
LEFT *Mary Tudor as princess; she was queen from 1553 to 1558.*
OPPOSITE ABOVE *A medal struck in 1554 to mark the temporary return of England to the Church of Rome.*
OPPOSITE BELOW *A coin showing Mary Tudor and her husband, Philip of Spain.*

advantage that she had no temptation to gain power or territory on the Continent as he had had. On the other hand, she was more interested in the oceanic voyages, which made England's fame, than Burghley was; in geographical exploration, colonization and the opportunities of planting English stock in North America. In all these matters she was personally interested, and invested in many of them.

The granddaughter of Henry VII, who was his own finance minister, the queen – along with Burghley – made the financial health of her small country a prime concern. Together they made a partnership impossible to surpass, or to circumvent. The prosperity and expansion of the age indeed rested upon the restoration of the value of the currency, after its dangerous debasement and the galloping inflation which had disrupted society in the middle decades of the century. With internal peace maintained by Elizabeth's government, society gained a sense of security such as it had never known, and this provided the ground for the confidence and achievement of the brilliantly creative Elizabethan age.

Fundamental to this was the religious settlement, which must be regarded as on the whole remarkably successful (when one compares it with the religious conflicts and wars which convulsed Europe) and which was the best that could be arrived at in the circumstances. It was not new: it was a return to the Edwardian course, which was itself a development of the Henrician Reformation. Elizabeth's archbishop – after the unfortunate demise of Archbishop Cranmer at the hands of her sister Mary – had been her mother's chaplain Matthew Parker, a moderate man. Most people, as usual, moved with the times. As sovereign, the apex of society and the arbiter of social order, the queen was naturally conservative of it and would have preferred a rather more Catholic mixture than that which she had to settle for. But having settled for it, for the rest of her long reign she stood by it as its chief guarantor – against the new Counter-Reformation Catholicism coming in with the Jesuits and seminary priests, from their exile abroad and also against the divisive Puritan minority, which aimed at carrying the Reformation further and bringing the Church under lay control.

The Elizabethan *via media* (middle way) was that best conceived to unite the nation (or divide it least), as the Puritan Revolution in the next century was to prove. The queen herself, who had an instinct for the consensus of the nation, held to this unifying concept and strove to enforce it, in religious as in other matters. When France, the Netherlands and much of Germany were paralyzed by religious conflict and division, England maintained essential unity, keeping extremists, Catholic or Puritan, out on the fringes. This achievement was an essential condition of the grand success of the age in other spheres.

From the beginning Elizabeth's government set itself to build up the real resources of the country. A search was instituted to find calamine, the ore from which bronze could be made. Whereas the country had previously had to import gunpowder and munitions, it was now rendered independent and by the end of the century had become the chief exporter of cannon in Europe. German mining experts were brought in to

ready waiting to resume that course and make the success of Elizabeth's reign were really Edwardians – Cecils, Bacons, Russells, Herberts; while, if Mary had not burned him, Cranmer, who had baptized Elizabeth, might have continued as archbishop to crown her.

ELIZABETH I was the most famous woman ruler in modern history, along with Catherine the Great of Russia (whose private life offered some contrast with that of the Virgin Queen). It is sometimes questioned what was Elizabeth I's personal contribution to the life of the age, her precise historic rôle. In the first place, hers was the ultimate decision on the issues of high politics. She usually saw eye to eye, though not always, with her chief adviser, William Cecil, Lord Burghley, her leading minister for forty years from 1558 to 1598. He was the spirit of the administration – indeed she called him her 'Spirit' – who supervised affairs in detail: particularly the economic and financial well-being and development of the country; relations with Parliament and public opinion; intercourse with foreign powers, the realm of foreign policy; and ultimately the European war which Spain unleashed as the spearhead of the Counter-Reformation, with the resources of American silver to back her overbearing power and interference in the internal affairs of other countries.

Elizabeth I took a personal hand in all these matters, if in different proportion. As a woman she was far less concerned in military matters than her father had been; it was a notable

develop mineral resources: tin in Cornwall, lead in Derbyshire and Cumberland, copper in Anglesey. An increase of coal mining and production followed in the Midlands, and most of all on Tyneside, which supplied London with sea-coal.

To increase the fisheries and shipping two compulsory fish-days a week were instituted. This notably increased the numbers of fishermen around the coasts. This encouraged the great maritime expansion, provided reserves of men for oceanic voyages, and ultimately created the navy which beat Spain.

A turning-point in relations with Spain was reached in 1569, with the return of Hawkins' third voyage from the disaster inflicted upon it by Philip II's viceroy of Mexico. This was a quasi-official voyage, in which the queen invested to sound out the possibilities of England sharing with her Spanish ally in the trade of the Caribbean. The Spanish colonists needed the trade, especially the slaves from Africa which had been imported from as early as 1502: Hawkins was merely attempting to share in an existing trade. His attempt was treacherously overthrown, causing heavy loss to himself and his backers, including the queen. Scores of English seamen were condemned to the prisons of the Spanish Inquisition; Hawkins' second in command, Robert Barret, was burnt in the market place at Seville. A young captain who escaped the tragedy was Francis Drake: for the rest of his life he worked his revenge, to become a name to conjure with – in Spain, too, where an epic, *La Dragontea*, was devoted to his fabulous career.

In this decisive year 1569 Spanish treasure-ships were driven in to the ports of Plymouth and Fowey by stress of weather and Huguenot privateers. They carried the money supplies for Alba's army which was engaged in suppressing the Netherlands' resistance to Spanish rule. The money had been borrowed from Genoese bankers. Elizabeth felt impelled to borrow it; it was ultimately repaid; but meanwhile Alba's troops mutinied for want of pay – and Spain never succeeded in re-establishing her hold in the Netherlands. Relations with Spain had been friendly during the first half of the century; they now turned to hostility 'beyond the line' – i.e. in the New World, where neither Elizabeth nor her seamen ever accepted the Spanish claim to monopoly and exclusion of others – and to cold war in Europe, leading eventually to the long open war of 1585–1604.

This crisis in foreign relations coincided with the prime internal crisis of the reign in the years 1569–72.

Mary Queen of Scots, Henry VII's great-granddaughter, had taken refuge in England from her disasters in Scotland – perhaps the greatest of her many mistakes. More French than Scottish, she was a catspaw of French policy and, as queen briefly in France, had put forward her claim to the English throne. Her mother, Mary of Guise, had ruled Scotland with French interests at heart, using French troops. The first success of Elizabeth's government was their expulsion from Scotland, after a short campaign, by the Treaty of Edinburgh (1560). On her return to Scotland Mary Stuart strengthened

The Armada Portrait of Queen Elizabeth I, with the Spanish Armada in the background.

her challenge to the English succession by marrying Henry, Lord Darnley, another of Henry VII's great-grandchildren. The marriage produced the infant James (ultimately to succeed to Elizabeth's throne), but foundered in Darnley's murder, by Mary's connivance. English interests naturally demanded the support of her opponents – to Elizabeth's distaste ; but Mary Stuart constituted a dilemma from which the English queen could never free herself.

Driven out of Scotland, Mary became the 'second person' – such as Elizabeth had been to her half-sister Mary Tudor – to whom the opposition and all discontented elements looked for an alternative. Elizabeth had experienced the danger of this eminence in her own person, when Mary Tudor sent her to the Tower of London and wished to execute her. Elizabeth had no intention of marrying, though pressed to it again and again by Parliament. Her cousin, the Duke of Norfolk, proposed to solve the problem of the succession by marrying Mary Stuart. Elizabeth said that within a month of such a marriage she would be inside the Tower again.

In 1569 the two leading northern earls, Northumberland and Westmorland, with a number of Catholic gentry, broke into rebellion. The rising was put down with much severity – Elizabeth's cousin, Lord Hunsdon (later, as lord chamberlain, a patron of Shakespeare's Company), distinguished himself in the field. In 1570 Pope Pius V made the grievous mistake of excommunicating the queen of England and absolving her subjects from their allegiance. This meant an agonizing decision for those who chose to remain Catholic ; the majority remained loyal, but the exiles, from whom seminary priests and Jesuits were recruited to re-convert the country, were propelled into the position of traitors, the Catholic minority being divided on the issue.

Norfolk, an incompetent conspirator, was caught red-handed in collusion with the papal agent, Ridolfi, and broke his pledged word to Elizabeth not to pursue the plot to marry Mary. Among the conservative nobility and even on the Privy Council Norfolk had a party with him. Only the staunch and undeviating stand of Elizabeth and Cecil together enabled them to surmount the challenges from so many quarters and combat so complex and long-drawn-out a crisis, internal and

Den VIII february werde onthalst Maria Stuart Schots Coninginne's terwende Roomsch Catholyck Hebbende gesocht veel onrust aen te richten Haer selven meer ter te maecken van Engelant dwelck Haer wanden Eael ofte parlement belamelyck swerde vertoont, Anno 1587.

Metren XIII fol. XIII en XIIII. v

external. But they had the support of Parliament, representing the gentry and middle classes over the country.

Parliament demanded the execution of both Mary Stuart and Norfolk, who admitted his treason. After long hesitation Elizabeth yielded Norfolk, to spare a queen's life in Mary Stuart: we need not think that it was a case of preferring a cousin on her father's side to a cousin on her mother's (she preferred the latter). The decision was a political one. The resolution of the crisis was marked by the elevation of Cecil to the peerage as Lord Burghley. The queen wanted to make him an earl: the politic Cecil would accept only the lowest step in the peerage. Henceforth the new deal would go forward unchallenged.

IN THE 1570S THE VOYAGES were resumed, to places further afield; improvements in shipbuilding and navigational instruments, in which practical seamen and shipwrights took a hand as well as cosmographical experts and mapmakers, extended the range of exploration. The English were concerned to find a way of their own to the riches of Far

OPPOSITE *The execution of Mary Queen of Scots in 1587, in Fotheringay Castle.*
ABOVE *William Cecil, Lord Burghley, on a mule, riding in his garden.*

Eastern trade, if possible by the discovery of a passage by the North-West or the North-East.

Three voyages under Frobisher – in the second of which the queen invested – explored the strait between Labrador and Greenland. Other voyages coasted Hudson's Bay. The fine navigator John Davis penetrated as far north as 83°N into Davis Strait. He was eventually killed in an affray with pirates in Far Eastern seas off Singapore. Will Adams ultimately reached the coast of Japan, where he was taken into favour by the Shogun but regarded as too valuable an acquisition to be allowed to return. He was profitably employed in improving Japanese shipbuilding and piloting voyages to Siam, Cochin China and the Loo Choo Islands. Having acquired a Japanese wife and family he died in the odour of approbation and prosperity, leaving a provision for his English family at home; his tomb still exists on the hill overlooking the harbour of Yokusaka.

Sir Richard Grenville planned a voyage into the Pacific to search for the unknown southern continent, Terra Australis, but it was given to Francis Drake to make the voyage, with the queen as prime investor. It paid some 1400 per cent, through the capture of a treasure ship by which Drake recouped his and Hawkins' losses in the 1560s. The voyage across the Pacific and round the world made a tremendous sensation, for it was the first circumnavigation from which the commander returned safe and sound, with many new additions to geographical and botanical knowledge. In the course of it Drake took possession of Northern California under the name of New Albion, and made an agreement with the Sultan of Ternate for the English to enter the valuable spice trade. Most of the proceeds of the voyage went on subsidizing the Dutch resistance to Spain in the Netherlands; some went into founding the Levant Company, which promoted trade with the Near East through the Mediterranean. From that, in 1600, sprang the East India Company, out of which developed Britain's trading empire in the Far East in competition with the Dutch, and eventually British rule in India.

The first oceanic openings to Russia via the White Sea and Archangel had been made by the Edwardians. These were now followed up regularly by the Muscovy Company; trading and diplomatic exchanges were full and frequent. Sir Anthony Jenkinson won the confidence of the Tsar Ivan the Terrible, who allowed him to push trade as far as the Caspian Sea. Doctors as well as traders were sent to Russia; Ivan affected generous sentiments towards the Virgin Queen, who reciprocated with presents and advice. In consequence the Kremlin today possesses the finest collection of Elizabethan silver gathered in one place, and the only English coach of the time to survive. The Elizabethan accounts of sixteenth-century Russia, with the documentation of the voyages, offer a prime source for its history.

In the 1580s attention came to be concentrated on the question of English settlement in North America, since Spain was in occupation of Central and South America. Advocacy of colonization fell to the remarkable geographer, Richard Hakluyt, known to us today for his collecting and editing *The Principal Navigations, Voyages and Discoveries of the English*

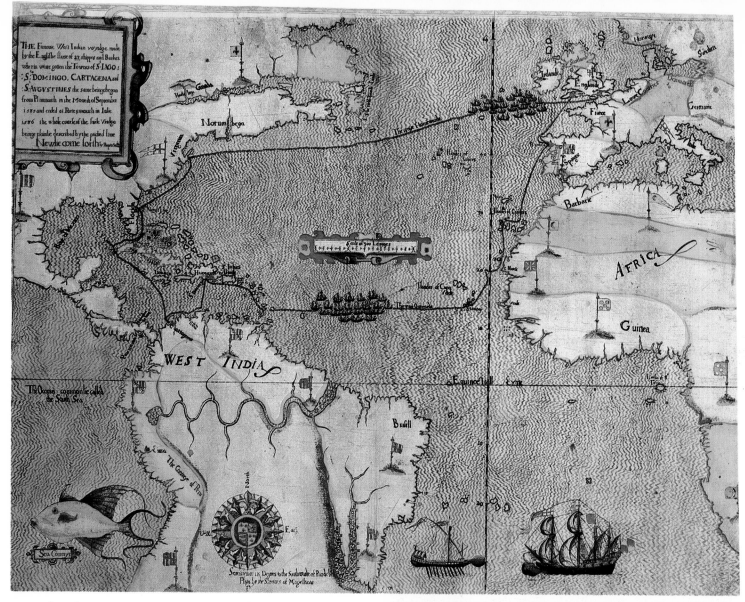

Nation, a classic or, even more, an epic of its kind. He acted as adviser to many of the commanders, such as Sir Humphry Gilbert, a principal advocate of American settlement, who took possession of Newfoundland in 1583. When he was drowned on his way home, his half-brother, Sir Walter Ralegh, took up the campaign, with the backing of the queen, who lent the name of Virginia to the promised English sphere of North America, between the French St Lawrence and Spanish Florida.

In 1585 Ralegh's first colony was planted on Roanoke, the coast of North Carolina. Though it lasted no more than a year, all the rest flowed from the experience garnered then: knowledge of the conditions of life, climate, natural products, American Indians, potentialities for the future. This was gathered into a book by Thomas Hariot, a leading scientist, algebraist and anthropologist; maps and depictions of the scene were made by John White, first of English water-colourists. Further attempts to make settlement were frustrated by the outbreak of war with Spain. It was not until

ABOVE *A map of Francis Drake's Caribbean campaign, 1585–6.*
RIGHT *Sir Francis Drake, who sailed round the world in 1557. He was knighted by Queen Elizabeth on board his ship, the* Golden Hind.
OPPOSITE *This Indian cotton wall-hanging depicts the English in India in the Elizabethan age.*

LEFT *In the 1580s English settlers began to colonize Virginia (named for Elizabeth, the Virgin Queen). One of them was the artist John White, who painted many water-colours of the native Indians, including this one showing Indians fishing.*
BELOW *Exploration during Elizabeth's reign reached many continents. This drawing shows Englishmen and Eskimos in a skirmish.*

peace was made in 1604 that the first permanent colony was established at Jamestown in 1607 – it might more appropriately have been named for Elizabeth I, who had given so much more active support – and further small settlements shortly followed in North Virginia, which was to become New England.

INTERNAL DEVELOPMENT AND EXPANSION were hardly less marked than external. The religious conflicts let loose in the Netherlands and Northern France brought numbers of desirable immigrants, with their superior skills and their capital, mainly Flemish and French Protestants. They introduced the new draperies, finer cloth manufactures, into East Anglia and Kent; canvas, glass, and paper making; the iron industry of the Weald of Kent and Sussex throve with their help; hops were introduced from Flanders. Useful immigrants crowded into London, bringing more sophisticated trades and accomplishments: printers, jewellers, doctors, painters, sculptors, musicians. Place was allotted them in the churches, and sometimes former monastic churches were handed over to them, like Austin Friars to the Dutch, or a chapel in Canterbury cathedral to the French Huguenots. These contributions to the creative amalgam of Elizabethan society are still witnessed by the names of writers and artists: Dekker and Deloney; Grimald, Bryskett, Florio, the Ferraboscos.

From the beginning the Elizabethans, led by a brilliant and sparkling young queen, meant a new deal, recovery and consolidation after the miseries of mid-century, and exemplified humane 'lenity', the watchword of which they were proud. This is again witnessed, as Sir George Clark writes, by 'the great codifying Statute of Artificers [craftsmen] or Apprentices ... the most comprehensive legislative plan for the economic life of a country that any European government had made.' It co-ordinated law and administration dealing with employment in the towns, the scarcity of agricultural workers, and provided controls for wages and prices – tasks so familiar to twentieth-century governments.

Sixteenth-century circumstances were simpler and more personal; social responsibility rested in the hands of the gentry

During Elizabeth's reign the stocks, shown here, were a common form of punishment.

all over the country, in the upper middle class in the towns, and in the Church, particularly in parish administration. An immense increase in secular philanthropy was visible, in the foundation of schools, hospitals and almshouses for the poor and aged. For the able-bodied who would not work but preferred to live at the expense of others, or took to crime, Elizabethan society had no sympathy. The struggle for survival was tough; everywhere there was disease, recurrent plague and occasional famine, a high rate of reproduction and infant mortality. Everywhere death was familiar; there were no illusions about the human condition.

By the end of the century twenty years of war had produced much dislocation, unemployment and want. A codification of the Poor Law (1598–1601) provided as best society could for those genuinely in want, and dealt severely with malingerers and parasites on others. A considerable literature regarding criminals, thieves, cutpurses, tricksters, and such gay company vividly describes this fringe of society, particularly in London.

PARLIAMENT REPRESENTED THE COUNTRY as a whole, or at least its politically conscious governing classes. The increasing power, social weight and numbers of the gentry led them to demand an increasing number of seats in the Commons, while they largely took over the representation of the boroughs. The executive remained, as it always had been, the Crown, i.e. the monarch aided by the Privy Council formed of its leading and ablest advisers, with its secretariat and adjunct bodies through which it operated – already an embryo civil service. London, under its lord mayor and corporation, with its twelve chief livery companies, its guilds and parochial administration, was practically self-governing. With the influx from the country and from abroad it grew rapidly to a population of some 220,000 by 1600. From the decline of Antwerp, in the conflict raging in the Netherlands, London largely profited, commercially, financially and culturally.

Parliaments were called at national junctures and crises, to consult the opinion of the country and its localities – counties and towns – and to provide the money by taxation for the government's purposes. Thus the Elizabethan religious settlement was agreed by Parliament, as Henry VIII's Reformation had been. Further Parliaments gave the government support and resolved the crisis of 1571–2; and they were called on more frequently from 1584 to provide money for the war with Spain. Careful finance had built up a reserve to meet the necessities of war when it came; but it was nothing like enough to meet the strain. The resources of the Crown itself were called upon, and large sales of remaining Church land were made. Though the governing class prospered, the resources of the Crown diminished: this was to have revolutionary consequences in the next century.

The open war with Spain was entered upon after grave consideration, as the consequence of the Treaty of Greenwich, in 1585, with the Dutch. Their historic leader, William the Silent, had been assassinated in 1584, as other Protestant leaders had been in France and Scotland; the Netherlands were in imminent danger of becoming wholly subjugated to

The defeat of the Spanish Armada, in 1588.

Spanish power. This constituted an obvious threat to England's security, which could be countered only by entering openly into war. The government published an appeal to European opinion, declaring that its object was in no sense territorial acquisition but the safeguarding of the liberties of the Netherlands – to which an army was dispatched under Leicester.

England was militarily unprepared, as so often in its later history, but the navy was at its highest pitch of efficiency. When Philip II opted for the great gamble of the Armada of 1588 (he was hoping for support within England), the small country was keyed up to resist invasion, musters drilled and beacons organized in every county. The week-long contest as the Armada progressed slowly up Channel in the stormy summer of 1588 was something unprecedented in naval warfare – a contest between two ocean-going fleets in terms of manoeuvering and gunnery, instead of the previous practice of grappling and boarding, which had merely been an extension of land warfare. In a series of actions the Armada was beaten off and demoralized before the final action off Calais, whence it fled into the North Sea, to make its way home round the coasts of Scotland and Ireland. Altogether, only one-third of its complement of ships and men ever got back.

In the next year, 1589, the English reply – combined naval and military operations against Lisbon – was a fiasco, though it sustained few losses. Two further armadas were sent against England in 1596 and 1597, but only reached the western approaches, to suffer severe losses from storms. Meanwhile, the English war effort achieved spectacular success with the capture of Cadiz in 1596.

Military operations spread to the Continent. From early on individual contingents joined the Dutch resistance to Spain; an army under Leicester was sent to their support, and large loans advanced. As the years wore on amateur soldiers became professional; the English learned modern warfare from their enemies and produced able generals in the de Veres. The Dutch state would not have come into being but for English help. Similarly the Protestant cause of Henry of Navarre, who was to become Henry IV of France, desperately needed aid; forces were sent to Normandy and Brittany, along with subsidies. It is astonishing what the growing resources of the small country achieved.

The chief strain upon them was Ireland. Ireland was more important strategically to England than the Netherlands were to Spain. No English government could afford to leave its country exposed to an enemy on that flank. Elizabethan policy in Ireland wavered to and fro, government mostly preferring to leave the English interests of the Pale around Dublin and friendly feudatories, like the Ormond clan, to manage for themselves. Everywhere around the rim of North-Western Europe the more concentrated nation states were expanding into the fragmented Celtic world – from the Scottish

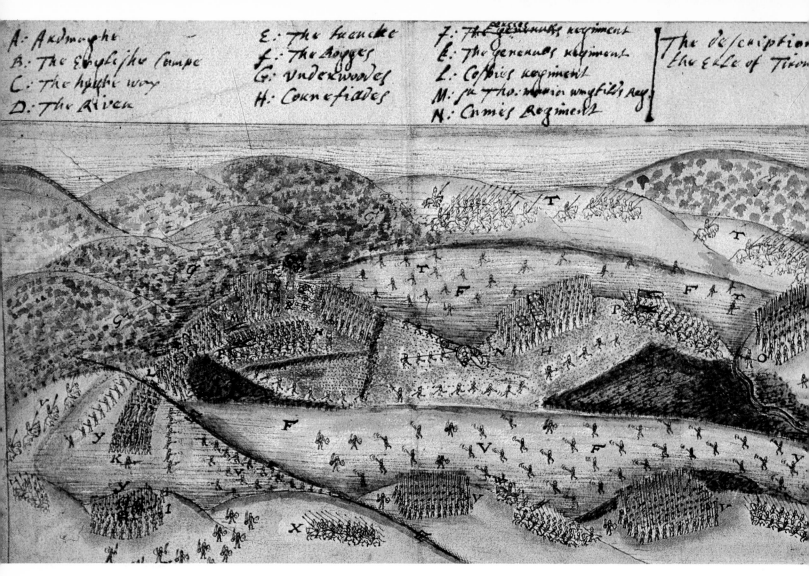

Highlands and the Isles to Ireland, Wales and Cornwall, as also in Brittany.

Ulster had remained the least penetrated and irreducible of the Irish princedoms. The last O'Neill attempted from there to build up a wider resistance movement, penetrating into Munster to join up with a Spanish force sent in aid. This move was defeated, but wearing down resistance took some years and exhausted the Crown's revenues. The subjugation of Ireland was a strategic necessity, but not an enterprise of profit; it was the grave of reputations, and of many men, good and bad, who lost their lives in it.

EXPANSION, WHICH WAS THE ORDER OF THE DAY and the essence of the time, has left permanent marks in literature and art, in the realm of the intellect and even dawning science. The English language itself underwent an immense expansion along with the experiences of those who spoke it. The vocabulary of Shakespeare was twice that of the average educated person today. Sir Philip Sidney – whose father had been an ardent expansionist and able colonial administrator in Ireland – formed the conception of creating a literature which could compare with that of Italy. He set the models for this in both verse and prose, and forwarded the campaign by his patronage. This was carried further by the prime poet of the age, Spenser, and his friend Ralegh. Spenser's *Faerie Queene* embodies the chivalrous and ethical ideals of the age

in a work half romance and half epic, as Ralegh's prose works, particularly his monumental *History of the World*, express its combination of realism with high imaginativeness.

Above all, Elizabethan drama and music speak to us today. This was the golden age of English music; all the world sang or played, while the summits were occupied by such spirits as Byrd, Shakespearean in grandeur and depth, the haunting airs of Dowland, the obsessive, tormented mastery of the keyboard of John Bull, a whole company of madrigalists and composers of music, secular and sacred.

The drama was a national activity, which expressed the unity of the nation under the pressure of war and the confidence engendered by its tumultuous experiences. It is enough to cite the name of Shakespeare. A comparable spirit, of a more intellectual cast, was Francis Bacon, who set a new model in prose with his *Essays*, made equal contributions in law and natural philosophy, and pointed the directions in which science was to develop in succeeding centuries.

In the plastic arts England was yet to learn from the Latin countries, though the Elizabethans characteristically achieved a prolific development in portraiture. Still more, in architecture – with such creations as Hardwick Hall, Longleat and Wollaton, Burghley and Theobalds, Holdenby and Hatfield House – they created a style expressive of the fantasy and soaring imagination of the age.

ABOVE *A map of an Irish campaign in Elizabethan times.*
OPPOSITE *A detail from the funeral procession of Elizabeth* I.

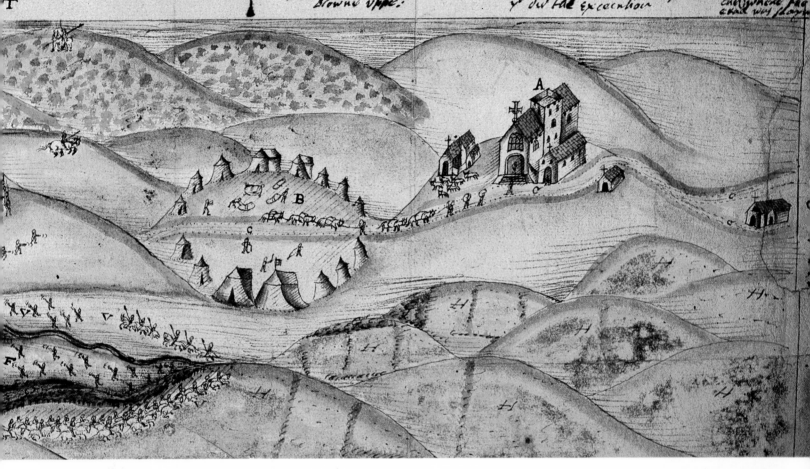

the Army wch was defeated by ... of August 1598

P. Billings Reg:
Q. Troupes of Horse
Q. Artillerie
R. 4. Barrels of Powder Blowne vppe.

S. the fallen Bogges
T. Odonnells horse and foote
V. Tirones horse and foote
X. the Traytors and horse yt did the execution

Y. The Hill ... house where execution
Z. the pace the ... to the ... where ... was slayne

The Chariott drawne by foure Horses vpon which Charret stood the Coffin couered wth purple Veluett and vpon that the representation. The Canapy borne by six Knights.

Chapter 4

Revolution and Reaction

JAMES I, WHO REIGNED FROM 1603 TO 1625, was no fool, as he has sometimes been represented; he was in fact a clever man, well educated, with an international outlook. After his difficult and some-times dangerous early years, during which he was kept in Stirling Castle for safety, he had made a success of his rule in Scotland; and, as he reminded Parliament, he brought to England the dowry of a kingdom. The union of the two kingdoms had been the objective of English policy for centuries, and this was the best way in which it could have come about to the satisfaction of both sides. Great Britain – the new name was James's own characteristic choice – now became the foremost Protestant power in Europe.

Perhaps naturally, with the extraordinary mixture of stocks from which he was descended – Scottish Stuarts, Welsh Tudors, French Guises and Valois – James never hit it off with his English subjects, as Elizabeth I had done. And James was understandably jealous of the fame of his great predecessor, as all his Stuart descendants were. He could emulate neither her dignity, nor her style – he was, in fact, curiously undignified and much too friendly for a sovereign. Nor did his subjects appreciate his lofty ambitions. In religious matters he was genuinely ecumenical: he desired a more Christian spirit among the quarrelling Protestant sects, and he wished for better relations with Rome and Catholicism abroad and at home. He considered the English Church to offer prospects of a genuine middle way. Similarly, he ardently desired peace in Europe, a drawing together of Catholic and Protestant powers. No soldier, and with a dislike for military men, James's greatest ambition was to be thought of as a peace-maker.

This did not render him popular. But it is the clue to his prolonged and over-optimistic negotiations with Spain for a marriage (with a handsome dowry) for his elder son, Prince Henry, over which he drew a blank after years of effort. On

OPPOSITE *A painting of Charles I made during his trial in January 1649 by Edward Bower.*
ABOVE *A later impression of Civil War soldiers.*

the other side, he married his daughter Elizabeth to the German Protestant Prince Frederick (from whom the present Hanoverian line in Britain descends). Frederick, by accepting the crown of Bohemia, against the will of Habsburgs and Catholic Europe, as also his father-in-law's advice, pre-cipitated the Thirty Years' War in Europe. He was expelled from Bohemia by the new emperor, Ferdinand II, and the Catholic princes of Germany, while a Spanish army overran his German territory. His wife became 'the Winter Queen' celebrated by the Caroline poets, for she was a brave, spirited woman, who had much to put up with. She bore a fine family of sons to fight for Charles I in the Civil War.

Thus James died in the end a disappointed man, defeated in his hopes. But he managed to give the country a longer spell of peace than it had enjoyed since Henry VII, during which it went ahead and prospered as never before. One still sees the evidences in the great Jacobean mansions all over the country, such as Hatfield House and Audley End, built by his ministers.

A showdown with Sir Walter Ralegh – one of the few men James actively disliked (the dislike was returned) – announced that the Elizabethan age, with its career of warfare, armadas and glory, was indeed over. Ralegh who, already despairing of favour, foolishly involved himself in a plot to displace James, was condemned to death but kept in the Tower, where he wrote his great *History of the World*. Let out in 1617 for a voyage to Guiana, by which he hoped to repeat the exploits of the Elizabethans, he turned to plundering the Spaniards, who demanded his execution under the old suspended sentence. In life a much-hated man, his execution made him a hero – and one more notch in the unpopularity of the Stuarts.

A positive upshot of all the Elizabethan effort, upon peace with Spain in 1604, was the founding of Jamestown in Virginia in 1607. The second charter of 1609 turned this into a national effort; hundreds of people put their names down as 'venturers', from the top to (almost) the bottom of society. People felt that it was a challenge to the nation to plant English stock in North America, as the Spaniards had planted theirs in Central and South America; that the future of the country was at stake – as indeed it was. The wreck upon

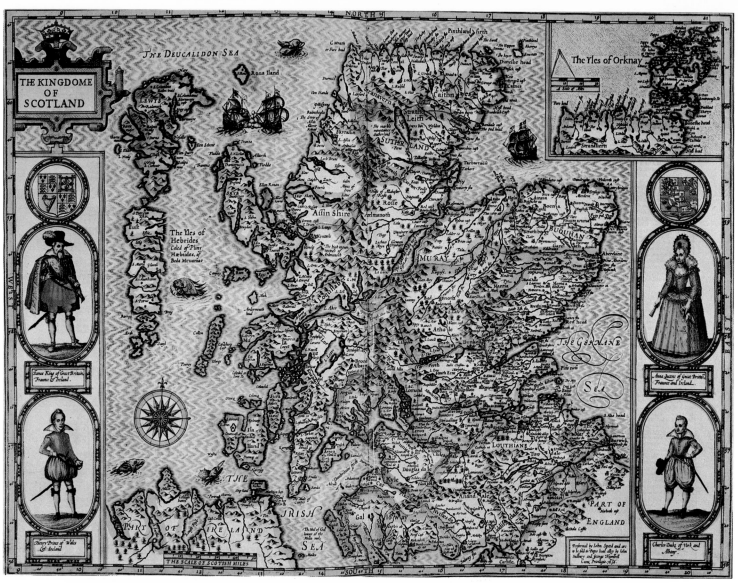

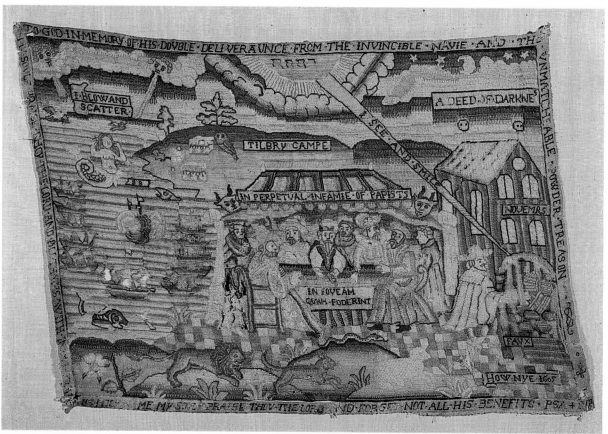

Bermuda of the flagship carrying colonists, inspired Shakespeare's *The Tempest*. His former patron, Southampton, took an active interest in the colony as treasurer of the Virginia Company, 1620–4. The colony had acute difficulties in surviving – this was the 'starving time' – and there was a fierce Indian massacre in 1622. Thousands died in the early years, and few venturers ever saw their money back; but colonization henceforth went forward, never faltering, and shortly similar efforts followed upon the coast which was to become New England.

A permanent achievement of James's wish to favour the Puritans – he was himself a Calvinist in theology, which Elizabeth, though a protestant queen, had never been – was the Authorized Translation of the Bible into English, a monument to Elizabethan English. It was to have historic consequences, not all of them favourable, for the future of religion in Britain. The king's hopes of an understanding with the Catholics (his wife, Anne of Denmark, became a secret convert) were exploded by the Gunpowder Plot of 1605. A band of young Catholic fanatics engaged themselves to blow up king, royal family and Parliament at its state opening. Guy Fawkes was caught red-handed with a heavy store of gunpowder ready for the purpose. This set back the hopes of the Catholics for toleration for a century; it left a legacy of suspicion and hatred which added further fuel to the fires of religious dissension so typical of the time.

Meanwhile James had little success with his Parliaments, with which he was not in tune either by temper or sympathy. He told the Spanish ambassador that on coming to the country he found the institution in existence, by favour of his ancestors, and that there was nothing he could do about it. As he saw it the function of the Commons was to supply money when needed for the exceptional purposes of government, but it was the business of the government to govern. Initiative and executive authority lay with the king, who created his ministers; policy was not Parliament's business.

A tradition of opposition had been growing up in the Commons, particularly from Puritan-minded gentry who wanted to push the Reformation further and bring the Church under their control. Both monarchs and the Church resisted this growing tendency, and this later precipitated the Civil War. Now the Commons were prepared to push their claims further, and challenge the prerogatives of the Crown. The Commons insisted on shielding MPs from arrest under due operation of the law, and controlling their own membership.

Trade was increasing and prices were rising, for James's reign was a period of economic prosperity till towards the end. The government's right to increase customs duties, with a new Book of Rates, was challenged. More important, prolonged negotiations to put the Crown's revenue on a settled basis, the Great Contract, which might have averted the Civil War, failed. The proposal was to end the Crown's antiquated and uncertain feudal calls for money in return for a regular revenue from Parliament. Into this project the far-sighted Robert Cecil, now Lord Salisbury, entered with hope. He had deserved well of the country for the skill with which he had engineered James's smooth accession, bridged the transition, directed the peace with Spain and effectively run the country. But neither king nor Parliament would come to terms, and an historic opportunity was lost.

Until his death in 1612 Salisbury controlled the administration and kept things on a steady course. After that they deteriorated, and troubles accumulated. The Dutch would hardly have won their independence from Spain in the first half of the century if it had not been for English support, in men and money. Now they were the first commercial and maritime power in Europe, taking far the larger share of the herring fishery off the long east coast of Britain. In the East Indies they were determined to exert their monopoly of the rich spice trade of the Moluccas, so profitable to the magnificent Dutch East India Company, and to keep the English out. In 1623 occurred the 'Massacre at Amboyna': the Dutch rooted out a small English settlement in the Moluccas, tortured and executed ten Englishmen and their following.

An early 17th-century drawing of Westminster Hall with the Courts in session. The judges are sitting under the canopies, and the lawyers can be identified by their long gowns with wide sleeves.

OPPOSITE ABOVE *A map of Scotland, 1610. The borders are decorated with portraits of James I and his family.*
OPPOSITE BELOW *A prayer-book cushion worked to commemorate* LEFT *the defeat of the Armada in 1588, and* RIGHT *the discovery of Guy Fawkes's Gunpowder Plot in 1605.*

The English were thus brutally warned off; the English East India Company was to keep to the mainland of India – with historic results for the future of that country. Amboyna generated bitter feelings for a generation – until Cromwell made the Dutch pay handsome compensation for it, after the successful First Dutch War.

The government's failures were made worse by trouble from Parliament, for after Salisbury's death it lost cohesion. Opposition was given intellectual leadership by an indefatigable lawyer of equal learning and avarice, Sir Edward Coke (he built up an estate of nearly sixty manors), who regularly attacked the Church and its judicial courts, and was an ardent proponent of common law. With his out-of-date learning in the law he constructed a view of the past – partly mythical, still more propagandist – which questioned (wrongly) the prerogatives of the Crown, putting forward Magna Carta as the true charter of English liberties. This was widely believed, as it accorded with many people's interests, and had growing influence.

The Parliament of 1621 was bent on trouble. It took the initiative in an attack on monopolies, by which the Crown raised some money, and passed an Act which laid down the principles that still rule today, allowing monopoly in the case of new inventions, for example. It impeached a harmless monopolist, Sir Giles Mompesson, and went over to the attack on the most exalted minister, Francis Bacon – Coke's great rival, at last lord chancellor. Coke, mean-spirited as always, had his revenge: Bacon was ruined, for accepting bribes and presents on too large a scale, principally through his factotum, John Churchill, ancestor of the famous Churchills.

In his last years James lost his grip on affairs. His place was taken, disastrously, by the younger generation in the form of his favourite, the glamorous George Villiers, whom he made duke of Buckingham, and Prince Charles, heir to the throne since his elder brother's death. They went against the old king's better judgment in their journey to Madrid to try to clinch the marriage with the Spanish Infanta. This romantic escapade ended, of course, in fiasco. No marriage was to be had: a Spanish Infanta would never marry a non-Catholic.

The disillusioned romantics returned humiliated to push for war with Spain, and that was a popular move with Parliament, which voted a large sum for the purpose. The young men plumped for a French marriage for Prince Charles with Henrietta Maria, then fifteen, sister of Louis XIII, in return for naval help to reduce the Protestant stronghold of La Rochelle. This was not popular.

In the midst of these preparations, in March 1625, James died. His disappearance made no difference to the conduct of affairs, which for some time had been in the hands of the two inexperienced young men. The opposition did not hesitate to say – and Milton was to repeat it – that they had poisoned the failing king, when their fault was that all three had been only too fond of each other. Charles I (reigned 1625–49) and Buckingham paid bitterly for their inexperience. After so long a peace the expedition they sent to attack Cadiz in 1625 was ill-prepared and worse led; it was an utter failure, and

George Villiers, 1st Duke of Buckingham, the influential favourite of both James I and Charles I.

thousands died of disease. Charles met his first Parliament in these discordant circumstances. All the help they would give was to impeach Buckingham, who was saved by the dissolution of Parliament.

Next year Great Britain found itself in the almost impossible situation of a war with both Spain and France (mainly through difficulties over the marriage treaty). Buckingham now reversed himself to lead an expedition to relieve La Rochelle – another fiasco followed by the death of troops through spreading disease.

Parliament's anger mounted. For a popular cause it was prepared to grant money – but it demanded in return the Petition of Right, by which Charles conceded to all its demands: no forced loans, no billeting of soldiers and sailors, no martial law except within an army in wartime, no arbitrary imprisonment without cause shown. This was an important step in the acquisition of constitutional liberties.

At Portsmouth, where he was preparing yet another expedition to retrieve honour, Buckingham was assassinated, and the repressed and introvert king seems to have nursed a residual resentment against the English for this murder.

The architect and designer Inigo Jones introduced the complete classical style from Italy into England. The Queen's house at Greenwich exhibits the perfection of his style.

Parliament now turned its attention to harassing his religious preferences and chosen ministers, thus assuming the right to dictate beliefs. The lead was taken by an impetuous Cornishman, Sir John Eliot, with impassioned oratory. He went beyond the bounds in having the speaker held down while a resolution was put against the king's High Church Anglicanism; any man contravening it was 'an enemy to this kingdom and commonwealth'.

It was an illegal act, portending the conflict that brought on civil war. Eliot was sent to the Tower, where he would never capitulate and, a consumptive, died three years later. The king refused the request to bring his body home to Cornwall: 'Let Sir John Eliot be buried in the parish where he died.' Thus Parliament obtained its first martyr in the struggle for liberty or, rather, for power. For his part the king had had enough of parliaments – his reign had had an ominous beginning – and did not summon another until forced to by events ten years later.

THE NEXT DECADE was one of peace and prosperity, and civilized progress under the auspices of a cultivated king and Court, while the Thirty Years' War raged on the Continent and ravaged Germany. In the late nineteenth century,

Bismarck said that the scars from this war could still be seen in his time: the Germans were left behind in the race. In England persecution for witchcraft ceased – to be resumed by the Puritans of the Civil War, as it was continued by their allies in New England. Charles and Archbishop Laud would have none of it.

The genius of the architect Inigo Jones brought back from Italy the full inspiration of the artistic Renaissance, expressed in the Queen's House at Greenwich and the Banqueting House at Whitehall – from a window of which the king was to step out to his execution in 1649. Jones prepared a design which would have given Whitehall a palace comparable to the Louvre or the Escorial. He and the dramatist and poet Ben Jonson collaborated in the splendid Court masques, which enabled Charles to forget the facts of politics for a time in a fantasy world remote from hard realities. He formed the most splendid collection of pictures and works of art ever assembled in England – to be dispersed by the Puritans of the Commonwealth. (One sees his Titians and Mantegnas today in the Louvre and the Prado.) He gave his patronage to Van

Van Dyck's painting of the Earl of Pembroke and his family, at Wilton House. Van Dyck was court painter under Charles I and executed many portraits of the king and his family.

Dyck, in whose paintings one sees that destroyed world of elegance and distinction portrayed, and Rubens produced fine paintings for him.

Charles was a complete contrast to his father: he was, above all, refined, but he had less political sense. He recruited to his service a remarkable administrator, Wentworth, better known as the earl of Strafford, though he did not make full use of his talents at the centre of government until too late. He kept him in his native North, as president of the council, to administer the region from its capital at York. Then he gave Strafford the most difficult assignment of all – to govern Ireland. There he ruthlessly enforced order, making enemies on every hand, built up an army, some economic progress made.

Upon the Flight of the Northern Earls – the absconding of the heads of the tribes of O'Neill and O'Donnell to Rome – James I had tried to fill the gap by planting Scottish colonists in Ulster. This added a further element of religious dissension, in the form of the Scottish Presbyterians, to the conflict between the Catholic Irish and the Protestants of the Pale.

Charles had complete confidence in the other great servant of the Crown, Archbishop Laud – and, for all Laud's eminent qualities, this was a mistake James I would not have made. Laud's High Anglicanism aroused the fury of the Puritans, and he attracted enemies on every hand. He was the son of a Reading clothier, who had risen entirely by his own abilities – and this was a reason for the aristocratic jealousy of him when he came to be a power in the state as well as the Church. He had an admirable record at Oxford, where he had new buildings erected at St John's College, became Chancellor of

the university and eventually the greatest benefactor it has ever had. His gifts of Oriental manuscripts to the Bodleian library made Oxford the centre for these studies for the next century. From the University Press, which Laud nursed, came the leading works in this field. His administrative energy showed itself in his drafting a constitution for the university which ruled it up to the Victorian age.

Transferred to leadership in the Church, he dedicated himself to repairing some of the damage done by the Reformation, restoring churches, recovering misappropriated tithes where possible, aiming at order and decency in ritual, encouraging music and the arts. In these aims he was

ABOVE RIGHT *The ceiling of the Banqueting House at Whitehall painted by Rubens in Antwerp. The centre panel is* The Apotheosis of James I.
RIGHT *Charles I dining in public at Whitehall Palace.*

completely at one with the cultivated king, though he was hampered by the unwise support of the queen for Catholicism. Charles and Laud were convinced Anglicans, with a firm philosophic outlook. They wished to impose external order, not to pry into people's consciences and beliefs, as the Puritans did; intellectually, Laud's Anglicanism was more tolerant. His social sympathies were with the poor – and this further antagonised the upper classes.

These currents ran together to make him a prime target for boundless criticism and abuse; his betrayers, such as the odious lawyer Prynne, were very properly punished. But this made them martyrs. Rather than subscribe to uniformity, thousands left the country in the 1630s to form the nucleus of New England – and set an example to the world.

When Laud accompanied the king to his second coronation in Scotland, he was shocked at the devastation the Reformation had wrought in cathedrals and churches there. He encouraged the production of a Scottish Prayer Book, in line with the English liturgy. Its first reading in Edinburgh produced an outburst of mob hysteria, which gathered force across the nation. The governing class fell in with it out of self-interest, and signed a National Covenant; an army was recruited, and the king, isolated, was taken by surprise.

It took him some time to realize that he had a revolution on his hands, and he had not the wherewithal, money, arms or popular support to deal with it. The forces he took up to the Border in 1639 and again in 1640 were quite inadequate. The Scots had a disciplined fanatical army, which invaded the North of England and camped there until paid to go away. This necessitated the calling of Parliament, which alone could raise the cash. Henceforth, the Puritan leaders moved in accord with the Scots in a sinister dialectic – advance and retreat, alliance and conflict. No one could foresee that it was the beginning of a twenty-year-long upheaval: the Puritan Revolution, culmination of decades of agitation for power in Church and state.

The crisis was inflamed and made all the more dangerous by the Irish following the example of the Scots and rising in rebellion in 1641, beginning with a massacre of English and Scots intruders into their island. This outbreak aroused hysteria in England and sharpened the demands of the Parliament which the king had at length been forced to call. A long catalogue of the enormities of royal government in the past decades, the Grand Remonstrance, was driven through by the ability of John Pym. Largely propaganda, the kernel of the matter was the demand that the king should appoint ministers such as Parliament should have 'cause to confide in'. This was in essence a demand for ministers responsible to Parliament – a constitutional innovation pointing to future developments, but a long way ahead.

Negotiations to this end broke down through acute mistrust on both sides. Moderates saw that the Parliamentarian leadership was driving towards taking over government from the Crown. The Grand Remonstrance was passed by only a small majority. One MP of whom much would be heard, Oliver Cromwell, said that if it had not been passed he would have sold all that he had and left the country

for New England. Years later, an opponent of his who became a great historian (Clarendon) recorded: 'So near was this poor country to its deliverance.' Such was the spirit mounting on both sides propelling it into civil war.

What gave the king a party was the attack on the Church. The Puritans intended to take it over and establish something like the Presbyterian discipline of Scotland. This was not in keeping with the character of the English people, as events were to show. The English Church, with its Prayer Book, had now established itself in the hearts and minds of people after three generations. At Westminster, mob pressure was applied to force the king to sacrifice Strafford, who was brought to the block by the political power of Parliament. This was a fatal blow to the prestige of the Crown. It was followed by the impeachment of the archbishop, who was also sent to the

The first reading, in St Giles's, Edinburgh, of the new Scottish Prayer Book, in line with the English liturgy, produced a riot.

Tower. There he waited patiently a couple of years for execution. His martyrdom ultimately won the battle for the Church, as did the king's for the monarchy. But a sea of bloodshed, anarchy, disorder and actual famine was to be crossed before this reasonable consummation was reached.

ONE SHOULD SYMPATHIZE with Charles I's difficulties in conducting the government of three disparate kingdoms with their differing social structures and religious persuasions. He had no civil service to carry out the decisions of government, which was in consequence haphazard and inefficient. He depended on the ruling class of nobles and gentry. The consensus between the king and the governing class had broken down. This is the simple clue to revolutions, abdications and such in our history: from Edward II to

Richard II and Richard III; with Charles I and James II, to our own time with Edward VIII. Each lost the confidence of the governing class and in consequence was deposed or disposed of.

In the Civil War the governing class split in two: those who were for king and Church, against those for Parliament and Puritanism. Regional and class differences entered into the confrontation: the lesser gentry were envious of the great landed nobles, who were mostly Royalist. The middle classes of the towns, the manufacturing areas with their small craftsmen and artisans, in sympathy with Puritanism, were for Parliament. Parliament had two overwhelming advantages, which should have enabled them to win the war earlier: the City of London, with its dominating resources in cash, trade and credit; and the navy. (The navy had been built up largely from Ship Money, taxation which earlier had been confined to coastal counties but was, reasonably, extended inland. This was made out to be a grievance, though the sums were trifling – mere chicken-feed compared with the taxes and excise Parliament imposed to fight the war. John Hampden, a cousin of Cromwell, was regarded as a hero because he refused to pay; he died later for his convictions, mortally wounded on Chalgrove Field.)

TOP *Thomas Wentworth, Earl of Strafford, by Van Dyck.* LEFT *The king could not save his loyal servant from his Parliamentary enemies, and he was put on trial in Westminster Hall.* ABOVE *The execution of Strafford on Tower Hill.*

71

At the beginning the Royalists had the advantage in the spirited cavalry of their young gallants, led by Prince Rupert, a son of the Winter Queen. After the drawn battle of Edgehill (1642) the king nearly reached his capital but was turned back, and he never came within striking distance again. Next year the Royalists had success with their western army, which won a series of victories and captured Bristol, then the second city in the kingdom. In 1644 Parliament lost an army in the West, though this was more than balanced by their decisive victory at Marston Moor.

Superior resources were bound to tell. In 1643 Pym called in the Scots and their army to decide the issue – as they had done at Marston Moor – in return for cash and the imposition of the Presbyterian Covenant in England. Meanwhile Cromwell was organizing the resources of eastern England in the New Model Army, with which he was victorious in the conclusive battle of Naseby in 1645.

Parliament had won. But what to do with the victory? How to cash it in a tangible, lasting settlement of the issues in dispute? In simple words, who was to have the power, how was it to be organized, in what forms? The governing class had split on these issues, the authority of the Crown had plunged; with the lid taken off the top of society, anarchy threatened; after years of fighting, living off the land, neglecting cultivation and work, want and actual famine stalked together.

The victors now split apart. Parliament exercised civilian authority, but was jealous of its army; but Oliver Cromwell was the one army commander to have also a voice in Parliament. The king tried to play one off against the other.

ABOVE *A romantic 19th-century impression of Charles I's relative, Prince Rupert, at the battle of Edgehill.*
RIGHT *Two scenes depicted on a window in St Chad's Church, Farndon, Cheshire, made in 1660: top Royalist troops at the siege of Chester and bottom a Cavalier at the siege.*

The army offered him surprisingly moderate terms. He refused, hoping to get a better offer from Parliament and preferring a parliamentary settlement as more constitutional and offering more chance of permanence. Simultaneously he was negotiating with the Scots, one section of whom, under the Duke of Hamilton, invaded England on his behalf. Royalist risings took place in various parts of the country, in South Wales and Essex, where Colchester Castle held out against strong forces. Hamilton's ill-equipped forces, invading by the western route, were caught hopelessly strung out at Preston by Cromwell's swift march across the Pennines and destroyed.

Now Parliament, too late, came to terms with the king, who had attempted to escape from the army's control but was imprisoned at Carisbrooke Castle in the Isle of Wight. The army's resentment was intense. The day after Parliament's acceptance of the king's offer, Colonel Pride was posted at its door to purge the House of some 140 of its Presbyterian members. Already one-third of the House had withdrawn as Royalists. Only a Rump Parliament of under a hundred remained as a figleaf of constituted authority to carry out the army's wishes.

What to do with the king?

He was brought to a so-called 'trial' in Westminster Hall by the pressure of the army leaders – though everybody else recognized its illegality. The commander-in-chief, Fairfax, refused to attend; his wife publicly protested that he had more sense than to be there. The trial enabled the king to recover popular sympathy for his regal bearing, his dignity in distress, the tragedy of his personal life; he was able at last to appear as

LEFT *The frontispiece of a Royalist book describing early events in the Civil War.*
ABOVE *A playing card satirizing the Rump Parliament, the few who were left after Colonel Pride in 1648 had expelled all the Members who were out of sympathy with the army.*

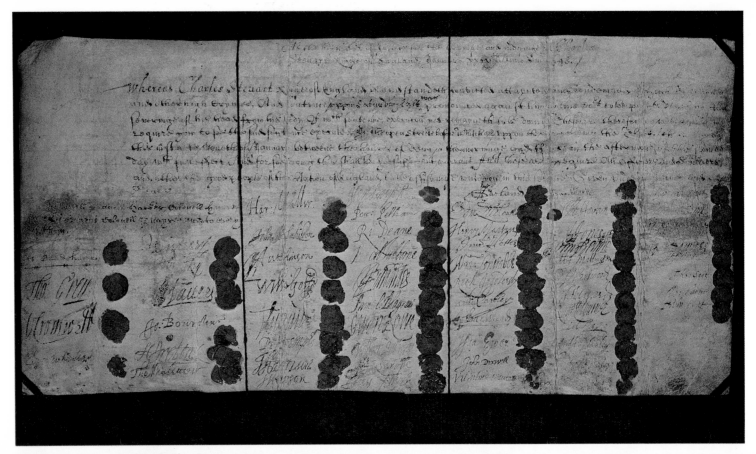

TOP *The death warrant of Charles I, signed by 59 regicides.*
ABOVE *An imaginary reconstruction of the execution of Charles I in 1649. Charles stepped out to the scaffold from the windows of the* Banqueting House at Whitehall, *and confronted death with courage and dignity.*

the defender of the liberty of the people. This was true; a military dictatorship was to come out of the confusion, though not immediately.

It does not appear that Cromwell made up his mind about the king's execution till the last moment. He could not trust Charles, and no doubt reflected that at a turn of the tide the king would have him by the neck for all that he had done. The king's execution, on 30 January 1649, sent a thrill of horror throughout Europe. In England its consequences were more lasting: his blood ran forever between the English people and the triumphant Puritans. The horror at his martyrdom ultimately saved the monarchy, as Laud's eventually did the Church, when things returned to normal.

Meanwhile a highly abnormal state of affairs prevailed – a political revolution was embarked upon. The monarchy and House of Lords were abolished, and England was declared a Commonwealth. A Council of State drawn from the small minority of Rump Parliament and army ruled through its pertinacious committees, more efficiently and interferingly than ever the Privy Council had done. The country was heavily taxed; prodigious fines were imposed upon all Royalist opponents, whom the Puritans called 'malignants'. The estates of the Crown were taken over, those of the Church sold; a considerable transference of land to new owners took place, and many Royalist gentry were ruined. The Puritan grandee Sir Arthur Hazelrig took over the bishop of Durham's place at Auckland Castle; the Puritan Cornelius Burgess made himself cosy in the deanery of Wells; Levellers like John Wildman built up estates out of confiscated Royalists' properties. Such were Whig foundations.

It was indeed a revolution, and there was still trouble ahead.

Ireland was up in arms and out of all control. The Catholic Irish operated under the lead of a papal emissary, but could not subdue the Anglo-Irish Pale under Ormonde. The situation was hopelessly complicated, not less so when Ormonde allied himself with the Catholic Confederates: all depended on the resolution of the crisis in England. In the summer after the king's death, 1649, the Puritan Commonwealth sent over Cromwell with a powerful army to conquer Ireland. This he did, with his characteristic daemonic energy, given a sharper edge by memories of the Massacre.

The conquest was followed by a rooting-out of native Catholic landlords, and the planned settlement and colonization by Cromwellian soldiers, a number of them Welsh, like the Bowens and Joneses, and others, like the Guinnesses, who were to become even more famous. When things settled, the new régime did well for Ireland. In due course she was granted, like Scotland, thirty seats in the British parliament, and free trade with Britain. This was a foundation for better things, and peace was enforced.

Scotland was a harder nut to crack; it was more disciplined, with an army of its own under competent leadership. The nation was affronted by the execution of their king; they proclaimed his son king as Charles II; he accepted their terms, subscribed to the Covenant, and was preached at to repent the sins and the 'whoredoms' of his Catholic mother, until the young man wondered whether he should not repent that ever he was born. It had certainly been a mistake to accept the invitation, as his English advisers thought, but it was a step in his political education. No wonder he emerged as a cynic. A great gentleman himself, he later said that Presbyterianism was 'no religion for a gentleman'.

The Scots prepared once more to invade England, this time to place on the throne the son of the king they had helped to displace. Cromwell was sent against them and, in difficult circumstances, won a resounding victory at Dunbar in 1651. Scotland was still, however, unconquered. Charles II was crowned at Scone, and in 1652, glad to escape from restraint, made a dash with a scratch army down the western road to Worcester, hoping to raise West Country Royalists. They were too exhausted to rise; however, the small army fought

A 19th-century impression of the battle of Dunbar, 1650.

gallantly against Cromwell's, outnumbered by two to one. The young king was lucky to escape. After a series of hardly credible adventures – which, in later years, he was fond of retelling – he made his way across country, sometimes recognized, never once betrayed, to the coast of Sussex and a ship for France.

The fundamental factor now was that the whole governing class was alienated. Puritan rule was that of a small minority, and it depended upon a victorious army, of whose power it was jealous, with which it was in disaccord, and which it proceeded to offend. The Presbyterian grandees of the Rump Parliament did not wish to raise the money to pay the troops – and indeed the country was hard pressed to pay for its extravagances since 1642. (Many must have sighed for the good old days of royal government again.) The Parliamentary politicians were mostly stiff-necked Presbyterians, who hated toleration. The army contained many different sects; its sympathies were mainly Independent.

In all these cross-currents Oliver Cromwell stood at the centre, at the strategic crux. A victorious general, he was also a Member of Parliament – a special exception had been made for him, no one knows why. Socially conservative – for he was

A contemporary painting of Oliver Cromwell.

a gentleman of family, with a widespread cousinage to back him – he was religiously a reformer, sympathetic to the sects, and he talked their language. No one of good judgment could mistake his nose for politics, He was a dynamo of energy, a tremendously forceful personality, of unquestioned morals, a good family man with an affectionate nature. His emotions were strong and liable to carry him away; his religious convictions remained firm, while he was surprisingly tolerant, within the bounds of Protestantism. He had a compulsive gift for speaking which, rough and untutored as it was, overwhelmed his audience. He was the man for the moment.

The Rump of a Parliament proposed to do nothing about providing a settled constitution or submitting themselves to a newly elected assembly. (A freely elected Parliament would immediately have recalled the king.) The Rump proposed to sit in perpetuity, a perfectly unrepresentative minority government. Cromwell came to one of his sudden resolutions and, provoked beyond endurance, called in his musketeers and cleared the House: 'Take away that bauble!' (the prestigious Speaker's mace). Charles I had never done anything so drastic. The unceremonious dismissal was quite popular. Henceforth it was naked military dictatorship, plain for all to see.

Charles I had never been able to unite his three kingdoms; they were now forced into union by military power.

The army leaders drafted a written 'constitution', the Instrument of Government, which was really a return to rule by a monarch, under the title of lord protector. Cromwell filled this office for the next five years with comprehensive ability and raised the country's prestige abroad with its large army and navy. He ended the war with the Dutch on terms advantageous to England. He used England's new-found power to protect Protestants abroad, and he joined France in a war against Spain. The Puritans had been the empire builders all along. Blake's navy won victories in the Mediterranean, into which England now penetrated in force. In the Caribbean a strongpoint was won in Jamaica and, on the mainland of Europe, Dunkirk, in place of Calais lost by Mary Tudor, which the Elizabethans had so longed to recover. In may ways the time of Cromwell was a return to the age of Elizabeth I, for whom he gallantly expressed much respect.

He was a great Englishman, which Charles I was not. But he could never make his rule popular with the country, for all his 'great heart' – to which even his opponent Clarendon paid tribute. His régime was in the nature of things temporary, opposed as it was by the entire governing class, the two wings, Parliamentary and Royalist, feeling their way to coming together after their foolish scission. After the rule of anarchy, the motto of the possessing classes would be: 'Never again!'

The Protectorate effectively ended when Oliver died in 1658, worn out by his exertions. He had fought not only over all England, but Wales, Ireland and Scotland too. He was given the funeral of a prince in Westminster Abbey.

At once the quarrel between the political Republicans and the army, which Oliver himself had not been able to resolve, broke into the open. His son Richard, 'Tumbledown Dick', who occupied his father's seat for a few months, abdicated. The country might have fallen into anarchy if it had not been for the wisdom and patience, the sheer canniness and policy of keeping silence of General Monk, commander of the army in Scotland. There he had ruled with as much success as possible over a population resentful of defeat. He now marched south to fill the vacuum of power, watching the moods of the people and the demands of a complex situation after so long a period of unsettlement: a constitutional hiatus.

Monk came from a West Country Royalist background, and he saw early on that only a return to the ancient settled constitution of king, Lords, and Commons would fill the bill. The problem was how to get this accepted without bloodshed, with both the army and the Republicans still embattled. With much diplomatic skill he played his game, making his moves with caution – still more so his contacts with the exiled King Charles II and Court in France – until the Restoration was seen to be inevitable. The formula that suited both sides was a freely elected Parliament; all along it had been obvious that a freely elected Parliament would restore the king. The triumph of the king's principal adviser, the earl of Clarendon, was to get him restored without conditions.

Nevertheless, it was inevitable that the restored monarchy would be a constitutional one, jogging along in harness with Parliament – the one solid gain from all the agony and destruction of civil war and revolution.

Charles II returned from France and made his entry into London on 29 May 1660. The country in general was in a

delirium of delight at the Restoration, with bonfires everywhere, bells ringing, and wine running from conduits in the City. The Puritan prophet, Milton, his hopes for a millennium all falsified, hid himself. Some of regicides – the late king's murderers – fled to New England, others to Switzerland; those who remained faced imprisonment and execution in turn.

Charles II, a man of twenty-five, was experienced in every way, a contrast to his sad, refined father. He took after his Bourbon grandfather, Henry IV of France, in his good humour and friendliness – and in his insatiable appetite for women. Six foot tall (his father was a small man), very dark, he was a clever, rather indolent man, with a gift for popularity. Sceptical about religion, cynical about people, he was more interested in the new scientific experiments of the period and gave active patronage to the Royal Society, which had just been formed. He was a man for his time.

Stepping ashore at Dover in the glad May of 1660 and presented with a large Bible by the Presbyterian mayor, he said that it was what he most cherished. (He had learned his lesson in Scotland.) Tolerant and easy-going by nature, with a secret leaning towards Catholicism, he was in favour of a comprehensive Church to include Puritans, who had been lately dashed from power by a tide of reaction. Clarendon, an orthodox Anglican, also favoured including them.

Some former Puritans, like Cromwell's brother-in-law, the remarkable Wilkins – a key man in the formation of the Royal Society – allowed themselves to be comprehended and became bishops. The more stiff-necked refused and left the Church, to tread the diminishing corridors of Nonconformity. Thus the Church was restored in fairly full panoply, with its historic order of bishops under Juxon, who had attended Charles I on the scaffold and buried him at Windsor in silence, but for his

TOP *Charles II dances at a ball at the Hague, shortly before his return to England in May 1660.*
ABOVE *Charles II.*

77

tears, on that snowy February day in 1649, when the Prayer Book was forbidden. Now it was restored, as were the full rites and ceremonies of the Church for which Laud had died, along with the lands and estates of bishops, deans and chapters. Some twelve hundred ministers refused to accept the situation, and went out into the dark to serve their private congregations.

In reality what was restored was the rule of the governing class. Such a reaction against the doings of the past twenty years swept the country that an overwhelming majority of Royalists were returned to the 'Cavalier' Parliament, which was kept in being until 1679. They were standing no more nonsense from people of differing beliefs. It was the gentry of the House of Commons who enacted a repressive code against dissenters, inflicting various disabilities upon them in local government, education and the universities, and restricting their meetings. It was perhaps a fair return for what others had suffered during their brief hold on power; but a reaction all the same. Henceforth the alliance between Church and governing class held; the social structure in every parish was firmly based on the rule of both squire and parson. The lesson of the Puritan revolution had been well learned.

The reaction was to be observed in other ways. Dissenters were excluded from the universities, and they were not to teach school without licence from a bishop – which was rarely forthcoming. From Elizabeth's reign up to the Civil War there had been a remarkable expansion in the founding of grammar schools. A surplus of black-coated clerics for whom there were not enough jobs was one factor in Puritan unrest. Educational opportunity was now diminished; schools entered into their long decline up to the nineteenth century. It is fair to add that the great poet of the age, John Milton, and the leading prose writer thrown up from the people, John Bunyan (or Bunnion), were both dissenters. At the bottom of the social scale, in the parishes, the poor received short shrift; they were put to work, and were not allowed to move about as vagrants.

What enabled the country to recover quickly from the wounds of the Civil War was the remarkable increase in trade, industry and general prosperity. The country was full of energy and vitality, ready to resume its march overseas. The

BELOW *A map illustrating John Bunyan's literary masterpiece, the* Pilgrim's Progress.
OPPOSITE *A reconstruction in a museum of a room of the 17th century.*

first and most popular act of the Restoration was to disband the army and navy which the revolution had created and by which it maintained itself – it had been a heavy financial burden.

Forces were built up on a small voluntary basis, beginning with the Guards (Grenadier and Coldstream, and the Life Guards). Charles II's marriage to Catherine of Braganza brought a prodigious and significant dowry: Bombay and Tangier, nearly a million in cash and an alliance with Portugal. Unfortunately it brought no children, and this was to raise acute problems. Advance was resumed in the West Indies, and in America with the founding of Carolina. A new Navigation Act encouraged English shipping and increased England's share in the carrying trade, of which the Dutch had the lion's portion. There followed a renewed maritime war, in which the less well equipped Restoration navy was less successful than under the Puritan Blake. In 1665 London was paralysed by an appalling outbreak of plague; in 1666 followed the Great Fire, which consumed the old City. In 1667 no battle fleet was sent to sea. The Dutch sailed up the Thames

LEFT *A later impression of the Great Fire of London, 1666.*
ABOVE *Sir Christopher Wren, with his most important achievement, St Paul's Cathedral, in the background.*

estuary, burnt four ships of the line, and towed away the *Royal Charles*. Some people sighed for Old Noll (Oliver Cromwell) again.

Nevertheless the Dutch too were in difficulties, and peace was made on a reasonable basis. England gave up Surinam in South America, to receive New Amsterdam, renamed New York in honour of the king's brother, the Duke of York. Shortly his friend, the Quaker William Penn, the son of an admiral, founded Pennsylvania, thus completing a chain of colonies along the sea-board from Newfoundland almost to Spanish Florida.

AT HOME THE HONEYMOON OF CHARLES II and Parliament was breaking down. Parliament kept Charles on a tight rope for cash, and in 1670 he made the Treaty of Dover with Louis XIV of France; in return for a subsidy he was to join in an attack on the Dutch. The secret clauses were more disastrous: Charles was to declare himself a Catholic at some favourable time (it never came), but as English suspicions of this were confirmed Charles lost the people's confidence and never regained credibility.

He began his campaign for personal power with a Declaration of Indulgence – toleration for dissenters and Catholics alike. Though this was reasonable in itself, the governing class was determined to maintain the Anglican monopoly. A Test Act was introduced to exclude non-Anglicans from all office, civil and military. Many dissenters qualified for office by 'occasional conformity'; but the Duke of York had to resign office as lord high admiral.

The upshot of the war with the Dutch surprised everyone, and had lasting consequences. An internal revolution in the

Netherlands brought young William of Orange to power. The overwhelming French forces there were arrested by opening the dykes and flooding the land. Henceforth William of Orange dedicated his life to combating the growing and intolerable ascendancy of Louis XIV in Europe. This new factor brought about a re-alignment of forces, and the English were forced to re-think their foreign policy. Henceforth there was to be no more war with the Dutch; the chief threat to everybody was the France of Louis XIV, supreme on land, now bent on becoming a sea power too.

Charles II continued his covert relations with his cousin Louis XIV, aided by the French mistress the latter sent over as a go-between, whom Charles made Duchess of Portsmouth. To win Protestant support, he consented to the marriage of his niece Mary, presumptive heiress to the throne, to William of Orange, who thereupon became a factor of the first importance in English politics.

The growing mistrust of Charles II's personal policy, corroborated by his brother James's open Catholicism – a liability in an essentially Protestant country – broke national unity and created intense party conflict. Whigs and Tories came into being, the Whigs wanting to exclude James from the succession, or at least place restrictions upon him at his accession, until the Protestant Mary should come to the throne. Party conflict broke into mob-hysteria with the discovery of the Popish Plot, fomented by Titus Oates. This was made the utmost use of by the extreme Whigs, led by the clever party organizer, Shaftesbury. He headed the campaign to exclude James from the throne, but made the mistake of opting for Charles's eldest bastard, the light-weight Duke of Monmouth for king, whom he could manipulate, instead of

ABOVE *William Penn, founder of Pennsylvania, signs a treaty with the Indians there – a 19th-century engraving.*
RIGHT *A satirical print of a 17th-century Quaker meeting.*

adopting the moderate solution of backing Mary and William of Orange, who was Charles I's grandson anyway.

The reality behind the Popish Plot was that James had become an uncompromising Catholic. In the course of it some thirty-five innocent persons were brought to the block. A reaction was bound to come, for which Charles waited patiently and played his cards skilfully.

What helped him most was the determination to avoid civil war, not to allow party conflict to get beyond the point of no return. Three new Parliaments met in these crucial years, 1679–81. Charles sat them out, dissolving each in turn, outlasting and outwitting them. The strain was terrific; that, and the constant pressure of affairs with women – his bastards he created dukes – brought on a stroke. He could afford to take his last years more easily, for he did not summon a Parliament again: he preferred to rely for his finances on subsidies from France. So did some of the Whig leaders. It was in Louis XIV's interest to keep England divided, and thus the vital task of resisting his domination of Europe fell to William of Orange, watching and waiting in Holland, which he had saved.

Charles II's last years saw plain political reaction, as the Whig politicians had so shockingly overplayed their hand. Shaftesbury fled to Holland, where he died. Republican supporters were executed. The City of London, the Whig stronghold, was brought to heel. Throughout the country the charters of the boroughs were remodelled to keep out malcontents; this was important, for the borough corporations returned the largest number of members to Parliament. The opposition was quelled; all was set fair for James II's accession.

JAMES ASCENDED THE THRONE with much good will, after the persecution he had endured for his religion. He proceeded to throw it all away, as his cleverer brother had foreseen he would. ('Nobody is going to kill me to make you king, Jamie.') Charles gave him three years to outlast his welcome – which proved exact.

James's hand was strengthened at the beginning by the idiotic enterprise of Monmouth, who invaded the country with a handful of followers to try to make himself king. He called out the last remnants of the supporters of the Civil War in the West Country – Somerset, Dorset, East Devon. They were mainly dissenting artisans and small farmers led by their ministers, and they were quenched in the mud and blood of Sedgemoor. James took his revenge on them: some 150 good fellows were hanged, and 800 sent into slavery across the Atlantic. The totally irresponsible, though beautiful, Monmouth deserved what he got.

Just as had happened with Wyatt's rebellion against Mary Tudor, this abortive rising led only to reaction and determined the monarch to proceed on a full Catholicizing programme. He dismissed his ablest minister, Halifax, who had saved him from exclusion, and he also dismissed a Parliament that was willing to compromise and admit non-Anglicans to some offices. The king preferred to act on his own absolute authority, on the advice of a Jesuit, Father Petre,

James II, king from 1685 to the Revolution of 1688.

who was admitted to the Privy Council, and of Sunderland, who illegally went to Mass while he was a minister.

No real believer in toleration, the king put Catholics, of whom there was but a tiny minority (some 100,000) in the country, into a privileged position. Places in government, commands in the army and navy, the governorships of the Tower and of Portsmouth, military and naval bases, were given to them with obvious intention. The Catholic Tyrconnell was made ruler in Ireland. A large army was assembled on Hounslow Heath to overawe London, where the governing class was not overawed but affronted. Consensus was broken. From this time, said an old Catholic peer, 'I date the ruin of my religion.'

James now offended the universities, strongholds of Anglicanism, making a Catholic dean of Christ Church at Oxford, expelling the fellows of Magdalen for refusing the king's nomination (quite illegal) of a Catholic president. (The College still celebrates James's defeat and the return of the excluded Fellows.) Similar pressure was tried upon Cambridge and the Inns of Court, to meet with similar resistance.

James now came out, on his own authority, with a full Declaration of Indulgence, toleration for dissenters and Catholics, against the law as laid down by Parliament. The

Church was commanded to read this manifesto challenging its own monopoly from the pulpit on two consecutive Sundays. The archbishop and six other bishops who declined to do so were sent to the Tower and prosecuted for seditious libel. Never were bishops so popular. On their acquittal even the army on Hounslow Heath cheered – 'Do you call that nothing?' said James, frustrated and enraged.

Beyond all hope – for, like his brother, James had had a venereal infection – the queen produced a son. This was the last straw: people could put up with James's antics in the interval before the accession of his Protestant daughter Mary, but the country would not endure a Catholic dynasty in perpetuity. Only armed intervention from abroad could turn the scales: apparent power was with the king. William of Orange was asked to intervene, and the decisive invitation was signed by five of the great nobles and the bishop of London.

William made his preparations with maximum skill and efficiency, disguising his intentions and objectives. Because of the Catholic Louis XIV's intolerable arrogance the Protestant crusade gained the support of the pope. Above all, William had luck with him. A Protestant wind bore his armada down Channel safely to Torbay; it was not intercepted by the royal

A detail from a broadsheet of 1688 celebrating the arrival of William of Orange, and relating the events which led to his invasion of England.

navy, which was riddled with disaffection. William was taking no chances: he brought the largest disciplined forces ever to land on English shores, 11,000 foot and 4000 horse. James's forces were still larger, but he could not rely on them. There might have been a confrontation, but William was anxious for a walk-over, without bloodshed. This happened. James's ablest soldier, John Churchill, deserted him – in all probability because he had been frustrated of his ambition to decide the issue. William kept all the cards in his own hands. The king, overcome by fainting fits and nose-bleeds turned back to London, leaving the initiative to William. In James's absence the Princess Anne had deserted him, to join the northern forces marching south.

James's nerve broke and, in panic, he fled from London, throwing the Great Seal into the Thames. He had already sent

William of Orange landing at Torbay on November 5, 1688.

his wife and son abroad; on a second attempt he too got away safely, with his illegitimate son by Arabella Churchill, the Duke of Berwick, leaving a vacuum for William and Mary to fill.

In these circumstances the 'glorious' Revolution of 1688 was a very moderate and sensible affair, without bloodshed. The essence of it was the restoration of consensus between king and Parliament, between executive and legislature. The prerogative of monarchy was in essence unchanged; and in essential matters William exercised greater authority than his father-in-law had done. The monarch would continue to govern and to choose his ministers, but henceforth would not be able to dispense with Parliament or the laws. Awkward problems of conscience were raised for those who believed in passive obedience, mainly Churchmen. Actually the revolution was followed by a measure of toleration for dissenters; even Catholics were not persecuted, merely tolerated. The widest possible support for the new and more sensible régime was secured by making William and Mary joint sovereigns, with the understanding that William would exercise power.

This he at once proceeded to do by bringing England into the coalition against France. The aim of his life was to reduce

A jewellery box of 17th-century English design, made of steel and brass.

the over-mighty power of Louis XIV, and his chief purpose in taking over power in England – which he did not much care for, and where he was never popular – was this European ambition. The ambiguous policy of Charles II and the fatuity of James II had betrayed England's interests in allowing the France of Louis XIV to achieve a dangerous ascendancy, and become a threat to others. William at once declared war, with England now in a position to help in his design.

He had to fight for his throne in Ireland. Within a matter of months Louis XIV propelled James back into Ireland, with the hopeless idea of recovering the kingdom he had so foolishly thrown away, using Ireland as a base. There James restored Catholicism to full power – no toleration for Protestants, who were forced into hiding or prison (like the famous Archbishop King of Dublin). Again William was taking no chances; like Cromwell before him he embarked on the re-conquest with superior forces. William won the decisive victory of the Boyne in 1690 – James rode from the field before it was decided. It took two more years before Ireland was subdued.

The Stuart kings had been anxious for a measure of equity in the treatment of Catholic Ireland. There was no equity now: it was a conquered country. A further dispossession of Catholic landlords left two-thirds of the land in the hands of Protestants – a foundation for the Anglo-Irish ascendancy

which lasted up to the revolution of our time.

In Scotland the Restoration period had been marked by the conflict between Episcopalians and Presbyterians for control of the Church. For most of the period the country was ruled by the able and cynical ex-Presbyterian Lauderdale, who well understood the foibles of his native country. With the Revolution of 1688 – besmirched, however, by the lugubrious episode of the Massacre of Glencoe in 1692 – the issue was finally decided against Episcopacy in favour of Presbyterianism, itself in keeping with William III's Dutch Calvinism. Thus Presbyterianism became the established Church in Scotland; in England, the High Church position was undermined by the facts of the revolution, which encouraged the growth of a sensible Latitudinarianism.

Thus was unity – by force of circumstances, by force itself and with much sense and some reason – once more achieved in the three disparate kingdoms. It meant unity of power for Britain to go ahead in the world.

Chapter 5

Social Stability and Progress

THE REVOLUTION OF 1688 ACHIEVED SOME-
thing unique. As Sir George Clark, a leading
historian of the period, says: 'It had created a
constitutional monarchy. England was the only
country in the world where an elected assembly
shared the work of government with a king, in accordance
with mutually acceptable principles of co-operation.' It
proved an extraordinarily stable foundation for progress at
home and overseas, expansion of trade, industry and wealth,
the astonishing achievement of a maritime and commercial
empire from the base of a small island outpost on the fringe of
North-Western Europe. It was in a strategically favourable
situation at the European end of the shortest Atlantic crossing
– and it made the most of it. As the New World prospered and
grew, so did Britain.

The small country became the envy of Europe, particularly
for its constitutional arrangements, so much admired by
reforming spirits like Montesquieu and Voltaire, who only
wished that they could be applied in France. England's duel
for primacy with France was to last for more than a century,
and was concluded only by the battles of Trafalgar (1805) and
Waterloo (1815). It was very remarkable that a country only
one-third the size and population of France should have been
able to defeat her, the leading country in Europe. Britain was
able to resist her superior power and resources only by allying
herself with other powers – principally Holland and Austria –
also threatened by French supremacy.

This was the policy of the Grand Alliance initiated by
William III – after Holland's appalling experience of the
aggression of Louis XIV. This remained the sheet-anchor of
British policy up to our time, when it served the comparable
aim of saving Europe from the worse tyranny of the Kaiser's
and Hitler's Germany. The policy had been foreshadowed by
the Elizabethan resistance to the intolerable power of Philip
II's Spain, when England allied herself with the Dutch and
Henry of Navarre to withstand and defeat it.

OPPOSITE *William III.*
ABOVE *A miniature of the joint sovereigns William and Mary.*

William III had saved Holland by his long struggle from
1672 to 1678. As king of England he fought Louis XIV for
another nine years. He was no military genius, but he had
indomitable courage and persistence; his arduous life, in spite
of frail health, gave him greatness of spirit. It also made him a
dour man, not very lovable – but much loved by his loyal wife,
Queen Mary II, though he gave her no children; and by his
closest Dutch friends, Bentinck and Keppel. Not unnaturally,
he trusted the Dutch more than he did the English. An
undercurrent of sympathy for the Stuarts caused trouble for
decades, and was to erupt into two Scottish rebellions in 1715
and 1745.

Britain could not have been successful without her allies,
and these were kept happy, more or less, not only by common
interest but by her financial power. The Bank of England was
founded; funds from trading surpluses facilitated long-term
borrowing; liquid capital grew, with financial technique to
manage it. The prosperity of the City of London soared, and
the moneyed interest grew more powerful in government. In
politics the City was largely Whig, a prime source of strength
to the party. The Tories represented the country interest,
mainly of the lesser gentry.

William was not good at managing Parliament (who could
have been?); but he got his way in what he most cared about,
the war against Louis XIV, and in this Parliament supported
him. Sea power was the key to British strategy – and Louis'
great minister Colbert built up a powerful fleet. England did
not win command of the Channel till the battle of La Hogue in
1692. Meanwhile, year by year, William pursued his ding-
dong struggle on land in the Netherlands. He gave no chance
to the latent military genius of Marlborough (John Churchill),
for he did not trust him. Marlborough resented the chief
commands being given to William's Dutch, and went into
opposition – at one point he was sent to the Tower. But the
future was with him, through his wife Sarah's power over
Princess Anne, heiress to the throne after William. (The
popular Queen Mary died in 1694 of small-pox, a terrible
scourge at the time – it almost wiped out Louis XIV's
legitimate family.)

Upon the Peace of Ryswick, 1697, the prime European question was now what would happen to the vast Spanish Empire in Europe and overseas at the death of the last Habsburg king of Spain, Charles II, who was childless? Annexed to any other power, it would raise the spectre of a European supremacy again. Having been fought to a standstill Louis was willing to pocket his pride and negotiate the matter with William. Two attempts were made to settle the issue peacefully by partitioning the inheritance. The first broke down on the death of the agreed candidate; the second on the obstinacy of the Spaniards, who would have no partition.

William's strength was failing, but before his death in 1702 he had provided for the future. In 1701 the Act of Settlement legislated for the continuance of a Protestant succession to the throne after Anne, whose only living child had no promise of life. To achieve this, Parliament had to go back beyond the Catholic descendants of Charles I – to the royal houses of Bavaria and Savoy, both closer in legitimate line – to the granddaughter of the Winter Queen, the Electress Sophia of Hanover, and her son George. These Germans, lucky because they were Protestant, were the ancestors of the present royal house.

A combination of circumstances renewed the war with France. Louis XIV decided to accept the whole Spanish world-empire – in Europe, Central and South America, the Caribbean and the Philippines – for his Bourbon grandson, Philip. On the death of James II he recognized James's son as king, thus raising the issue again which had been settled at Ryswick. This roused Parliament to support William's renewal of war. He had already made his peace with Marlborough and designated him as his successor in the field – though no one could have expected the combination of military and diplomatic gifts Marlborough would reveal.

QUEEN ANNE, WHOSE REIGN, 1702–14, was almost wholly occupied by the War of the Spanish Succession, was always popular, and deservedly so. She was more English than any monarch had been for a long time, and rather pointedly drew attention to the contrast with her predecessor, whom she detested. (William was no lady's man, and had had no manners; but he had artistic taste and built Kensington Palace and part of Hampton Court.) As a granddaughter of an English commoner by origin, Clarendon, she had a fund of commonsense and devotion to duty, was a good conventional Anglican, and had her feet solidly on the ground – whereas the Stuarts, some of them light-headed, were apt to be too royal.

Marlborough went abroad to make sure of the Grand Alliance with Holland, Hanover, Prussia and the Austrian Empire, aiming to obtain the Spanish inheritance for a younger Habsburg, the Archduke Charles, second son of the emperor Leopold. The alliance held good through all the strains of a long war – with the aid of subsidies. The war began ominously with a French lunge at Vienna, the heart of the empire, with the aid of France's ally, Bavaria. It was countered by an unprecedented march by the allied army under Marlborough's command to the banks of the Danube. At Blenheim in 1704 a disaster was inflicted upon the French, which ended their designs in Germany. It confirmed Britain in the leadership of the alliance, and Marlborough's prestige was signalized by the building of Blenheim Palace, a national monument to Britain's military glory – a smaller rival to

INSULÆ

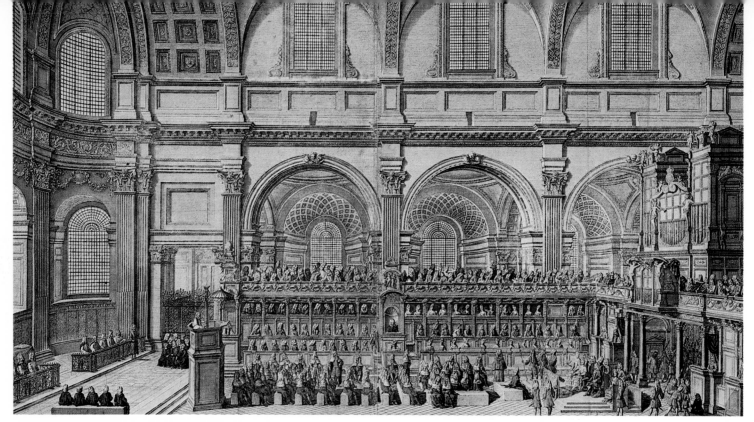

Versailles. Two years later, with the decisive victory of Ramillies, Marlborough swept the French out of the Netherlands.

The allies were committed to clearing the French out of Spain, but in 1707 at Almanza, Marlborough's nephew – James II's son – the Duke of Berwick decisively lost the allies' hopes of winning Spain for the Archduke Charles. None of the allies was willing to compromise at this point, though Louis XIV was. The war went on. Meanwhile Gibraltar was captured, and a valuable base in Minorca for blockading France from the south.

At home party unity lasted long enough to pilot through an act of constructive statesmanship, the Act of Union with Scotland, 1707 – a triumph of commonsense and mutual concession. Scotland kept her own religious and legal establishment, and was to be represented in the joint

Queen Anne receives the Act of Union with Scotland from the Duke of Queensberry, in 1707. Sixteen Scottish peers and forty-five MPs were to sit at Westminster as a result of this Act.

The Thanksgiving service held in St Paul's Cathedral to celebrate the victory at the Battle of Ramillies.

Parliament by a dozen peers and forty-five MPs. The Scots were admitted on equal terms to the home and colonial trade, and this led to the development of an industrial belt between Edinburgh and Glasgow, which became a leading port for Atlantic trade. The Scots took the familiar road south to contribute their energies and abilities in the professions, law and medicine, in trade and government, and more and more in the colonies and empire overseas.

The strain of the war exacerbated party feeling. The Tories began to lag in supporting the war: they wished to confine it to war at sea. Most of the money for it was raised from land tax, which fell heavily on the country gentry. The City, commercial interests, and the moneyed men in general profited by it and increased their hold. Their slogan was 'No peace without Spain', which in effect meant no peace at all. In 1709, with France utterly exhausted and suffering, Louis XIV was prepared to make every concession – except drive his grandson out of Spain. The Whigs, now in power, failed to take the opportunity. Marlborough had continued to win victories: Oudenarde in 1708, Malplaquet in 1709. Now he was ready to force the French frontier and march on Paris to instal a responsible constitutional monarchy similar to that in England. That would have saved France a great deal of trouble later, but in those circumstances it was a dream.

For at last the mood of the country had changed – Queen Anne interpreted it rightly in turning to the Tories, who won an immense majority in the election of 1710. The peace was a long time negotiating; when it came, the peace of Utrecht 1713, it not only provided handsomely for British interests but also established peace between Britain and France for the next thirty years. Spain's external dominions in Europe went to Austria, which took over the southern Netherlands, thus removing the strategic threat from a French occupation. Spain itself and its overseas empire remained in Bourbon hands, but the Spanish Bourbons were never to acquire the French Crown. Britain made gains overseas, commercially inspired: Hudson Bay for the fur trade; Newfoundland settlements for British fishermen; Nova Scotia, with a fine harbour at Halifax; St Kitt's in the West Indies for sugar. An *asiento*, or concession, to import nearly 5000 Africans into the Spanish colonies over the next thirty years was to lead to much trouble and later war with Spain.

The Tory government intended a commercial treaty with France which would have been beneficial to both; but they lost power with Queen Anne's death, and the Whigs dropped the treaty. Nevertheless a fair understanding was maintained with France for the next two decades, much to the benefit of both countries. The Tory party was ruined by its internal confusion with regard to the succession, and the in-fighting of its leaders, the ambiguous Harley and the brilliant but irresponsible Bolingbroke. One wing of the party was Jacobite, and would have liked to place the queen's half-brother, James Edward, on the throne. It is possible that if he had been prepared to

become an Anglican he might have made it; but, like his father, he was too stupid for that. The queen herself could not bear the Elector George of Hanover, who had failed to propose marriage to her when both were young – which would have saved much trouble.

So George I (reigned 1714–27) succeeded, with Whig support, really a Whig king, and the Tory party was ruined. The king was competent and an able military commander; but he knew not much English, and his heart – what there was of it – was bent on Hanover and Northern Europe. He brought with him his German mistress, with her fingers in the public purse; his wife he kept in life-long confinement at Celle for *her* affair with a lover. It is hardly to be wondered at that in his second year in England, 1715, the Scottish Highlands broke into romantic rebellion under the lead of the Stuart Pretender. It was a hopeless affair, and led only to the executions of a few Jacobite peers and the imprisonment of other prominent supporters.

A detail from Sir John Thornhill's representation of the triumph of the family of George I, in the painted hall at Greenwich.

THE STORY OF BRITAIN in the eighteenth century is fundamentally that of an extraordinarily successful society, with its internal problems solved, going ahead under a tough and able aristocracy to resounding achievements at sea and on land overseas, to the creation of an empire, the First British Empire. It was not, however, a closed society: it was open to talent, which could rise in it (Nelson, for example, was a parson's son). Moreover, the commercial community, particularly in London, was gaining more influence with Parliament and government.

This was to be seen in the War of Jenkins' Ear which flared up in 1738, in response to the popular outcry against Spanish interference with British trade-runners into the Spanish monopoly in South America. The British were bent on breaking into it, the Spaniards on keeping everybody out. There was a further source of dispute with the founding of

The paintings and caricatures of William Hogarth give a vivid picture of life in London and the provinces in the 18th century.
LEFT *Four Times of Day – Morning.*
BELOW *The Election – Chairing the Member.*
OPPOSITE BELOW *The Madhouse (or Bedlam), from* The Rake's Progress.

Georgia, the last of the chain of thirteen Atlantic colonies all down the coast of North America. (It was an unlucky number.) Georgia was founded in 1732 – named for George II – deliberately to head off the Spaniards in Florida and the French in Louisiana.

Sir Robert Walpole, who presided over prosperous Georgian England as prime minister from 1721 to 1742, was opposed to the war. He said that 'now they were ringing their bells, soon they would be wringing their hands'. Walpole had been called upon to get the country out of the mess of the South Sea Bubble, the international crisis excited by speculation on prospects of overseas trade. During his long period of power he did much to establish the new régime and set the model for the office of prime minister, dependent on a parliamentary majority. As Clark says, 'Great Britain was the first modern state in which the government had to carry out its tasks with the general consent of a governing class' – expressed through Parliament.

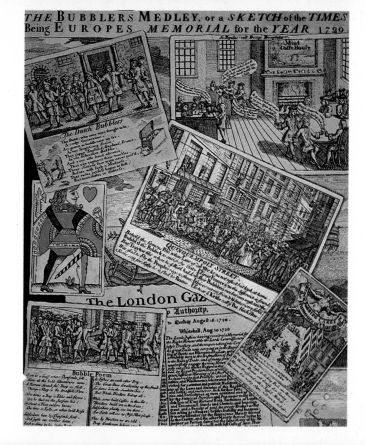

RIGHT *A collection of satirical prints relating to the South Sea Bubble.*

Eighteenth-century aristocratic society worked in agreement with the people, unlike on the Continent, where it operated at their expense. British institutions were a success not only at the top, with government, but all the way down to the local level, where the county communities had an active existence, with much healthy voluntary effort in sport, road-making, founding hospitals. It is true that a reactionary spirit prevailed in the laws regarding the preservation of game, and higher property qualifications were imposed on both MPs and JPs to maintain their positions. But popular spirit was never repressed – and often expressed itself in riots and window-breaking at the houses of unpopular politicians, until in 1780 the Gordon Riots went beyond all bounds in burning and destruction. There was no police and over this last riot the king himself, George III, took charge in restoring order. In the towns the industrious middle class was prospering; in the countryside, the farmers. The landscape was shaped and planted by several generations of improving landlords, building their mansions – some of them palaces – and decent country houses, surrounded by their parks. London burgeoned into well-regulated and proportioned squares; it had the first daily newspaper in the world from 1702. The country was further knit together by a new road system, the turnpikes with their toll-houses we still recognize along them, the first such network since Roman times.

LEFT *Sir Robert Walpole, Prime Minister for twenty-one years.*
BELOW *The battle of Culloden, 16 April, 1746, at which The Duke of Cumberland's forces defeated Highlanders under Bonnie Prince Charlie, whom they outnumbered two to one.*

AN EXACT VIEW OF THE GLORIOUS VICTORY
HIS ROYAL HIGHNESS WILLIAM DUKE OF CUMBERLAND
BATTLE OF CULLODEN IN SCOTLAND

The war with Spain over commercial-colonial objectives merged into another struggle with France for power: the War of the Austrian Succession, in which the indomitable Empress Maria Theresa held on to her throne. Spirited little George II, as elector of Hanover, won regard by fighting on foot, at sixty, at the battle of Dettingen. The British and their allies were defeated two years later at Fontenoy, 1745 – the year of the second Highland rebellion on behalf of the Stuarts. Though the Young Pretender, Prince Charles Edward, held court in the palace of his ancestors at Holyrood and his scratch army reached as far south as Derby before turning back, Stuart hopes were extinguished for ever at the battle of Culloden by the Hanoverian Duke, 'Butcher' Cumberland.

The duel with France overseas was unresolved. In India the French, under the brilliant Dupleix, meant to form an empire, and won a dominant position in the South, capturing Madras from the British. At the peace in 1748 this trading-post of the East India Company was returned. Meanwhile the French entertained a vast imperial design in North America, linking

European ladies wearing clothes made from Indian textiles.

Canada with a chain of forts down the Mississippi with Louisiana. This was intended to cut off the British Colonies from expanding west; though they were in no state to do so yet, the colonies were alarmed, and this necessitated the war waged by the home government primarily on their behalf.

This was the Seven Years' War (1756–63), in which Britain reached the height of her power. It began badly with the loss of Minorca and the French advancing in North America, where General Braddock's expeditionary force had been cut to pieces beyond the Alleghanies. The Whig oligarchy was showing itself nerveless in the conduct of war, until popular opinion and the support of the City brought a non-party man to wage it. This was William Pitt, grandson of a redoubtable governor of Madras, a man of a fearless, imperious spirit, whose oratory inspired Parliament and the nation: 'I know that I can save my country – and that nobody else can.' It was the spirit of Winston Churchill, remotely connected by family, in 1940.

Pitt proceeded to carry out his boast, for he grasped the essence of the world strategy necessary to contain France, and then defeat her in detail. Sea power gave mobility; but he understood the effective combination of land power and sea power, fleets and armies, as few war leaders have done, and possessed the perceptive eye to select the right men for the job. He chose Hawke and Boscawen at sea, and young General Wolfe for Canada.

Pitt's appeal was not to the oligarchy, which had always disregarded him and tried to do without him, and which in his heart he despised – for he was an unquiet spirit, impossible to deal with, except on his own terms – but to the people at large, who instinctively responded. As Trevelyan says, in his *History of England*, 'he evoked the spirit of freedom to save the Empire:

To glory we call you, as freemen, not slaves,
For who are so free as the sons of the waves?

The song conveys the spirit in which the Navy and the Empire won the decisive war against France on the high seas, in Canada and in the Ohio valley.' Trevelyan adds, in his own idiom, 'that victory decided that free institutions instead of despotic institutions were to dominate North America.' A more sceptical generation would conclude that that was inevitable anyway – and yet the issue had to be fought. A decisive element in all this, it must not be forgotten, was the sheer fighting spirit of the British tars (or sailors) in these wars: in spite of press-gang recruiting, harsh treatment and hard tack, beatings and all, they were tough and indomitable. The actual design of the French ships (like French taste in general) was in some respects superior; it was the gunnery and courage of the British sailors that made the difference.

Pitt grasped that France had to be held in check on the Continent, and his policy was 'to conquer Canada in Germany'. But by the 'reversal of alliances', a diplomatic revolution, France had won over Britain's historic ally, the Austrian Empire. There was nothing for it but to support – and save – Prussia, surrounded as she was by three great enemies, France, Austria and Russia, and holding off each in turn. Subsidies were poured out to keep Frederick the Great fighting in the field, though his survival was almost miraculous. He himself knew what he owed to Pitt: Great Britain had been 'long in labour, but had at length given birth to a man'. Frederick became a popular hero in Britain: hence the many 'King of Prussia' inns.

Soon the victories began to register, especially in the extraordinary year 1759, when Horace Walpole said the churchbells were threadbare from ringing out victories. Utterly decisive was the battle of Quiberon Bay, where Hawke destroyed the French Atlantic fleet. In combined operations Wolfe captured the Canadian capital, Quebec. Across the mountains the Ohio valley was cleared: Fort Duquesne became Pittsburg, named after Pitt. French possessions in the Caribbean fell to sea power; French power disappeared from North America. In India too the issue was settled, largely by a fighting spirit equal to Wolfe's, that of Robert Clive. He had begun, as a servant of the East India Company, by resisting

Robert Clive, or 'Clive of India'. He began his career there as a representative of the East India Company but became famous for his victory over the French at Plassey in 1757.

French power in Southern India. In 1757, in Bengal, he fought against vastly superior native forces and on the plains of Plassey in 1757 settled it that the British would be the superior power in the sub-continent. That power was only a commercial one, and the home government did not want to take on the responsibility of empire. It had, however, to fill the vacuum, and that posed a prime problem for British policy henceforward.

The immediate problem was – how to make peace? The war was won, but Pitt was unwilling to stop there. His strategic perception, amounting to genius, told him that France, relying on the Family Compact between the Bourbon powers (France and Spain), would call Spain to her aid in her emergency. Pitt, more imperious than ever, staked everything on attacking Spain before she was ready – and resigned when he could not force the government to follow him. Unfortunately he proved right: Spain declared war. It made no difference, the momentum of Pitt's drive continued.

Meanwhile the old king George II had died in 1760, at an advanced age and with few honours, and was succeeded by his grandson, the young George III. Pitt was the man for war,

hardly the man for peace, and the Peace of Paris, 1763, was made without him, much to his disgust.

It was a reasonable enough peace: Frederick the Great was left with the Silesia he had raped from Maria Theresa, thereby starting the previous war; he resented Britain's separate peace with France so much that she could not call on his support in her next hour of trial. Britain returned key-islands in the West Indies, of far greater value then for their sugar supplies to Europe and of much strategic importance, to France in place of (not very profitable) Canada. But the acquisition of Canada had been a prime objective of the American colonies and of Britain on their behalf.

The war left Britain with what could now properly be described as an empire, like that of Spain – except that it was mainly a trading and maritime empire, very disparate and with no apparent linking thread. There was a common sovereignty – the king-in-parliament – and it was subject to the Navigation Laws, protecting and nourishing its shipping and maritime power. Economic imperialism prevailed within it, i.e. the overseas possessions were to provide materials for home industries. The industrial development in the colonies was small; they made a prime field of export for the growing manufactures of Britain – in return the home country prohibited the growing of tobacco crops at home, for instance, for the benefit of the colonies.

So prodigious a settlement indicated trouble; so worldwide an ascendancy could not be supported for long by a small island power. Britain was left to all appearances in control of the whole of North America. Other powers could not be expected but to take advantage of the first signs of trouble. Moreover, the new system – it must have gone to the heads of some at least of the governing class – was contrary to the principle of Britain's security: not to be so powerful as to be a threat to others, but to form the keystone of a Grand Alliance against any other power that was. Now Britain's ascendancy had become a threat to others: in the next two decades she was riding for a fall.

Pitt's opposite number in France, Louis XV's minister Choiseul, said on Britain's annexing Canada, 'Now she will lose the American Colonies.' The threat to them removed, the colonies would need Britain no longer. Here was the cloud, not clearly discerned, that yet hung over politics until the outbreak of the American Revolution.

CONTEMPORANEOUSLY WITH BRITAIN'S RISE TO POWER the Continent was beginning to take more notice of her intellectually. Though Elizabethan plays and music had been performed in the Netherlands, Germany and Denmark, Francis Bacon's philosophic outlook, his vision of the way experimental science would develop, had had little influence abroad. With the foundation in 1660 of the Royal Society, through which the government supported scientific investigation, it began to flower and flourish. Sir William Hervey's discovery of the circulation of the blood in about 1616 took a generation to sink in to people's minds and enter general thought. Sir Isaac Newton made fundamental discoveries in optics and mathematics in the latter half of the

The death of Captain Cook, discoverer of Australia and New Zealand. A painting by John Clevely of his murder by Hawaiian natives.

century, leading on to the theory of gravitation as explanation of the structure and consistency of the cosmos. For the next two centuries up to our own time, with the appearance of Einstein, his views held the field – as Pope wrote:

> *Nature and Nature's laws lay hid in sight:*
> *God said, Let Newton be! and all was light.*

Newton's work raised Britain's prestige as much as Pitt's, and was much more unquestioned and lasting.

No less influential, in a more questionable sphere, was John Locke, the philosopher of the moderate Revolution of 1688, at the end of James II's reign. He thought that society rested upon an implicit contract between sovereign and people, ruler and ruled, and that, when the government broke this understanding, the people had a right to change it. The relevance of this to the circumstances of 1688 was obvious, and it would be appealed to by the American revolutionaries on their way to becoming Founding Fathers of the United States.

Locke was not so penetrating or so original a mind as Thomas Hobbes, who was more disturbing and uncon-

ventional. His emphasis on force in society, the necessity of sovereign power to hold it together, the brutal facts of the struggle for survival, his contempt for religious belief, his nose for humbug in all its forms, was very unwelcome to the English. Swift, too, was a writer who, with his searing view of human beings, his naked view of society without any illusions, had a universal appeal beyond other contemporaries.

Chapter 6

The Age of Revolutions

GEORGE III, OF THE FOURTH GENERATION OF his family in this country, was the first of them to speak English like an Englishman. Indeed, under the influence of his Scotch mentor, Lord Bute, he said in his speech on accession to the throne,' Born and educated in this country I glory in the name of Briton.' Unlike his predecessors, he was a nice young man; conventionally chaste and virtuous, he was always popular, through all his troubles and trials, with the great and growing heart of the middle classes and the country at large, but less so with the aristocracy. He had a poor opinion of politicians, their party spirit, their vanity and unreasonableness, and he had a German preference for experts and professionals. He was also a man of cultivated interests, being one of the foremost book-collectors of the age – his Royal Library forms the nucleus of the British Library. He loved music, particularly that of Handel, who became the 'family composer'. He patronized the arts – employing Reynolds and Gainsborough, Copley and Benjamin West (both Americans) – and sciences, making a particular friend of the atronomer Sir William Herschel, since he was interested in this subject himself. He was genuinely religious, anxious to promote the best men in the Church – the grazier's son, John Moore, was his personal choice for Archbishop of Canterbury. He had much to put up with from politicians and from his family, particularly his sons.

It is difficult to account for the feverishness of politics in the 1760s and 1770s. The inexperienced king's efforts to resume the just rights of the Crown and achieve some stability had the reverse effect, until he found a sensible prime minister in Lord North. An authority on the period, Richard Pares, used to think that much of the quarrelsomeness of politicians was due to their diet: they ate far too much meat and drank too much port. Pitt, who suffered agonies from the gout, was ordered by

his idiotic doctor to eat pounds of beef and drink gallons of port; when George III advised a moderate diet, like his own, Pitt as usual would not take telling. During this period there seemed to be wanting some principle of cohesion to keep politicians and nation together; Burke endeavoured to define one in his writings on Party (in 1770 he wrote *Thoughts on the Causes of the Present Discontents*) – but in vain.

Then a spanner was thrown into the works by John Wilkes, the Radical reformer, a man of scandalous morals, whom the virtuous House of Commons objected to having as a Member. Four times he was elected by the devoted electors of Middlesex, and four times ejected. The enthusiasm his case generated among his following had an important consequence: it gave the start to the political Radicalism which was to be of such significance in the next century. Meanwhile it had combustious and splintering effects at Westminster, where the politicians would not come together to form a stable government with a dependable majority in Parliament.

The personality of Pitt was an even more disturbing factor than the king's, and he was more autocratic. He would accept no principle of combination other than submission to himself. The result was that, when he consented to return to office in 1766, his Cabinet was a thing of shreds and patches. Even so, he could not get his own way. He seems to have seen into the heart of the problem of what to do in India: leave commercial matters to the East India Company, while the responsibility for territories taken over should be assumed by the Crown. This was thought too drastic a solution, and he was defeated; the problem remained. Whether owing to frustration or no, Pitt, who had become Lord Chatham and thus lost his command of the Commons, had a nervous breakdown while still holding nominal office. The king begged him to return to duty – in vain; his government gradually disintegrated. After this experience George III would never entrust Pitt with office again; when he recovered his faculties he went into Opposition.

The American question now came to dominate politics. Unrealized by either side, the colonies were approaching the political maturity which demanded self-government. They already largely ran their own internal affairs, though – after the Westminster model – their legislatures kept up a running fight with their executives, in their case the colonial governors. For all the Americans' excruciating concentration on politics, they had not been able to pull together at the Albany Conference in 1754, at which Benjamin Franklin put forward a plan to unify the colonies to face the French danger. The Seven Years' war, largely on their behalf, left Britain with a heavy burden of debt; it was reasonable to expect that they would help to carry it. In 1765 Parliament extended to America 'the familiar system of stamp-duties, which the British had copied from the Dutch'. The imposition was quite light, and Benjamin Franklin, the most eminent American of the day, saw no objection to it. But it was the first duty that had been imposed other than customs duties, and the Americans raised the age-long cry of 'No taxation without representation', and appealed to Magna Carta.

The Stamp Act was repealed the following year, with the agreement of George III. But revenue was needed and government tried to raise it by import duties, which were opposed both by the colonies and at home. In 1770 the concession was made of repealing all duties except that on tea. The East India Company had a surplus of tea to offer at an unusually low price, even including tax. But the imposition of the tax was a symbol of British oppression, and it was shortly followed by the Boston Tea Party, when a gang of rioters raided a ship's cargo of tea and emptied it into Boston harbour. Henceforth it became a patriotic duty for the Americans to drink coffee. Mob pressure was directed by such men as Sam Adams, a local collector of rates who was some two or three thousand pounds in debt, and had nothing to lose from revolution. Pressure was applied on the governor of Massachusetts, Thomas Hutchinson, himself a patriotic American, who was driven out of public life by the Radicals and forced into exile.

Puritan Massachusetts had always been ungovernable, and the revolution of 1688 had destroyed James II's hope of forming a more amenable Dominion of New England. The home government now took active measures, closing the port of Boston, suspending the colony's charter, and sending troops – who behaved well under the constant strain of insults and jeers; loyal citizens were tarred and feathered.

Other colonies now lined up to make common cause with Massachusetts, particularly in the South, which had little in the way of grievances, while the Middle Colonies were inclined to be neutral in the growing confrontation. The fact was that there was division within every colony, as there was at home, where some of the most eminent Englishmen sympathized with the Americans. The revolutionaries, as usual, were a minority; but they had the will-power and an objective – independence.

In 1774 an American Congress met in Philadelphia, the revolutionary precursor of the existing Congress. It was hardly to be expected in eighteenth-century circumstances that Great Britain would simply hand over to this body and evacuate – no other empire would have done so, Spanish, Austrian, or Russian. The American Revolution set the model

King George III by Alan Ramsay. Though Hanoverian by descent, he was English-born, the first in his line to speak English without an accent.

that the world was to follow, and the Declaration of Independence of 1776 provided a manifesto to inspire further essays in 'liberation'.

The war was in the nature of a civil war: the wealthier elements in most of the colonies, naturally conservative, were apt to be for maintaining the connection with Britain; while at home many people were pro-American; even the sympathies of some of the naval and military commanders, Keppel and the Howes, were with the colonies. The bulk of the backwoods country gentlemen supported the war. It was a tragedy that it was ever embarked upon; for, even if Britain had won, in ten or fifteen years' time, when she was engaged in a life-and-death struggle with the French Revolution and Napoleon, the colonies would have had to govern themselves and have achieved independence anyhow. The pity of it was that it came about in the way it did; it left an ill legacy. But it provided the new nation at its birth with a myth to sustain it.

It was the second of the civil wars within the bosom of the English-speaking peoples; the first had been in the seventeenth century, and had transmitted some of its Commonwealth thinking to the second. The third, the American Civil War of the nineteenth century, was the most terrible and deplorable of all.

Operations directed from across the Atlantic were difficult to co-ordinate, and the English regular troops were at a disadvantage against minute-men behind entrenchments, as at

OPPOSITE ABOVE *The English defeat at Bunker Hill, 1775, one of the early clashes in the American War of Independence.*
OPPOSITE BELOW *The battle of Princeton, 1777, by William Mercer.*

AN EXACT VIEW of THE LATE BATTLE AT CHARLESTOWN June 17th 1775.

In which an advanced party of about 700 Provincials stood an Attack made by 11 Regiments & a Train of Artillery, & after an Engagement of two hours Retreated to their Main body at Cambridge, leaving Eleven Hundred of the enemy Killed and Wounded upon the field.

Bunker's Hill in 1775, and in forest warfare – in effect against guerrillas. Disaster ensued at Saratoga in 1777, when General Howe failed to move up north to meet Burgoyne who was marching south down the Hudson Valley, and Burgoyne's army, isolated in the wilderness, had to surrender to the colonists. News of this decided France to enter the war on the side of the Americans, and transformed the situation.

Louis XVI's government had no interest in spreading ideas of liberty and self-government – France was merely taking her opportunity to get her own back; but liberal-minded aristocrats like Lafayette (a personal favourite with Washington), enthusiasts for liberty, equality, and fraternity, brought the idea back to France. Next year Spain joined in – no more anxious to see colonies set free, but to get back Gibraltar and Minorca. However, in the next generation Spain's colonies fought their own war of independence. One sees the world importance the American Revolution had; in a way, it was appropriate that English stock should follow the example set in the seventeenth century. The example was shortly to be taken up by others.

Britain was now fighting a world war, against half the world, across the oceans. Northern Europe, under the lead of the Empress Catherine of Russia, formed a hostile Armed Neutrality to stop the British navy's operation against trade with America. Britain retaliated by rounding up practically the whole of the Dutch merchant marine and outposts in America and Asia. For a time Britain lost command of the sea off the American coast to the French fleet, and this forced the surrender of Cornwallis' southern army at Yorktown in 1781. Thus was the independence of the colonies won.

George Washington and his generals at their decisive victory at Yorktown, 1781.

The fact was willingly recognized in Britain, except by George III, naturally enough, who did not wish to preside over the dissolution of the British Empire.

There remained the struggle in the rest of the Empire. Gibraltar, under siege throughout the war, was never taken. Communications with India were endangered by the brilliant commerce raider Suffren, but the dominant power maintained

itself by the courage and diplomatic skill of an imperial statesman of the first rank, Warren Hastings. Canada was saved by Carleton – though the Catholics of Quebec had no wish to come under the liberating influence of Puritan New England. Indeed the Quebec Act of 1774, giving full assurance for their religion to French Canadians, was made another grievance by the colonists. At length, in 1782, Admiral Rodney's great victory of the Saints recovered command of the sea, and enabled peace to be made on more favourable terms.

The Americans may not have won the war – the French had done it for them – but they certainly won the peace. Ironically,

Warren Hastings, governor-general in 1773, who championed England's growing interests in India.

in the event, France paid the heaviest price, with the French Revolution of 1789.

In Britain, the loss of the colonies brought a significant political change. Prime Minister Lord North, who was not to blame, was made the scapegoat; neither had George III been responsible for the war – merely for holding on tenaciously when he, like everyone else, was convinced that the loss of the colonies would be the end of Britain. As often happens in history, things turned out contrary to people's expectations: trade with the new United States actually increased, and Britain's industrial and trading expansion marched hand in hand with American expansion westward – now unhindered by concern for Indians.

The peace was made by the pro-American Shelburne, a left-wing Whig doctrinaire, who had a vision of co-operation with the United States – not justified in the event – for which he made large concessions about the frontier in the Middle West at the expense of Canada's future. This was never forgotten by Canada, where the English stock received a large recruitment of Loyalists who would not accept the new United States. They emigrated north in some thousands, United Empire Loyalists, to Ontario and the Maritime Provinces, where their resentment remained a factor to be reckoned with.

We must not overlook the greatness of George Washington, first President of the United States. In a real sense he was the father of the new country – descended as he was from ancient medieval stock in the North of England – not only for his military services but for his steadiness, courage, statesmanship. He was an improving landlord, the largest in Virginia, with a horde of slaves. (For the apostles of liberty, like Thomas Jefferson, were considerable slave-owners. And when Britain ended the slave trade in 1807, the Americans took that over also.)

George III offended American sentiment by employing Hessian troops, in the eighteenth-century manner, against the English colonists; but they in turn also employed Germans, French, Poles – and after all, he was Elector of Hanover. There was something in Chesterton's paradoxical summing up that it had been 'a war in which an English gentleman defeated a German King'.

REPERCUSSIONS FROM THIS HISTORIC EARTHQUAKE continued. In Ireland the Dublin Parliament, under the moderate leadership of Henry Grattan, won scope for independent action which might have led to better things. It repealed Poynings' Law of Henry VII's time, which subordinated Irish legislation to the approval of the English executive. The Dublin Parliament was still that of the Anglo-Irish Ascendancy, but the spirit of the eighteenth-century Enlightenment made for widespread toleration of Catholicism. Measures protecting Irish industries were passed – the cattle trade which gave Cork its prosperity, the glass making of Waterford, the linen industry of the North. The future looked hopeful.

In 1783 Chatham's son, the pro-American younger Pitt, took power with a programme of reform enough to fill a lifetime. The pity of it was that so much of it was frustrated. He took after his mother's family, the Grenvilles, in his dominant interest in administration; he had none of his father's genius for waging war, but the circumstances – the aggressive drive of the French Revolution – compelled him to spend most of his life combating it. He did inherit his father's spirit of lofty – and haughty – patriotism. 'England will save herself by her exertions and Europe by her example.'

His was an outlook in keeping with the new developments and needs of the age, especially the economics of the Industrial Revolution. Not for nothing had the young Pitt absorbed the teachings of Adam Smith's *Wealth of Nations*, published in the year of the Declaration of Independence, 1776. Adam Smith showed that opening industry to the vigorous challenge of competition would release economic energies and increase productivity and the nation's wealth. Pitt proposed a constructive scheme of free trade between England and

Pitt the Younger, Prime Minister from 1783 to 1801, and from 1804 to 1805.

Ireland, to the latter's advantage: accepted by the Irish Parliament, it was wrecked by the opposition of the English manufacturers. He was successful with a commercial treaty with France, reciprocally lowering duties, though it was opposed by Charles James Fox, anti-French for the purpose.

Fox argued that France was 'the unalterable enemy of England'; Pitt thought that 'to suppose that any country was unalterably the enemy of another was weak and childish'. When the French Revolution broke out, with the eventual threat of spreading to other countries, Fox said that the Fall of the Bastille was 'the best news since Saratoga'. What a thing to say, for a party leader who sought to run the country! For Fox, the descendant of both Charles II and James II – illegitimately, of course – was just as autocratic as George III. No wonder the provident king did not wish to entrust the treasury to a man who had gambled away a fortune of a quarter of a million, and was at one time bankrupt. Wonderfully gifted as he was, he was irresponsible; Pitt, ten years his junior, did well to keep him out of power so long as he lived.

Pitt reduced customs and excise duties – that on tea, for example, from 119 per cent to $12\frac{1}{2}$ per cent. This had a good effect in encouraging its consumption among all classes, instead of so much alcohol; good for revenue, it was also good

The RE-ELECTING of REYNARD,
or Fox the Pride of the Geese

for India, which grew it. Fox, during his brief tenure of power, had proposed an India Bill which, in effect, would have annexed the extensive patronage in India to the aristocracy, particularly of his own party. The Crown was much more representative of the general interest of both countries, and more impartial. Fox's brazen proposals were an important element in his overwhelming defeat in the country in 1784, which confirmed Pitt in power. Pitt's India Bill left political power to the Crown, very properly, while the East India Company appointed the officers to execute orders under a board of control. This dual system, a much more realistic and appropriate one, was found sufficient to carry on right up to the Indian Mutiny of the mid-nineteenth century.

On the other hand, the reformer in Pitt allowed the impeachment of the great pro-consul, Warren Hastings, and this was a grievous error. Perhaps Pitt could not help himself in the matter, but the seven-year-long persecution of Hastings was abominable, a blot on British history. Made governor-general in 1773, responsible for British power throughout the sub-continent from his base in Calcutta, he not only saved it but prevented the collapse of the states system. In the disintegration of the Mogul Empire, he saw that only British power could fill the vacuum. He had the courage to push forward British territorial responsibility in areas where there

'The re-election of Reynard', in other words the Whig statesman Charles James Fox.

was none, or where authority was breaking down.

One cannot make an omelette without breaking eggs, and some of Hastings' operations were open to question. (Though hardly to those of Burke, his prosecutor, whose cousin and housemate, William Burke, was up to his neck in speculation in East India stock; and Edmund Burke himself was not beyond reproach financially.) Hastings' authoritarian rule was beneficent to the Indian people: he took strong measures against dacoity (gang robbery), endemic in India – as later the Cornishman, Sleeman, devoted his life to suppressing the Thugs, the ritual murderers who strangled thousands along the highways.

Hastings had a deep interest in Indian culture; he learned Persian, consorting regularly with Brahmins and founding the Asiatic Society of Bengal. In this he was aided by a kindred spirit, a man of genius, Sir William Jones. From early Oxford days Jones was an Orientalist of distinction, noted for his translations from Arabic and Persian poetry. Jones had a passion for the East, and not only translated the epic *Sakuntala* but codified the whole of Indian Moslem Law. He then went into the more difficult field of Sanskrit and Hindu origins and lore – a closed book to the West. Winning the

confidence of the pundits, he uncovered the Hindu learning which had been submerged under the Moslem ascendancy of the Moguls, and resurrected and codified much Hindu Law before his death at the age of forty-seven. His was a prodigious achievement, and its ultimate effect was of historic significance: his work in recovering Hindu Culture, submerged beneath the Moslem, lay at the root of subsequent Indian nationalism. Perhaps it was no coincidence that Jones, with his enthusiasm and passion for learning, his deep sympathy with the submerged Indian culture, was Welsh; nor that a Briton thus initiated the eventual Indian resurgence.

Nor must we forget the labours of the missionaries, even if we no longer subscribe to the beliefs that inspired them to devote their lives to the well-being of the Indian people, and all that they did for the spread of education and medicine, language and literature. William Carey was a Baptist shoemaker, but, as Clark says, 'a born linguist. His grammars and dictionaries and translations' [into various Indian languages] 'represent almost superhuman labours. ... It did not occur to anyone to accuse him of spiritual imperialism'.

ABOVE *A British officer rides in procession in India in the late 18th century.*
RIGHT *The monument to the great Sir William Jones, Orientalist and lawyer, designed by Flaxman for University College, Oxford.*

Henry Martyn, a Cornish Evangelical, sacrificed his life for India – he died at thirty, but not before he had translated the New Testament and the Prayer Book into Hindustani, and the New Testament and Psalms into Persian. Handsome Bishop Heber of All Souls, Oxford, famous for his hymns, was only forty-two when he died, having travelled the length and breadth of India evangelizing, leaving accounts of his journeys and labours, establishing a college and schools.

A greater man than all these was John Wesley, founder of the Methodist church, whose life practically spanned the century: he was a man of orthodox Anglican belief, who yet established a world communion. A man of undoubted spiritual genius, he had tremendous energy and organizing ability. It is interesting that his first mission was to Georgia, and the Methodist Church was to have its largest following in the United States, though he was very much opposed to the American Revolution. He travelled incessantly all over the British Isles – his Journals give a vivid picture of eighteenth-century society – and in America, preaching, organizing, writing. Dr Johnson found him fascinating to talk to – only he never had time for a talk. His personality is venerated by millions still throughout the world.

WHAT ENABLED BRITAIN TO RECOVER so quickly from the appalling strain of a world war was the accelerating expansion of both Agrarian and Industrial Revolutions. There was a marked increase of population consequent upon a decline in the death rate. This was due not only to medical improvements, e.g. inoculation against smallpox, but to better nutrition. Improving landlords all over the country – such as Coke of Norfolk, Bakewell, Jethro Tull – increased the yield on crops by more scientific methods, better rotation and cultivating root crops for winter feed, so that cattle weighed more, and sheep produced more wool. Enclosures of private land on a large scale meant more efficient agriculture and more food. Much sentiment has been expended on the agricultural labourers who were rendered redundant by the enclosures. But more work was available in growing towns and manufacturing areas, to such an extent that there was a large immigration from over-populated Ireland and a more discriminating incursion of Scots.

The essence of the Industrial Revolution was the application of power to manufacture of every kind, first of water power, then of steam. These processes were complex, interdependent and widespread. In every region some of the landlords, from the dukes (e.g. Bridgewater, Devonshire, Bedford) downwards, acted as patrons to the actual inventors, operators, engineers, builders. To take only one example:

The death of John Wesley, founder of Methodism.

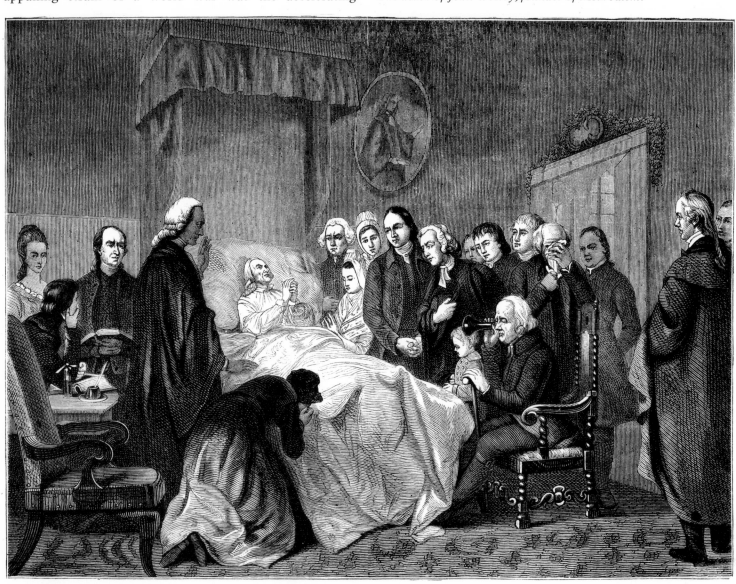

Cornwall, which led the world in the production of tin and copper, also led in the technique of mining, the development of the Cornish steam pumping-engine which cleared water from mines all over the world. (The biggest of these engines from a Cornish foundry pumped dry the Haarlem Meer and is now a national monument in Holland.) Mining development proceeded under the aegis of such landlords as Sir Francis Basset and Joseph Austen Treffry, entrepreneurs like the remarkable Williams family, and experts like Davies Gilbert, president of the Royal Society, allied to the inventive genius of Richard Trevithick, who produced the first steam locomotive.

The country was knit together by its new system of turnpike roads, with fast-running coaches, and a network of canals. This enabled the raw materials to be brought to where they could be most economically worked up. The same applied to coastal and oceanic shipping; coal from the South Welsh mines came across the Bristol Channel to Cornwall, which returned its tin for the tin-plate industry and smelting works of Swansea, which became the prime smelting centre in the world. American cotton was brought across the Atlantic to Liverpool, which grew into a great port, and on to Manchester and the towns of South Lancashire, which become the world's prime cotton-spinning region. The same happened in Yorkshire with woollens. The railways shortly followed, beginning in Tees-side. Metal industries centred upon

Sheffield and Birmingham; coal and iron in the Midlands, South Wales, the North Country and the industrial belt of Scotland. The engines invented by Boulton and Watt not only served Britain but went all over the world.

The discovery of china clay in Cornwall gave Britain a new industry in the manufacture of china ware, located in the Staffordshire Potteries under the lead of Josiah Wedgwood. America provided the largest market for these products, where one sees many fine examples in the museums. The grandest of Wedgwood dinner services was ordered by the Empress Catherine of Russia, where one can still see it.

No less a source of power was the application of the capital that was accumulating for productive developments. This meant a considerable growth of banking all over the country: here the reliable Quakers were to the fore. Of numerous examples we might cite John Taylor, of East Anglian Quaker stock, who, after a successful career as a mining engineer, turned to funnelling London capital into mining enterprises in Cornwall and West Devon, Wales and Derbyshire, and finally into the silver mines of Mexico.

It is impossible to do justice to the rush of energy released by these developments or the legion of creative capitalists, inventors, engineers and manufacturers, who made the new factory system, responsible for this beneficent revolution. The historian observes two conclusive points. First, the centre of

RAIL ROADS.

OPPOSITE ABOVE *A reproduction of the famous Spinning Jenny, designed by Hargreaves, which revolutionized the wool industry.* OPPOSITE BELOW *A satire on the first railway boom.*

ABOVE *The world's first iron bridge, at Ironbridge, Shropshire, designed by Abraham Darby of Coalbrookdale in 1780. It is still in use today.*

*A painting by Joseph Wright of Derby, showing children
and adults in awe before one of the age's new inventions,
the Air Pump.*

gravity within Britain moved north for the first time in history; the backward, underpopulated Highland Zone became foremost. This would have its political consequences all through the next century. Secondly, modern world civilization is industrial civilization: its foundation was laid, its basic methods worked out, in this small island.

IMMEDIATELY, INCREASING TRADE and the ebullience of the economy enabled the country to carry the large burden of funded debt from the American war. Revenue recovered, along with reduction of restrictive duties, so that in a few years Pitt was actually able to announce a surplus. It was just in time to counter the challenge, then the threat, finally the almighty danger, of the French Revolution and Napoleon.

Pitt began as a convinced parliamentary reformer; he proposed the reasonable, but pretty considerable, measure of disfranchising rotten boroughs, the redistribution of seventy-two seats to the counties, and widening the franchise, which would give votes to many small land-holders. Compensation was offered to borough-holders for their property rights. Vested interests saw, however, that this was but the thin end of the wedge and that Pitt meant to go further. The measure was defeated by a large majority. How many of Pitt's admirable intentions were aborted by the force of circumstances and the facts of political life!

The early stages of the French Revolution of 1789 were greeted with a fair amount of sympathy in Britain – people hoped, with some complacency, that France would at last settle down with a constitutional monarchy after the British model. The course of the Revolution put paid to these hopes. At the same time as it liberated the peasants from feudal subjection and gave them the land, it released mob fury against the aristocracy in the burning of *châteaux*, even cathedrals, and in the killings and drownings at Nantes. These excesses reached their height in Paris with the massacres in the prisons of September 1792, and the executions of Louis XVI and Marie Antoinette. The Jacobins of Paris and the leading cities governed by guillotine, and shortly the Revolution began to devour its own offspring – as we have seen the Russian Revolution do in our own time.

Europe was filled with Frenchmen fleeing from the monstrous régime of Danton, Robespierre and their kind – not only the royal family and aristocrats, but the higher clergy, for the Church too was under persecution. Men of genius like the writer Châteaubriand had to take refuge abroad. Others, like Condorcet, the philosopher of progress, or Lavoisier, France's greatest chemist, the discoverer of oxygen, or André Chénier, the brilliant young poet, perished on the scaffold.

It was natural that civilized people everywhere were shocked and alarmed, and that the reaction against it gathered strength. The Revolution and its repercussions, in one way and another, re-made the politics of Europe, not only its map. The consequences in the British Isles were profound. It not only put paid to all hopes of parliamentary reform for a generation but, as reaction gathered force in the course of the struggle, Radical sympathizers with the Revolution, the Corresponding Societies, were put down, subversive literature proscribed, fellow-travellers discouraged and, by legislation against combination in industry, trade unions prohibited. On the other side, the long struggle against France generated a strong current of national feeling to sustain it, a natural patriotism of which Nelson was the foremost, and most emotional, exponent.

Pitt, though less emotional, was not far behind him. He had no aristocratic illusions and his appeal was to the constantly growing middle classes. The young reformer became the inspiration of a new kind of Toryism, exemplified by such middle-class men as George Canning, the most brilliant of them; Sir Robert Peel, Lancashire cotton magnate and father of the later prime minister, who carried the first Factory Act to care for the health of young mill-hands; the staid and sober Huskisson, with his comprehensive knowledge of trade and industry; or Jenkinson who, as Lord Liverpool, led the new Tory Party long after Pitt's early death right up to the age of reform.

Pitt had no wish whatever to join in the war undertaken by reactionary Austria and Prussia against the French Revolution: he was bent on peace and progress and maintained neutrality. But the Revolution unleashed a new impetus in the most powerful nation in Europe. It applied conscription to a population still over twice the size of Britain's

and added that to the technical skill and discipline of the foremost army in Europe. The result was to be seen at the battle of Valmy in 1792, when the French revolutionary army rolled back the forces of ancient Europe and proceeded to conquer Belgium. This was always strategically the most dangerous spot, immediately opposite the Thames estuary, for Britain to have in occupation of an enemy power; but it was France that declared war in February 1793 against the two neutrals, Britain and Holland. Pitt expected the war to be short, but the renewed duel was to last for a generation.

As usual the war began badly for Britain which was unprepared militarily. Her attempts to intervene on land in the Netherlands, and on the French coast to help the Royalists in Brittany, were either incompetently handled or futile; while at Toulon, occupied for three months, the British were blown into the sea by the ardour and artillery of a young gunnery expert, Bonaparte. (If only the British had held on to Corsica earlier he would have been a subject of George III.) The navy reached its zenith in this war, under the highest leadership and a brilliant school of sea officers, while the French fleet, which had done well in the American war, was demoralized by the killing and discouragement of its officers in the course of the Revolution. Admiral Howe immediately won command of the Channel by the 'glorious First of June' 1794, when six

A famous cartoon showing Pitt and Napoleon 'carving up' Europe between them.

French ships of the line were captured and made a useful addition to the navy.

The year 1797 was the lowest point of the war. Bonaparte had over-run Northern Italy and made it a French dependency. Russians and Austrians were alike defeated; Switzerland and Holland became French-dominated republics; France advanced to the Rhine. The old nightmare of a Europe dominated by one great power, which could then subject Britain, had returned in a still more threatening form with the impulse of revolution. Hitherto armies had been comparatively small and war was waged mainly by professionals. Now the French armies were enormous; everywhere they marched they carried the standard of revolt against feudal and aristocratic privilege, so they always had a party with them in the country they invaded – and meanwhile they lived off the land.

Britain's safety line lay in sea power, and the traditional anchor of security, a grand alliance against the aggressor. This took the form of successive coalitions with Continental powers similarly threatened – and defeated in detail by Napoleon, until the advent of the fourth and final coalition of all the powers necessary to bring him down. Britain remained steady throughout the long ordeal, but sometimes for some years was fighting on alone. This was the danger point in 1797, when the British fleet mutinied at the Nore. The crisis was well handled by concessions and improved conditions, and the sailors sailed out happily to destroy the Dutch fleet at Camperdown, which otherwise would have been annexed to French resources.

In the next year, 1798, Napoleon was induced by the strain of megalomania which led to his ultimate undoing to invade Egypt, as a stepping-stone to India. (His brother Louis said of him: 'I know him well. He will blow the bubble till it bursts.') Napoleon conquered Egypt, but was followed by Nelson, a comparatively junior admiral, who, at the battle of the Nile, destroyed or captured every ship of the French fleet. It was a cardinal event in the war, for at one blow it restored British ascendancy in the Mediterranean, and enabled Malta, a strategic key, to be recaptured and friendly powers helped from island bases, e.g. the kingdom of Naples from Sicily. The victory enabled a second coalition to be formed, with Russia and Austria – defeated by Napoleon at Marengo. Russia and the Scandinavian powers now formed a hostile 'armed neutrality' against Britain's naval power; but this 'neutrality' was at once rendered worthless by Nelson's bombardment of Copenhagen and the destruction of the Danish fleet.

Sea power enabled Britain to mop up dependencies of hostile powers or those under French domination in the outer seas, in the West and East Indies; Cape Town and Ceylon were taken over to safeguard the strategic routes. The island

The battle of Copenhagen, 1801, a victory for Nelson. It was here that he put the telescope to his blind eye, to ignore the signal to withdraw.

A portrait of Nelson, one of Britain's greatest heroes, by Sir William Beechey.

of Penang had already been ceded, a gateway to Malaya on the way to China, supplied with much-required opium from India. In Southern India Tipoo Sahib undertook an energetic campaign to restore French influence, while the military power of the Mahrattas embarked on aggressive expansion in the North-West. A series of successful actions there demonstrated the military capacity of a young officer who was to become better known as Wellington. He was sneeringly described as a 'sepoy-general' (i.e. a commander whose experience lay with native troops) by Napoleon, who was to find otherwise on the field of Waterloo. Direct and indirect rule through the East India Company was now paramount throughout India; before the end of the war the company's monopoly of trade was ended and the market of the sub-continent thrown open to the products of the Industrial Revolution.

At home the most threatening repercussions of the French Revolution were felt in Ireland, always Britain's Achilles' heel strategically. In Ulster the Protestant Dissenters, full of revolutionary ideas first from America, then from France, formed the United Irishmen and prepared for armed rebellion. In Dublin a young disaffected Protestant, Wolfe Tone – a restless spirit who had a fascinatingly adventurous life, was incorrigibly idle at school, college and the bar, and ran off with an under-age girl – had a grand vision of union between Protestant Dissenters and Catholics to bring about an Irish Republic. 'To subvert the tyranny of our execrable government, to break the connection with England, the never-failing source of all our political evils,' was his declared objective: he was an eloquent Irishman.

He went to France for help, and in 1796 a large squadron of forty-three ships and 15,000 soldiers under the able republican Hoche – Bonaparte's rival – set sail from Brest. Disaster accompanied them, from poor seamanship, the indiscipline of the new revolutionary marine, and bad weather. Ships parted company; even so a section of the fleet, with 7000 men, arrived in Bantry Bay, without supplies, to be dispersed by a providential storm. Back to Brest! One does not know what might have happened if a large French army had landed. In 1798 a smaller force from France made a landing in the North of Ireland; during the action Tone was captured and committed suicide. In the South a larger rebellion of Catholic Irish broke out, but Tone's vision of co-operation with Protestants to establish a Franco-Catholic republic proved an illusion: the Loyalists joined with regular troops to defeat a rebel army of 15,000 in Wexford. Even so, another French force landed in the North and got across the Shannon before being forced to surrender. There followed severe repression: this was a stern necessity.

But what to do about Ireland?

Pitt was convinced that only a great act of statesmanship on the lines of the Union with Scotland could meet the situation. To allow Catholics the right to sit in Parliament, which would give them a majority in Dublin, could be safely granted at Westminster, where they would be a minority. His measure incurred every kind of opposition, and, already an exhausted man, he had great difficulty in getting it through both Parliaments. Ireland was to be represented by thirty-two peers (including four bishops), and one hundred MPs – more than twice the representation of Scotland. The royal prerogative would be restricted to keep the Irish peerage to one hundred, though Irish peers might sit in the United Kingdom House of Commons (as Castlereagh and Palmerston did). Financial arrangements fair to Ireland were made, and free trade established, though Irish woollens and cottons were to be protected against English competition for a term of years. It must be remembered that at this time – and until the great famine, largely due to over-population – Ireland's population was half that of Britain. She was correspondingly far more important then than later as an independent country.

The essential condition of success for the measure was to meet the claims of the Catholic Irish, which Pitt proposed to do. Catholics and other Dissenters should both be admitted to Parliament and office, the oath of allegiance being modified to accommodate them. Catholic priests and dissenting ministers would receive support, and the tithe system would be revised in their favour. Pitt at once came up against opposition in his Cabinet, and the Lord Chancellor Loughborough, of whom no good is known, betrayed the proposals to the king. George III was shocked and alarmed; he called it a 'Jacobinical' measure, and believed it contrary to his coronation oath. The Church came out in opposition, the archbishops working on the king's mind. A 'No-Popery' agitation, the product of centuries of past history, undermined Pitt's support in Cabinet, and he was unwilling to push George III, who suffered from recurring bouts of insanity. He himself, on the verge of a nervous breakdown, resigned after seventeen years of office; shortly after, the king had his breakdown all the same.

Once more the hope of a new deal in Ireland was fatally destroyed, and the consequences were as bad for Britain. For the Irish representation at Westminster added a large number of Tory backwoodsmen to the Commons, guarantors of reaction; Irish affairs, Irish problems and grievances, Irish agitation would bulk more largely than ever for the next century. Among other concessions to promote the Union Pitt had had to guarantee that the Protestant Church of Ireland, against the great majority, would remain established. The best hope of peace in Ireland thus remained politically impossible. The English Church was established in England; the Scottish Kirk in Scotland; why should not Catholicism, the religion of the majority, have been established in Ireland? It would have served, in its day, to keep order in the nursery.

AT THE TIME OF PITT'S RESIGNATION Britain was without an ally, and the war had reached a stalemate: the French had ascendancy on the Continent, the British on the seas. George III, having ruined the prospects of the Union with Ireland and recovered his senses, summoned a minister to his side whose intellect was more on a par with his own. (He never much liked Pitt's superiority of mind and manner.) The new prime minister was described by Canning:

> *As London is to Paddington*
> *So Pitt is to Addington.*

A peace was patched up at Amiens which was recognized as no more than a breathing space, for it left French domination of the Continent untouched, and Bonaparte proceeded to advance his position on the chess-board at every turn; and so the British refused to give up Malta. During the short interval bemused Whigs like Fox rushed to Paris to consult with the first consul, Bonaparte, who used his blandishments on his visitors to some purpose. Left-wing Whigs like Fox's nephew, Lord Holland, remained constant admirers of the military dictator in spite of everything; so too did a jaundiced Liberal like Hazlitt, who wrote his biography. Men of genius who had been enthusiasts for the French Revolution in their callow youth – Wordsworth, Coleridge, Southey – learned better by experience and became inspirers of a more philosophic Toryism. Sir Walter Scott, who understood so much of human nature – like Shakespeare – was always sensible and without

The young Wellesley, later to become the Duke of Wellington.

illusions about it. Edmund Burke, another Shakespearean spirit, had with the intuition of genius seen from the first that the hopes of 1789 would lead to military dictatorship. His *Reflections on the French Revolution* gave a lead to European thought on the subject, more influential than any English work since Locke.

Bonaparte's actions in the Mediterranean and the Near East, and his intrigues in India (which fascinated him), corroborated British suspicions about his lust for power, and the duel was renewed. Pitt, though ailing, was recalled to power, since his name was a host in itself. He was willing to bring in the widest support and include Fox, leader of the Opposition, but the king refused to have him. Others declined to serve, and Pitt was left to carry the burden virtually alone.

He devoted his last energies to forming yet a third coalition. In 1804 Napoleon, declaring himself emperor – with a remote reference to Charlemagne, as emperor of the West – was

preparing transports at Boulogne for the invasion of Britain. The crisis became a folk memory along the Channel coast of England, enshrined by Thomas Hardy in literature, especially in *The Dynasts*, and *The Trumpet-Major* and recalled again in unforgettable days in 1940.

All depended on the navy. When Nelson took leave of the prime minister in 1805 for the campaign that was to be his last, Pitt departed from his usual formality to accompany him to the gate of 10 Downing Street. Each knew all that was involved. At Portsmouth, when Nelson stepped into his boat to go out to the *Victory*, people knelt on the shore. They too understood. Off Trafalgar, Nelson met the combined French and Spanish fleets, which were heavier and more powerful. That did not deter him from heading a shattering blow at the centre, breaking the back of their line. By the end of the day French sea power was destroyed, though Nelson was dead.

Napoleon at once cut his losses and raced his armies to Central Europe to drive Austria out of the war at Austerlitz. Next Prussia was overthrown at Jena, and Russia at Friedland. The allies had not learned to coordinate, the

Gent, No Gent, & Regent !!

TOP *The death of Nelson at the battle of Trafalgar, 1805.*
ABOVE *A caricature of the Prince Regent, future king George IV.*

OPPOSITE *The Royal Pavilion, Brighton, inspired by the Prince Regent.*

coalitions to coalesce: Napoleon defeated them by swift, concentrated blows in succession. In 1807, when he signed the treaty of Tilsit with the Emperor Alexander of Russia, he stood at the height of his power, having come to an arrangement with Russia to a division of spheres of interest. He persuaded the Russians to come into the Continental System he was building up to exclude British trade from the Continent. The French Empire was extended, with its dependencies, along the mainland coast of northern Europe. British exports fell seriously; there was unemployment and want in various areas of Britain. Once more the reply was to wrest the rebuilt Danish fleet from falling into his hands.

Shortly after hearing the news of Napoleon's victory at Austerlitz in 1805, the first mortal blow at Pitt's third coalition, Pitt died, at forty-six: 'How I leave my country!' There was nothing for it but to call in the second man in politics, Fox, with the hopes he had nourished all along of making peace. He soon found that Napoleon had no intention of making peace except on his own terms. Shortly after, disillusioned at length, Fox died. The war was to continue;

but the Whig Ministry of 'All the Talents' was not at all talented at waging it. The reforming Lord Grenville rushed a special Act through Parliament to enable him, while prime minister, to enjoy by deputy his sinecure office of auditor of the exchequer at £4000 a year. Lord Ellenborough was made a member of the Cabinet, with doubtful constitutional propriety, while holding the office of Lord Chief Justice. They proceeded to tease the old king by raising the issue of Catholic disabilities unnecessarily. George III collected his last reserves of strength to replace them by another ministry.

The contest was George III's last political effort; he now went permanently insane, and his place was taken by the Prince of Wales as regent. He was the best of a not very satisfactory bunch, 'the first Gentleman of Europe'. He had exquisite, if extravagant, taste, built Carlton House, the 'stately pleasure-dome' of the Royal Pavilion at Brighton, and ultimately reconstructed Windsor Castle, filling his palaces with French furniture and works of art, an imaginative patron of Sir Thomas Lawrence and other painters. As a young man he had lent himself to the party purposes of Fox and the

Whigs; now that responsibility had come to him, he found that only the disciples of Pitt and the new Toryism could be relied on to hold on a firm course. For once more, on the break-up of the third coalition, Britain was left to fight on alone.

In 1808 an opportunity presented itself at last. Napoleon swept the Spanish royal family off the board like a pack of cards, made his reluctant brother Joseph king of Spain (at the royal palace in Madrid; 'Vous êtes mieux logé que moi' 'You are better lodged than I am.') – and for the first time came up against the strength of nationalism that was eventually to overthrow him. The British sent a small army under Sir John Moore to the assistance of the Spaniards; it was forced to retreat to Corunna by the large army Napoleon sent after him. The government at home did not give up, but sent Wellington to occupy Portugal: he dug himself in behind the impregnable lines of Torres Vedras, and, with constant naval support, could never be got out again for all the armies and marshals with whom Napoleon flooded the peninsula.

The Spaniards' contribution to the defence of their country was irregular and undisciplined, but distracting to the French: it took most effectively the form of guerrilla fighting all over the large country. This was was full of savagery, as we see from Goya's etchings and drawings. For the British the long-drawn struggle of the Peninsular War, 1809–14, recovered prestige for their arms and built up a gallant tradition in the annals of the army. It was a tough struggle with much bloodshed at the crossing of the Albuera and the storming of Badajoz (1812). For a century or more these memories were enshrined in folk-ballads, like the 'Bloody Albuera', sung in messrooms – as I remember sung on gaudy nights at All Souls.

Wellington played a cat-and-mouse game with the large forces the French had to deploy across the spaces of the Spanish Peninsula, advancing to deliver a blow, retreating to his triple lines when superior forces concentrated against him – exhausting them, never losing an action. Stage by stage the chess game was won: Fuentes de Onoro, Albuera, Badajoz, Salamanca, Vittoria – and the road was open for the invasion of France and the toppling of Napoleon.

For a turning-point was reached in 1809, when Napoleon attacked Austria, defeating her at Wagram, extracting from her her Italian provinces and a dynastic wife for himself in the emperor's daughter, Marie Louise. For the purpose he divorced his wife Josephine, who could bear him no children. At this point the cleverest brain in France, the ex-bishop Talleyrand, left him: he perceived that Napoleon no longer served the interests of France, but his own. This became still more evident with his most power-seeking folly, the attack on Russia and the march to Moscow; though he won the battle of Borodino in 1812, the Russians set fire to Moscow before abandoning it to him, and in his subsequent retreat in the severe Russian winter many of his troops died.

With this the long tide turned; for he had now aroused against him the nationalist sentiment of Germans by his punitive treatment of Prussia, and the profound feeling of the Russians for Holy Russia. Russians, Prussians, Austrians at length concentrated against him and gradually drove the French back across the Rhine, while Wellington crossed the

A cartoon by Rowlandson of Portsmouth Point in the early 19th century.

Pyrenees and won his way to Toulouse.

Napoleon abdicated in 1814 and was sent off to honourable imprisonment on the island of Elba. After a generation of such upheavals, the hammering out of peace terms and the settlement of the Continent was a complicated matter. Great Britain, the one power that had stood steadfast throughout, was in a central position: Castlereagh was sent abroad to represent the country and proved his greatness as a foreign secretary by his constructive, mediating policies. He and the Austrian statesman Metternich largely shaped the peace together. The Prussians were anxious to punish France and, backed by Russia, demanded the whole of Saxony, which would at once make them the dominant German power. Austria could not stand for this, and a crisis occurred.

Napoleon took advantage of this to return to France, where the Bourbon kings had been restored in the person of Louis XVIII, a fat and unwieldy man, but with a sense of humour. Louis XVIII fled at Napoleon's approach. The bulk of the nation accepted Napoleon's return, and during the Hundred Days that followed he collected a large army and massed artillery with which to confront the depleted allied forces under Wellington and Blücher at Waterloo in Belgium. Inflicting a reverse upon the Prussians, he made the mistake of detaching 30,000 men to follow what he supposed to be their retreat. This still left him with over 70,000 men, with a heavier

Mexico to annex one-half of Mexican territory – Texas, New Mexico, Arizona and California. The Southern dynasty of 'democratic' presidents – Jefferson, Madison, Monroe (of Welsh and Scots descent) – were hostile to aristocratic England.

The Americans did well at sea, inflicting heavy losses on merchant ships; invading Canada, they burned Toronto but were forced back by small Canadian forces, which fought tenaciously under effective leadership. In return the British burned Washington, though there was not much of it to burn – except the redbrick presidential mansion, which needed white-washing and so became the White House. After the signature of peace a victory was won at New Orleans against British regulars under Pakenham.

The peace that emerged from the Congress of Vienna in 1815, which settled Europe for a generation, was a moderate affair. France had to pay an indemnity for her final outbreak, and receive the Bourbons once more as kings at the hands of Britain. Paris was occupied for a time by allied troops under the command of Wellington, who provided a backbone for the returned dynasty. He enjoyed the favours of Mademoiselle George, of the Comédie française, who had also enjoyed those of Napoleon. Prussia got half of Saxony and its frontier was advanced to the Rhine; Austria got a dominant position in Italy; Russia got Poland, and Finland, which Napoleon had allowed to the Tsar Alexander at the Treaty of Tilsit. To bar French ambitions in the Netherlands, Belgium was joined to Holland, which was further strengthened by the return of her possessions in the East Indies, particularly Java.

Britain had no claims in Europe but she received from Denmark the island of Heligoland in the North Sea, which had been a useful post in the gigantic smuggling of goods with which Britain had countered Napoleon's Continental System. (As so often in history he, too, had been unable to square the circle. The lesson of history is that one should moderate one's aims.) Later Heligoland gave trouble, when it was handed over to Imperial Germany, and became an essential key in the development of her naval power. Malta was retained, as were Cape Town and Mauritius, along the route to India. France was to join Britain in the abolition of the slave trade. Since the Dutch East Indies were returned in friendly fashion, an empty island was acquired, upon which in time arose the greatest trading centre between India and China: Singapore.

On the whole, the clue to the success of the Vienna settlement was its aristocratic moderation, as against the excesses of the French Revolution and Napoleon's lust for power. 'Pourvou que ça doure' (Provided it lasts'), Madame Mère, his sensible old mother, used to say in her strong Corsican accent. It could not last, once the force of nationalism was aroused against him – the dominant force of the future.

Moderation was also the clue to Britain's success – otherwise others would have found her world-wide supremacy at sea intolerable. It gave her a blissful century of security in which to forge ahead on her own lines to achieve the most creative epoch in her history.

OVERLEAF *The Duke of Wellington at Waterloo, 1815.*

weight of artillery, against Wellington's mixed army of 65,000, of which the hard core was 27,000 British regulars.

The battle of Waterloo was very bloody – Wellington called it a very 'close-run thing' – and fell hardest upon the British, especially upon the officers, who suffered heavy casualties, to Wellington's distress. A cool, modest man, he allowed that the result might not have been the same if he had not been there. Napoleon was not his old self and made mistakes, of which Wellington took advantage. The French Marshal Ney sent thundering masses of cavalry to meet the deadly fire of the British squares, concealed behind the rise of hill. By the end of the day – Blücher keeping his word to be there to help the English – the Prussians began to join in on the French right, and turned doubtful victory into a rout. Napoleon fled back to Paris, abdicated a second time, surrendered to the British and was politely escorted to the island of St Helena. There the only harm he could do was to re-write his own legend in 'liberal' terms; this had a historic importance in paving the way in France for the Second Empire of Napoleon III.

In the last stage of the long struggle a distracting side-issue was a second colonial war with the Americans, who forced it on. Their grievance was the British insistence upon the right of search at sea, directed against trade with the enemy – since blockade was a chief weapon for a sea power in the struggle against Napoleon. Neither New England nor New York wanted war, but the Southern expansionists did; they aimed at annexing Canada – as shortly they were to force a war upon

Lithographed, Printed & Published by VINCENT BROOKS, 421 Oxford St. London.

Chapter 7

Recovery and Reform

THE LONG STRUGGLE WITH FRANCE HAD settled the historic issue: though France remained the first country in Europe, she was no longer to dominate it. Something like a Concert of Europe prevailed during the next few years, with a succession of conferences to discuss problems. The tone became more reactionary with Russia's Holy Alliance of 1815, in which England did not join – 'holy moonshine' Castlereagh called it; he was anxious to see that a Russian domination did not succeed the French one. When France intervened to restore reaction in Spain, Castlereagh's successor, Canning, promoted the struggle of the Spanish colonies in Central and South America to achieve their independence in turn. He summed it up as calling into existence the New World 'to redress the balance of the Old'. President Monroe proclaimed his doctrine warning off European powers from intervening in the New World; the reality behind this was that it was British sea power which kept them off.

At home there were severe problems: a quarter of a million men demobilized from the army meant unemployment; a succession of bad harvests produced the introduction of the Corn Law of 1815, excluding foreign corn until the price of British corn rose. Rick burnings in the country were followed by transportation to the penal settlements in Australia. Strikes in industrial areas, and smashing of machinery by the Luddites, were no help. A better solution was the model factory at Lanark, with schools, demonstrated by Robert Owen; he was something of a socialist, but more of an idealist.

Successive Factory Acts gradually improved working conditions, restricted hours of work, forbade women and children to work in the coalmines, and appointed inspectors to see to it. A big demonstration at Manchester in 1819 ended in the 'Peterloo Massacre', when soldiers fired on the mob, killing ten persons and wounding many – for there was as yet no police force, no civilian means of enforcing order.

Nevertheless, gradually, reforms were made: mechanics' institutes, working mens' colleges, and the foundation of University College, London, on a secular basis to challenge the Anglican monopoly of Oxford and Cambridge. The growing power of the middle class was to be seen in the accelerating energy of voluntary societies, out of which so much of the

OPPOSITE *In 1851, Prince Albert created the first international exhibition in history, to proclaim industrial progress and Britain's contribution to it. The Crystal Palace was designed by Joseph Paxton to house it; sited in Hyde Park, it covered twenty-six acres.*
ABOVE *The young Queen Victoria. Set in her bracelet is a portrait of Prince Albert.*
RIGHT *With the spread of industrialism, the Midlands and the North developed factories of many kinds, as in this view of 19th-century Leeds from Richmond Hill.*

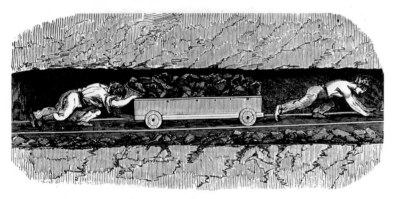

TOP *The interior of a pen-grinding factory.*
ABOVE *Small boys at work in a coalmine.*

good work of the nineteenth century was to come. The middle class believed firmly in individual initiative and enterprise – naturally enough it distrusted government intervention after the long reign of aristocratic favouritism and corruption. Lord Melbourne, a Whig prime minister, thought than an English gentleman was qualified to hold any office to which his birth entitled him. But underneath this sparkling façade – for Melbourne had aristocratic charm and wit – 'it was not long before men who were products of the Industrial Revolution stepped into leading places in parliamentary politics.'

Dr Arnold's appointment as headmaster of Rugby School in 1827 was a portent: the provost of Oriel said that he 'would remake the face of education in England'. He did set the model for reform of the old public schools and the foundation of new ones for the education of the constantly expanding middle class, the prime social force of the century. Arnold's influence was felt as far afield as India, throughout the empire and in the United States. His son Matthew Arnold's influence became still larger at home, in the sphere of elementary and secondary education. Middle-class power expressed itself in the marked growth of newspapers, of which the most influential was 'the Thunderer', *The Times*.

The reaction against the French Revolution and the long duel with it frustrated reform for two decades. The first breach in the old system was made by Catholic emancipation in 1829. Agitation for this had grumbled ever since its withholding ruined Pitt's hopes of the Union with Ireland. Granted now, it made little difference there, for the root of the trouble was over-population. At this time the Irish population, on a poor soil, a land largely of mountain and bog, increased by one million every decade, living mainly on potatoes. It was a crazy and dangerous situation. By the time of the terrible famine in the 1840s, when the potato harvest failed – as it did elsewhere, in the Netherlands, for example – Ireland, with a population of eight million, was the most densely populated country in Europe. This was at the root of everything – as in India today. It is true that there were other evils – absentee landlords for example; indeed, Ireland should have been a country of peasant proprietors, as it largely is today, with a population of some three million, as much as it can support.

It fell to Wellington to preside over Catholic emancipation which, as an Anglo-Irish Protestant, he had opposed for years. Though in politics nothing is so easy to eat as words, this operation caused him acute indigestion, and helped to split his party. His prestige helped greatly to carry it; but, the most famous man in the country and a devoted servant of the state, he was a failure as a politician, too rigid and unaccommodating. He was being left behind by a new world.

This was dominated by the question of parliamentary reform, which would open the floodgates of reform throughout the whole system. The simple social force behind it all was the pressure of the middle classes. The agitation for reform dominated the next few years, taking the form of propaganda, demonstrations, and riots (in one of which the centre of Bristol was burned). The governing class received a warning in the overturn of the Bourbon monarchy in Paris in 1830, and the revolt of the Belgians against the Dutch. This problem was safely dealt with by the establishment of an independent Belgium, guaranteed by the powers.

The Tories could not produce reform: this was left to a coalition of Whigs under Lord Grey together with the Radicals. Grey not only piloted through a complex measure, but conducted all the negotiations necessary to have it carried. Here the monarchy showed its usefulness; for there was always a heavy majority against the Reform Bill in the House of Lords. William IV prevailed on Wellington, the moderates and the bishops alike to let the Reform Bill through at the last moment, when the country was on the brink of disorder, and it was carried on 4 June 1832.

It was a victory for the middle class, not a triumph of democracy. As the historian Keith Feiling writes, 'It was the plain determination of the middle class which, more than mob violence, impressed Parliament: their huge but orderly meetings, the warnings received through Radical leaders, the refusal to act as special constables, resignations from the yeomanry, the overwhelming voice of the press and a firm lead given by *The Times*.' The new qualifications to vote added only some 250,000 voters, perhaps doubling the number in Britain (without Ireland). The redistribution of Parliamentary seats was more important, for at last the big Northern and Midland towns, the industrial areas, would receive political representation more in accordance with their economic and social power. But working-class votes were diminished, and disappointment and agitation over this led on to the Chartist movement, from 1838 to 1848, demanding six specific points of reform; but the working classes were not yet politically or educationally mature enough to share in power – nor would they be for a long time to come. What had happened was that 'the land-owning class had thus taken into partnership the middle-class manufacturers, tenant farmers, and skilled artisans'. This proved 'a first condition for all that was done in Victorian Britain'.

And the Reform Bill did release a vast impulse for reform, pushed forward and propagated by elect bourgeois spirits: Jeremy Bentham and his Philosophical Radicals, James and John Stuart Mill; Edwin Chadwick and Sir John Simon (the great Sir John), experts on working-class housing, sanitation and the Poor Law; Michael Sadler and Richard Oastler, Tory

A Chartist demonstration (in support of the 'People's Charter') being observed by Robert Peel's new police force, the Peelers.

This engraving shows the interior of the Field Lane night refuge for the destitute.

factory-reformers. '*Sanitas sanitatum*, all is sanitation,' sighed the cynical Disraeli.

Now much-needed reforms could go ahead. First the law, which was in a mess; some of the anomalies which Dickens exposed in his novels were ended and a more rational structure was given to the courts. The law had a long way to go, however, before it caught up with the progressive spirit of Bentham – in regard to sex, for example, where we have reached his enlightenment only in our time, not completely even so. The Church was tackled if gently. The archbishop of Canterbury's salary was reduced from £30,000 to £15,000 a year, quite sufficient for his purposes. The princely bishopric of Durham was reduced from £70,000 a year to provide an endowment for a new university based in the Castle. Surpluses were applied to raise the salaries of poor clergymen of which there were far too many, while some bishops and deans and chapters still had too much. This measure sparked off in 1833 the Oxford movement, under John Keble and John Henry Newman, which in time would re-make the face of the Church at home and overseas.

Next year followed the reform of the Poor Law, 'the most ambitious piece of social legislation which Parliament had ever enacted'. During the long war, poor relief had got into appalling confusion – no rhyme or reason in it, with a heavy burden on local rates, which varied; while sections of the people were demoralized, others went hungry. The gigantic mess was now mopped up by an administrative revolution under Chadwick's ruthless zeal. He arranged over 20,000 parishes into 600 'Unions', each with its workhouse and elected body of guardians supervised by commissioners at the centre. The measure was intensely unpopular, but it was better than having the localities bankrupted by poor relief on one side, or people starving on the other.

In 1835 municipal corporations throughout the country were drastically reformed and reconstituted, under the drive of a Birmingham Radical, Joseph Parkes. Over 200 old corporations were dissolved, and some 180 municipal corporations set up to be run by elected councils, all rate-payers having the vote.

Greatest of this spate of reforming measures was the abolition of slavery throughout the empire. William Wilberforce had never been content with stopping the slave trade – for when Britain ended hers in 1807, others carried on. She paid Spain and Portugal £700,000 to induce them to end theirs. France was made to stop hers by the peace. The Americans stepped theirs up. Now Parliament advanced the

enormous sum of £20 millions to compensate slave-owners for giving up their possession of slaves. This led to the decline of the sugar industry in the West Indies, which now could not compete with the slave-grown sugar of Cuba and Brazil. The example was not followed by the Southern States in the USA.

IN 1837 A YOUNG QUEEN came to the throne, Victoria, who was to reign so long as to give her name to the greatest age in our history. To begin with 'this new monarchy was very German, and by no means popular'. It did get rid of the encumbrance of the Hanoverian dynasty, but Victoria's marriage to her cousin, Albert of Saxe-Coburg, increased the monarchy's German inflexion. Coburg ambitions and the marriages of their numerous family made for a swarm of useful dynastic connections all over Europe.

The 1840s were remembered by the people as 'the hungry forties'. My grandparents in remote Cornwall handed on the memory: poor harvests, potato blight, crop disease, want and poverty – felt worst of all in Ireland, with its rapidly increasing population. Catholic emancipation admitted to Parliament a leader in Daniel O'Connell, who now went all out for repeal

ABOVE *William Wilberforce addresses an Anti-Slavery Convention.*
RIGHT *A poster announcing a slave sale.*

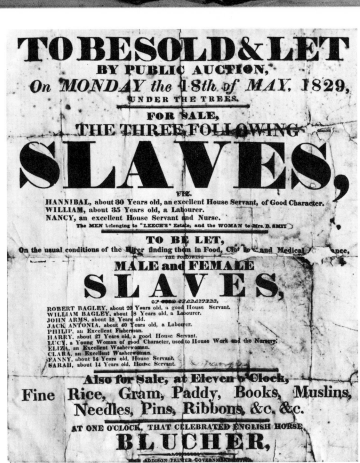

Queen Victoria drinking the health of the City of London at a Guildhall banquet in 1837.

of the Union. Meanwhile, a still more effective campaign for the repeal of the Corn Laws was mounted by the middle class in England. Its impetus was irresistible, for it had plenty of money behind it from Lancashire manufacturers, producing pamphlets by the million. There were hundreds of meetings, organized by the able Free-Trader, Richard Cobden; and the Radical, John Bright, became well known for his oratory.

The propaganda fell on the willing ears of Sir Robert Peel, the Tory prime minister who was really above party politics. With no glamour – his smile was described as like that of a silver plate on a coffin – he was a master of administration, the last prime minister to have a grasp of the work of every department. Throughout his ministry he engaged in dismantling the protection of goods, freeing over a thousand items from import duties – for industrial England could well stand competition from any source.

Peel's non-party spirit had its success in turning the corner of the Chartist movement, a parallel to the Anti-Corn Law League, which, since it was working-class and had few resources except mere numbers, was much less well led. All of the demands of the Charter for full democracy (except that for annual Parliaments) – equal electoral districts, the secret ballot, payment of MPs – were to come about by 1914: such was the set of the tide.

The repeal of the Corn Laws was enforced by the appalling

disaster in Ireland of the failure of the potato crop two years running, in 1846 and 1847, bringing disease and death on a scale that could not be dealt with. There were no railways in Ireland to transport food (even if enough food for eight million had been available). Nothing was more certain than that one day the potato crop would fail, and in 1846 three-quarters of it rotted in the ground. What government in the world could have dealt with such a disaster? No English government could have supplied poor relief to a population half the size of its own – when it did not undertake poor relief to its own, but left it to local rates. Many Irish landowners did what they could, but that was a flea-bite in the disaster to a nation; some relief measures were improvized – soup kitchens, and private philanthropy, but nothing would avail on such a scale.

Government was hampered by the fact that relief on a national scale would not have been possible in England either. Moreover, it was contrary to orthodox economic beliefs, which had thrown over economic nationalism ('mercantilism') for free trade, and the problem had the simple fact behind it that Ireland was disastrously over-crowded. Nearly a million died; another million emigrated, some to Britain, most to America.

In England too the consequences were shattering, but politically. Peel repealed the Corn Laws, and ruined the Tory Party. The opportunity to wreck the leading figure in politics was taken by the Tory backbencher Disraeli, whom Peel had rejected for office. Night after night Disraeli delivered

THE GREAT ANTI-CORN-LAW LEAGUE MEETING, IN COVENT GARDEN THEATRE.

GIVE US THIS DAY OUR DAILY BREAD

NATIONAL ANTI-CORN LAW LEAGUE,

is a Registered Member

Joseph Hickin Secretary

Registered by

TOP *The great Anti-Corn-Law League meeting in Covent Garden theatre.*
ABOVE *A pamphlet issued by the Anti-Corn-Law League.*

Meanwhile England was engrossed by railway mania. The constructive figures were those fine engineers George Stephenson, who began with the Stockton – Darlington and Manchester – Liverpool railways, and his son Robert, who built the Newcastle and Menai bridges. The entrepreneur George Hudson was partly responsible for the boom that bankrupted himself and others. However, by 1848 the country had 5000 miles of railway working; others, like Thomas Brassey, were launching out to build railways in France, India, Canada and the United States. In 1844 Gladstone carried an Act which created a third-class passenger service for the people at a penny a mile.

A more complex operation was that of Rowland Hill, whose campaign for a simple penny postage, prepaid and whatever the distance, ultimately won. Hitherto the postal service had been unbelievably complicated and inefficient. Efficiency, simplicity, utility were Utilitarian watchwords; many old-fashioned usages were ended and dead wood cut out. A reform with which Peel was personally associated was the creation of a Metropolitan Police force, civilian in character – hence 'Peelers'. This was such a success that in ten years it was extended all over the country. The Bank Charter Act of 1844 provided another sort of security, a sound currency on a self-regulating gold standard, after flighty fluctuations and many bank failures. As with the Elizabethan restoration of the value of the pound sterling, it proved a stable foundation for the prosperity of an age. This prosperity was exhibited to the world in the Great Exhibition of 1851, in the Crystal Palace, which was then in Hyde Park. All the world came to view and study it, packed with the useful products of the Industrial Revolution. It was a good idea of the prince consort's; a constant visitor was the 'Iron Duke' – Wellington – who little realized that he himself was a prime exhibit, an historic monument. Next year he was dead.

This was the age of steam, in which Britain led the world; along with locomotives, mine engines of every kind, threshing machines, steam was now applied to shipping. Samuel Cunard was a Nova Scotian of Philadelphian descent who developed the mail steamship service between Britain and North America – the famous Cunarders that held the blue ribbon for the Atlantic crossing for decades: speedier still when vessels were made of iron and propelled by screw, instead of paddles.

These developments made emigration of the first importance – not only of Irish, but of Scots, Welsh, Cornish, and even of the English. In the sixty years after Waterloo seven and a half million people emigrated from the United Kingdom: half to the United States; one and a half million to Canada; another million to Australia and New Zealand. This did no harm to the old country, but built up flourishing new communities of English-speaking stock overseas, to which they made essential contributions, and where they had wider opportunities and were able to better themselves. When Britain was in grave danger in the next century from the aggressive might of Germany, all these stocks sent their offspring – they came from Southern Africa too – to Britain's help. We do not forget that we owe our deliverance to them.

speeches against his leader, which rallied the majority of his party against him. Gladstone said in later years that nothing like it had been heard in Parliament: it had to be witnessed to be believed. Years later, too, Peel's daughter asked Disraeli, now a famous politician in his turn, why he had ruined her father. Disraeli replied blithely: 'I was a young man, with my way to make.' Peel himself wrote at the time: 'Thank God I am relieved for ever from the trammels of such a party.' Disraeli spent a lifetime picking up the pieces and reconstituting it, but was out of power most of his life.

RIGHT *The interior of the train shed at Euston, 1837, starting point for the London and Birmingham railroad.*
BELOW *The opening of the Liverpool and Manchester railway on 15 September 1830.*
Two new kinds of steam-ship: BOTTOM *A Thames steamer, moored at Gravesend, and* OPPOSITE BELOW *A larger steamer, suitable for Transatlantic crossings.*

IN PLACE OF THE AMERICAN COLONIES a second empire was growing up, of which the United States might almost be described as economically and culturally a part; for associations between the two countries were of the closest, and the more the States prospered the more did Britain. They were bound together by ties of all kinds, not only language and sentiment, but economic and political interest. Where political interest diverged was mainly over Canada. Canada too was expanding westward. The ambition of the imperialist US President Polk, who took half Mexico, made him claim a frontier line which would have cut off Canada from outlet into the Pacific: 'Fifty-four forty degrees or fight.' Ultimately a compromise of a frontier along 49° was effected, which retained British Columbia for Canada, though most of the Oregon country went, which had been opened up by the Hudson Bay Company, and most of the coast reaching up to Alaska.

The general development in each of the colonies followed that of the original thirteen: a movement at varying pace in rather different circumstances, as each approached maturity, towards self-government. Canada came first, where a nucleus of English-speakers in both the Maritime Provinces and Ontario was formed by Loyalists who would not accept the new United States. Two leaders in Canada's development were former Americans, Beverley Robinson, of Virginian stock, and Egerton Ryerson, who made Methodism a source of patriotism. It is thought that three-quarters of the population of early Ontario were American in origin. Nova Scotia led the way in achieving self-government, based on a majority in her assembly: 'we seek for nothing more than British subjects are entitled to, but we will be content with nothing less.' This summed up developments everywhere. Canada soon followed suit, though the over-riding problem remained the relation between French Quebec and the constantly growing provinces of mainly English-speakers to the west. When federation ultimately came in 1867, it profited from the recent experience of the American Civil War to make the central government stronger, and the provinces less strong than those in the American States, with their claim to secede.

Australia was transformed, first by capturing the world's market for the finest wool from immense flocks of sheep with unlimited pasture; second, by the discovery of copper in South Australia, to which the Cornish emigrated in thousands; third, by the assisted emigration of Irish; fourth, by the discovery of gold. The provinces took shape, and by mid-century achieved responsible government, with control of their lands and future development.

New Zealand was exceptional in that it sprang entirely from individual enterprise inspired by Gibbon Wakefield, expert on colonization, and his company – only just in time to prevent French occupation. Missionaries also took a hand, notably the Cornishman, William Colenso, first of New Zealand naturalists, who filled Kew Gardens with splendid flora from the new country. Unfortunately, greedy and uncontrolled land claims, and the selling of guns to the Maoris, whose land it was, led to a series of wars in North Island. South Island was more free for settlement, especially

by Presbyterian Scots – though the Anglican settlement of Canterbury won literary fame through Samuel Butler's writings, especially his Utopian classic, *Erewhon*. Within fifteen years of this migration the colony achieved responsible government.

In South Africa the situation was far more complex and difficult. Cape Colony was inhabited mainly by slave-owning Dutch farmers – the Boers. British rule was heading for racial equality, and the claims of blacks were put to Parliament by the Quaker Fowell Buxton's Aborigines' Protection Society, following upon the abolition of slavery. Meanwhile the British were penetrating Natal, where the famous Bishop Colenso (or infamous to those alarmed by his Biblical criticism) was to take up the cause of the Zulus. For, as the whites were expanding into the interior, various black peoples were swarming south. Resentful of interference with their ways and customs, confirmed by the Bishop's critical attitude to the Old Testament, which he was passing on to the Zulus, the Boers decided on the Great Trek into the interior – much like the contemporary trek of the Mormons to found their new Jerusalem, under Brigham Young in Utah. The Boers

British officers entertained by an Indian ruler, from an Indian print of about 1820.

A Zulu chief reviews his soldiers.

fought their way to the Vaal river and beyond, to found two new states: the Transvaal and the Orange Free State. One of the trekkers was young Paul Kruger of whom, as an old man, a great deal would be heard. The Boers gave much the kind of trouble to Britain as the Mormons gave to the United States: they had marched away to independence, but to the central authorities they were subjects or citizens absconding from authority. Moreover the Boer Trek had stirred all the black peoples into commotion. This exposed both Cape Colony and Natal to trouble: the government at home could not but take notice, though it was in an intractable situation, with conflicting advice; it tried various tacks, advancing and retreating, finding no durable solution.

India was a vaster question, more intimately bound up with British politics, since its government had become Britain's responsibility. Pitt had declared that schemes of conquest were repugnant to the nation, and no one at home wanted to take on the government of a sub-continent. The East India Company had been led on step by step to fill the vacuum.

Huge areas were misgoverned, like the Carnatic in the South; the militant Mahratta Confederacy was powerful enough to conquer the North, but for the British bastion in Bengal. The threat was countered by the hard-won war in which Wellington proved his ability, and ended by recruiting the Mahrattas as stalwarts for British rule.

The problem was to reach defensible frontiers. This led the Calcutta government to protect Bengal from the east by capturing Rangoon and advancing into Burma; pushing up the Ganges to the Himalayas and Kashmir; in the west to the Indus and the frontiers of Afghanistan. This involved several wars with the Afghans, always ready, as their precursors had been, to descend from their mountains and valleys into the rich and populous plains. Moreover, by mid-century the Russians had advanced five hundred miles, annexing all Turkestan, to the frontiers of Persia and Afghanistan. The continuous concern of the British Raj with the advance of Russian power – so much to the fore in Kipling's *Kim* – was not an idle fear; nor was the pushing of British power up to the North-West Frontier, and the position of the Indian Army there, without purpose.

By mid-century British supremacy, by direct or indirect rule, was asserted throughout India, and a splendid school of administrators grew up. British rule was undoubtedly beneficent; it provided impartial justice wherever its writ ran. But it ran up against the most sensitive area of all, people's age-long beliefs and customs. Suttee, the burning of Hindu widows on their husbands' funeral pyres, was suppressed: this was hardly popular, even with the widows, defrauded of their fondest wish to accompany their late husbands. When the Indian army learned that they were being forced to go against their religion because the cartridges of their new Enfield rifles had been greased with animal-fat, and that they needed the end biting off, and when they feared that they were to cross the ominous sea to campaign in Burma – they were ready to mutiny.

The Indian Mutiny of 1856–7 was essentially a military revolt. The main factor was the small ratio of British troops, further decreased by the demands of the Crimean War. The Indian Army was overwhelmingly located in India itself; while the British troops were dispersed, some in Persia, some in Burma, others strung out in the Punjab or along the Sutlej. The governor-general's urgent warnings about this were ignored by the East India Company, which itself would have to find the money to rectify the situation.

Thus the Mutiny concentrated itself at various centres, upon Lucknow, Cawnpore, Delhi. It did not affect India as a whole, and even in the affected areas the villagers sheltered British refugees from the terror – which showed what they thought of British rule. It was a ferocious ruler like Nana Sahib, who, after the surrender of Cawnpore, gave four hundred combatants a safe-conduct to go downstream to Allahabad, then massacred them as they reached the boats. When Havelock's relieving army drew near, he had two hundred women and children cut to pieces and thrown into a well, dead or alive. This kind of thing was not unprecedented

LEFT *The storming of Delhi by the 60th rifles.*
BELOW *'Troops hastening to Umballa', from a series of sketches made during the Indian Mutiny.*

or remote from the characters of some Indian princes, as we know from history and literature. All the same, an almighty revenge was exacted and atrocities were inflicted in return.

Most of India took no part in the Mutiny, however. The Punjab, only recently subdued, was so quiet that law courts and schools functioned normally throughout; the Sikh states remained firm; the Gurkhas gave invaluable help; several hundred sepoys served faithfully all through the siege of Lucknow. With the relief of Lucknow and the capture of Delhi, the worst was over. The grandest casualty of the Mutiny was the historic East India Company. In the following year, 1858, Parliament transferred government to the Crown, with a secretary of state responsible to Parliament, and the heroic John Lawrence of the Punjab as viceroy.

Yet things were not to be the same again: mistrust between the races had been engendered.

THE CRIMEAN WAR, OF 1854–6, is usually considered to have been a blunder: it certainly exhibited muddle and mismanagement, diplomatically and militarily. But the root of it was the Tsar Nicholas' intention to carve up the Turkish Empire, which he proposed to share – offering Egypt and Cyprus to Britain. It is likely that, if the strong-minded Palmerston had been at the foreign office, Russia would have been warned off and there would have been no war. On the other hand, if it had not been fought, the Russians would have taken over Constantinople. Palmerston was an aristocrat whose bluff no-nonsense personality endeared him to the middle classes; but he was disliked by the queen, for personal reasons. The inept conduct of the war forced him back into office – like Churchill in 1939.

The war showed up appalling inefficiency and incompetence in the last area of aristocratic privilege, the army, where little had been changed since Waterloo. The worst ineptitude and neglect was in regard to the welfare of the troops, medicine and nursing: some 2500 men were killed during the Crimean War, but many of these died of disease, the Russian winter helping. Here again the situation was remedied by voluntary action, led by a famous woman, Florence Nightingale, who devoted the rest of her life to pioneer welfare work, nursing and hospital reform.

Together the British with their French allies hung on to the Crimean peninsula, the Achilles' heel of Russia, through two Russian winters – through Inkerman, Balaclava (the Charge

'Quiet Night at the Batteries' – a picture of life during the Crimean War of 1854–6.
OVERLEAF *The Charge of the Light Brigade at Balaclava in the Crimea, 1854.*

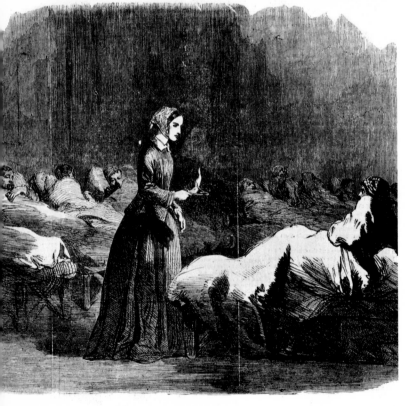

TOP *This early photograph shows British and French troops in camp during the Crimean war.*
ABOVE *Florence Nightingale, the 'Lady with the Lamp', at the army hospital at Scutari in the Crimean War.*

of the Light Brigade, celebrated by Tennyson), and the siege of Sebastopol (in which Tolstoy served). At length the great fortress fell, in 1855, and the death of the Tsar enabled peace to be made. The French bore the brunt of the war, the British got the fruits of the peace: Russian designs on Turkey were held up for another twenty years, and the Russians accepted restrictions upon their naval power in the Black Sea.

The American Civil War of 1861–5 was a far more terrible affair – the first modern war, in which railways, photography, newspaper reporting were all made the most of. Its effect upon Britain was serious. The ending of cotton supplies from the Southern States put half a million people out of work in Lancashire; much want and hunger ensued, which private charity could not cope with – any more than in Ireland. Yet the people never wavered in their support for the Northern anti-slavery cause. The sympathies of the upper classes were naturally with the South, which regarded itself as an independent nation with a right to its independence, as in 1776. However, Britain could not intervene in what was an internal affair. The victory of the North was a victory for democracy not only in America but also in Britain; it was a portent of the way things would go: the end of the aristocratic age.

This was brought home by Gladstone's first ministry, 1868–74, which registered his best achievements in Liberal reform. Graduating from a Peelite Liverpool background, he displayed a mastery of financial administration; his Budgets marked the final steps towards Free Trade. With the Victorian belief in individual enterprise – he was the Victorian age incarnate, even more than the queen herself – he pushed income tax down to fourpence in the pound, to release capital for productive employment. For a moment, income tax even reached threepence in the pound. No wonder production soared! The Crimean War had cost £70 millions – it was not even noticed in the high tide of Victorian prosperity.

As the leader of middle-class Liberalism, Gladstone tackled reform on every front – except the social, where he always remained an individualist, against collectivism. First, he tackled Irish grievances, disestablishing the Church of Ireland. Next, his Irish Land Act of 1870 established much improved conditions for tenant farmers. He could not achieve the impossible – the buying out of the whole Irish landlord class, to establish a land of peasant proprietors, such as Radicals like John Bright wished. It could not be done; for one thing, his own Whig supporters could hardly be expected to confiscate their Irish holdings. Gladstone regarded his Land Act as an instalment. Disraeli, with prophetic insight, saw the dismantling of the Protestant Ascendancy as 'tending towards civil war'.

Wonderful, if belated, progress was made in the sphere of education, so long held up by the quarrels between the religious sects. The property of the endowed schools was re-arranged and properly directed. Still more important were the reforms at Oxford and Cambridge, ending religious tests and releasing dormant college funds for university purposes. Nothing was more important than the grand Education Act of 1870, at last establishing a national system of education for the working classes. Piloted through by the Quaker, W.E. Forster, largely inspired by the Arnolds, it made the best of the existing Church Schools, filling the gap with national schools looked after by local school boards. Local patriotism was never released to better purpose.

The civil service, following the Anglo-Indian model, was now thrown open to recruitment by examination, instead of patronage and privilege. The legal system was reformed and rationalized from top to bottom by the Judicature Act of 1873, in time to move into the grand new Gothic Law Courts in the Strand, another monument to Victorianism (like St Pancras, a design thought to have been rejected by Palmerston for the Foreign Office).

Most urgent of all were the army reforms of Cardwell, for the American Civil War and the German wars in Europe had revealed that a new epoch in warfare had opened. The British army was hopelessly out of date, geared only to small campaigns on colonial frontiers, where it was seen at its best. First, a short-service army was established, with trained reserves; 20,000 men were brought back from the colonies to form a hard core. Second, an army of 'territorials' was recruited, based on the counties but linked with the regular army, to form a reservoir into which local and regimental spirit could be channelled. The higher command was at last subordinated to the war office, the infantry re-armed with up-to-date rifles and the artillery strengthened. All this, under Mr G.'s (Gladstone's) eagle eye, was achieved without increasing the army estimates.

The need was obvious, indeed urgent. For Bismarck's irruption upon the European scene, piloting Germany to unification and empire by 'Blood and Iron', announced a new era in Europe, with Germany dominant, threatening and bullying everybody. First, war was forced upon Denmark in 1864, in which Germany took Slesvig and Holstein; then war was forced upon Austria in 1866, in which Germany annexed Hanover to Prussia and enforced the North German

Lord Palmerston outside the House of Commons in 1865.

Confederation. Lastly, there was the war of 1870–1, into which the failing Napoleon III was tricked and which ended with Germany taking Alsace and Lorraine and proclaiming the German Empire from Versailles. Not content with this, Bismarck threatened a 'preventive' war against France in 1875.

Bismarck might describe himself as satisfied: Germany certainly was not. This was the dominant fact in Europe right up to 1945. Bismarck's reduction of politics to brute force – he described parliamentary government as 'the Revolution' – put the clock back in Europe by a century. It was a European tragedy that Germany, the leading power in Europe, had been fashioned by Prussian militarism and exemplified its methods and standards; and that the empire which emerged from it was, literally, irresponsible, i.e. it was not responsible to a parliament or elected assembly representing its people at large with power to act. It was absolutist, and it was militarist. Bismarck despised all that Gladstone stood for: parliamentarism, democracy, liberal-minded pacificism, responsible self-government for peoples. Here were the two poles of European politics. In the eventual conflict between these two polarities Europe was torn apart, and lost its ascendancy in the world.

But which offered better hope for it?

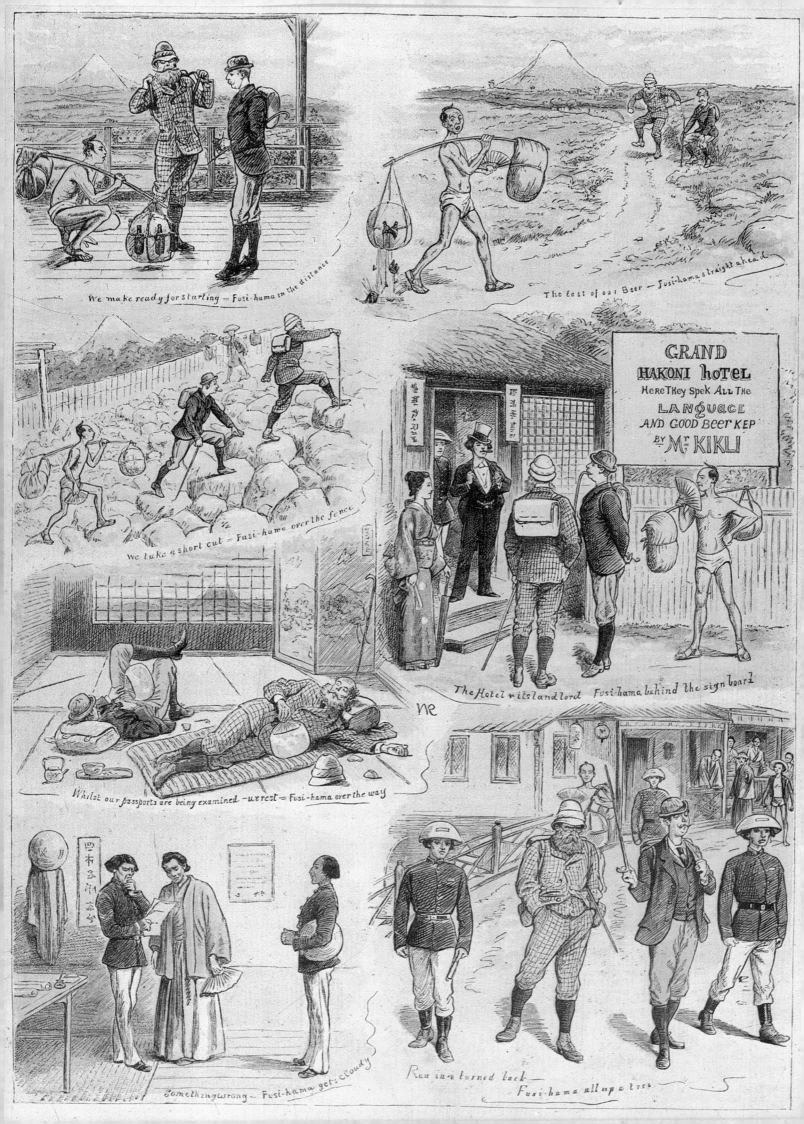

We make ready for starting = Fusi-hama in the distance

The last of our Beer — Fusi-hama straight ahead

We take a short cut = Fusi-hama over the fence

GRAND HAKONI HOTEL HERE THEY SPEK ALL THE LANGUAGE AND GOOD BEER KEP BY Mr KIKLI

The Hotel & its landlord   Fusi-hama behind the signboard

Whilst our passports are being examined — we rest = Fusi-hama over the way

Something wrong = Fusi-hama gets cloudy

Run in & turned back — Fusi-hama all up a tree

Chapter 8

Imperialism and Liberalism

AFTER THIS TREMENDOUS SPATE OF REFORMS Gladstone's government lost its impetus, as governments do. Disraeli saw Parliament sitting on its benches like 'a row of extinct volcanoes'. During a lifetime spent mostly in Opposition he had re-made his party, and accepted Free Trade including foreign imports – ironically, for it was during his government of 1874–80, that the railways and steamships began to bring in the wheat from the Middle West which competed with and gravely depressed British agriculture, particularly in the eastern counties. Gladstone had a blind spot – social legislation: here was a gap that Disraeli, the author of *Sybil, or the Two Nations* was keen to fill. Two Labour Acts came in 1875: one putting master and man on equal terms in matters of contract, the other allowing strikes and peaceful picketing. Factory and Public Health Acts consolidated codes of beneficial legislation, housing was now tackled for the first time by the state in a Workers' Dwellings Act which gave local authorities the power to pull down slums. Joseph Chamberlain set to work in Birmingham.

Gladstone had turned down the offer of a dominant portion of the shares in the Suez Canal, which had just been built; Disraeli accepted it, and with the good will of France, which had built the Canal, for he gave her firm support against Bismarck's threat in 1875. In the steamship age the Canal was a vital link in communications with India. The East appealed to the novelist in Disraeli, and the title he conferred upon his 'fairy queen', Victoria, of Empress of India, was a stroke of imagination which pleased her and the Indian princes.

It was a good thing that Disraeli was in power, instead of Gladstone, during the next round of Russian aggression against Turkey. For in 1877–8 the Russian army conquered everything up to the gates of Constantinople and imposed a treaty which handed over Bessarabia and the gateway into Armenia to Russia, and created a large satellite, Bulgaria,

OPPOSITE *Views of British tourists abroad at the height of the Victorian Age.*
ABOVE *A caricature of Benjamin Disraeli, Prime Minister and novelist.*
BELOW *The opening of the Suez Canal, 17 November 1869.*

"CRITICS."

(WHO HAVE NOT EXACTLY "FAILED IN LITERATURE AND ART."—See Mr. D.'s New Work.)

ABOVE *A famous Punch cartoon of Gladstone and Disraeli inspecting each other's literary works.*
ABOVE RIGHT *The Four Courts, Dublin.*

which would dominate the Balkans, Constantinople and Greece. In this crisis Disraeli played his cards very close to his chest, for there was much opposition in England to his imperial moves: the fleet was sent to the Bosphorus, Indian troops to Malta, reserves were called up. Everybody thought he meant war, and he lost two members of his Cabinet. However, he did not mean war, but he meant to win the peace.

Old and frail as he was, Disraeli was the dominating figure at the Congress of Berlin, 1878: '*Der alte Jude, dass ist der Mann*', ('The old Jew, that is the man') said Bismarck. And he succeeded in wresting the fruits of victory from Russia without losing her friendship, and in saving the Turkish Empire; if Russia obtained Bessarabia and the gateway to Armenia, Britain got the right to occupy Cyprus. It was a clear diplomatic victory and it kept the peace between the powers for nearly forty years. He was content to claim on his homecoming that he had achieved: 'Peace with Honour'. In two years he was dead, and his novel, which was to portray the paradoxical career of his rival, Gladstone, remained unwritten. His successor, Lord Salisbury, said of him: 'Zeal for England was the consuming passion of his life.' It was a tribute both to the man and to the country.

In 1880 Gladstone initiated modern electioneering with his Midlothian campaign, a direct appeal to the electorate – thus adding one more mortification to the existing ones of political life, as Lord Salisbury observed, with distaste, to the queen. She had now taken completely against Gladstone and thought him a mad old man – he was certainly an old man in a hurry, and past his best. He swept in with a majority, but the Liberal government of 1880–6 was hamstrung by problems and failed in most spheres. In Ireland another Land Act advanced the interests of the tenant farmers against the landlords in 1881. Strenuous efforts were made for a settlement with Parnell, the morose and sinister Irish leader, the 'uncrowned king of Ireland', who invented tactics which held up business in Parliament and government in Ireland. Nothing but an Irish Parliament (Home Rule) would satisfy him. Lord Frederick Cavendish, sympathetic to the Irish cause, was sent over as chief secretary; shortly afterwards he and the under-secretary, the Irishman Burke, were murdered in Phoenix Park.

There appeared no end to the misery, though a fundamental fact was that Ireland was less important now from the point of view of its population: three million to Britain's thirty. Gladstone convinced himself that nothing but self-government – his solution for small nations all over Europe – would do, and produced a Home Rule Bill which split his party. The aristocratic Whigs opposed it as 'Liberal Unionists', as powerful in propaganda as they were in property; but so too did the Radical wing under Joseph Chamberlain, who combined Imperialism with social Radicalism. Chamberlain had announced a full Radical programme which anticipated Lloyd George and the twentieth century. It was distasteful to Gladstone, and so was Chamberlain. A middle-class man, yet

with an Oxford High Church background, Gladstone's tastes were aristocratic; Joe Chamberlain was a vulgar business man, a Nonconformist and not a very nice personality. Gladstone gravely underestimated him; for he was to become the most dynamic man in politics, a Birmingham party boss whose party machine was the model for the future.

Chamberlain was all set to become the Radical leader after Gladstone, with a programme to anticipate Socialism. These prospects were ruined by the problem of the unending Irish question in British politics. Gladstone's first Home Rule Bill was thrown out by Parliament – no Home Rule Bill could win a majority in Britain – and the rule of Liberalism, with its promise for the future, was ended for the next two decades. Chamberlain threw in his lot with the Tories he had fought most of his life – 'Judas!' was the cry with which he was usually heckled. His driving force was deflected into Imperial objectives, where he did almost as much harm, and tariff reform (protection), which split the Unionist party in turn.

It seems now that Gladstone was right in pressing on for self-government for Ireland; it is also probable that he was premature, the conditions not yet making it possible. The House of Lords stood in the way, and he did not provide for the growing opposition of Ulster to Home Rule in any form. ('Home Rule is Rome Rule,' i.e. Catholic rule, was their slogan; well, it was. How to solve that problem has baffled

ABOVE RIGHT *Gladstone introduces the Home Rule Bill for Ireland in the House of Commons.*
RIGHT *Sir John Millais' portrait of Gladstone, Prime Minister four times between 1868 and 1894.*

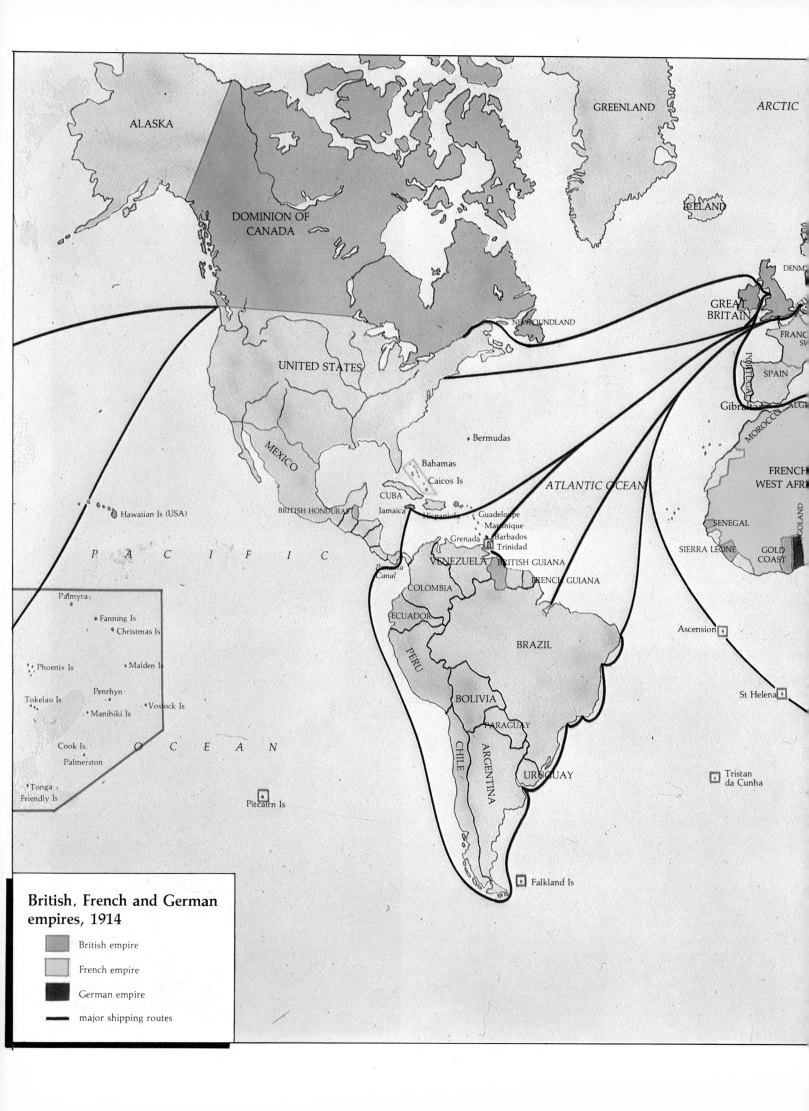

ALASKA

DOMINION OF
CANADA

GREENLAND

ARCTIC

ICELAND

DENM

GREAT
BRITAIN

FRANC

NEWFOUNDLAND

PORTUGAL

SPAIN

UNITED STATES

Gibraltar

ALG

MOROCCO

• Bermudas

MEXICO

Bahamas

ATLANTIC OCEAN

FRENCH
WEST AFR

Caicos Is

CUBA

Hawaiian Is (USA)

BRITISH HONDURAS

Jamaica

Hispaniola

Guadeloupe

SENEGAL

Martinique

TOGOLAND

Grenada

Barbados

SIERRA LEONE

GOLD
COAST

PACIFIC

Trinidad

VENEZUELA BRITISH GUIANA

Panama
Canal

FRENCH GUIANA

Palmyra

COLOMBIA

• Fanning Is

ECUADOR

• Christmas Is

BRAZIL

Ascension

• Phoenix Is

• Malden Is

PERU

Penrhyn

St Helena

Tokelau Is

• Vostock Is

• Manihiki Is

BOLIVIA

OCEAN

PARAGUAY

Cook Is.

CHILE

Palmerston

ARGENTINA

Tristan
da Cunha

• Tonga
Friendly Is

URUGUAY

Pitcairn Is

Falkland Is

British, French and German empires, 1914

British empire

French empire

German empire

major shipping routes

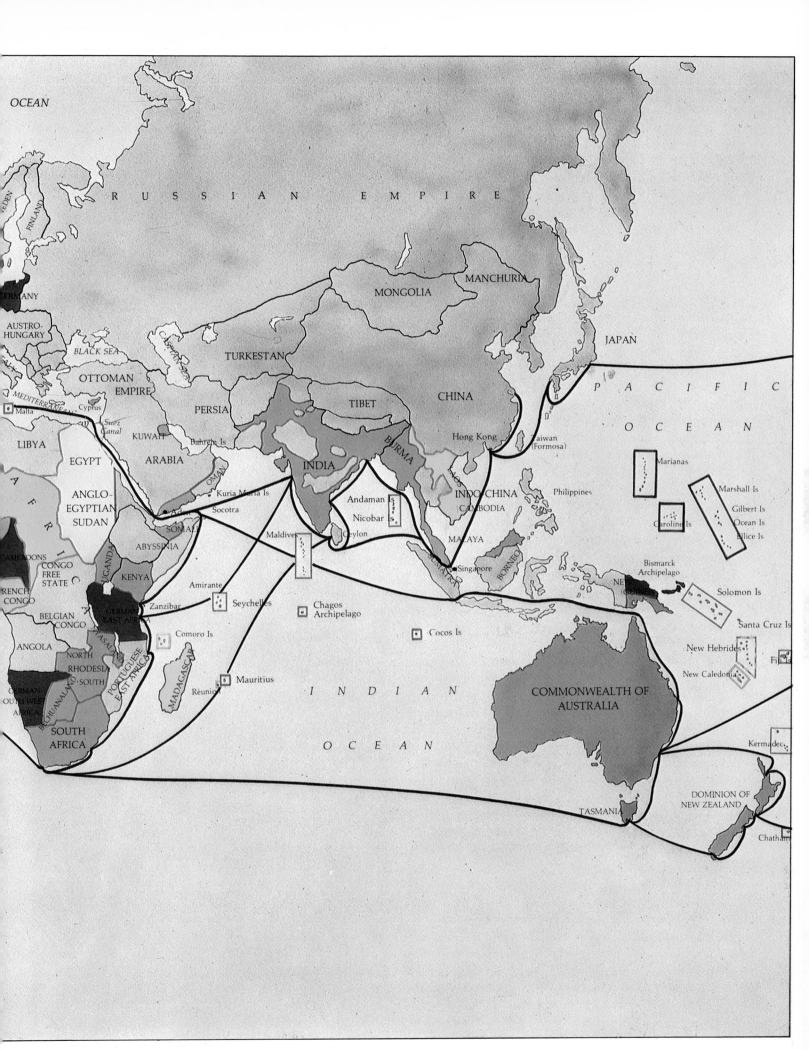

people to this day.) The tragedy of the next forty years was that the Irish question became an envenomed party issue in Britain, and Parnell played this card for all he was worth. He was caught out at the height of his power by the facts of his private life, which were not unknown to politicians, but were treated with characteristic Victorian censoriousness when they came out. Kitty O'Shea, the wife of Captain O'Shea, a follower whom he used in some of his negotiations, was his mistress. An element of political blackmail probably entered into it.

These revelations ruined the hopes of Irish nationalism for a generation. It split Parnell's party in two: there were embittered rows between Parnellites and Anti-Parnellites, and they continued after Parnell died. In Ireland the Catholic Church was against him, in England the Nonconformists. Gladstone – whose own benevolent and well-meaning relations with prostitutes were risky enough – disclaimed him. Such was Victorian hypocrisy.

GLADSTONE HAD NO WISH for further responsibilities abroad; he was the reverse of an Imperialist – he was a 'Little Englander', as many Liberals were. But circumstances were against him; his withdrawals were even more disastrous than his reluctant assertions of power. And a feeble foreign secretary was no match for the malign genius of Bismarck, who – with no real interest in colonial problems himself – was now engaged in needling Britain on every front. He encouraged French colonial ambitions, not only to deflect attention from Alsace-Lorraine, which he had annexed, but also to encourage conflict with Britain. He secretly arranged with Russia and Austria to close the Straits of Bosphorus to British warships. In 1884 he proclaimed a German protectorate over South-West Africa. He annexed Togoland and the Cameroons, and rallied the French to oppose Anglo-Portuguese priority in the Congo. A German colonial company with official backing probed East Africa, while claims were advanced in the Pacific, in New Guinea and Samoa.

The new dominant power in Europe was bent on becoming a *Weltmacht* (world power) in double-quick time. Bismarck was adept at using French hostility towards Britain over Egypt and the Sudan to hustle Britain in Africa and the Pacific. German haste and methods precipitated the question of the partition of Africa as the chief preoccupation on the international scene. It was fortunate that it fell to Salisbury to wrestle with the problem, for he was Bismarck's match – cool and wise, moderate but firm, with a clear eye as to British interests and strategy.

Gladstone and his Liberal Cabinet's muddles and disasters alarmed the nation, especially over Egypt and the Sudan. Imperialism was not a British phenomenon only: as Clark writes, 'Between 1880 and 1900 something of the sort appeared in all the industrialized countries of Europe and in the United States.' Perhaps there was something in the laborious analysis being made by the man who was to become the most influential of the many exiles to whom Victorian England gave shelter – Karl Marx. He called the phenomenon 'economic imperialism'. But expansion was not only a phenomenon of industrialized countries – the largest example of it was that of backward Russia, expanding thousands of miles across Siberia to the Far East, and along the whole of her southern border into Central Asia. And the United States were to force a war upon Spain, as they had done upon Mexico, to acquire Cuba and the Philippines.

British interests in Africa flowed mainly from commerce and sea power, from the astonishing achievements of exploring and missionary enterprise, which went largely together, and from a long history which created obligations and responsibilities, not always to the liking of government at home – as with India. Clark writes: 'Annexation might be the best means of protecting the natives against one another. It was the only means of protecting them against oppression by Europeans.'

British sympathy for Africans – and it was reciprocated – stands out again and again in the record. Consider the fidelity of Livingstone's natives, as they carried his dead body hundreds of miles through jungle and forest to the coast. David Livingstone was a Victorian hero, and characteristic of his age: a doctor inspired by a passion for humanity, he had a marvellous career as an explorer. In the course of it he did more to discover East and Central Africa than anyone. George Grenfell, a Baptist doctor, gave his life to exploring the Congo

Livingstone's last journey.

without reinforcements. Great anxiety prevailed in Britain; Gladstone was forced to take action, but too late: when they arrived, in January 1885, the popular hero was dead, and the garrison had been massacred. The queen was furious, and so was the country. But the Sudan was evacuated. Not until 1898 at Omdurman – where young Winston Churchill served – was the Sudan recovered, to become a model of administration so long as it lasted, i.e. until the final abdication and the handover.

British penetration of Africa was thus propelled by natural forces, in some cases to prevent slave trading, for which purpose Lagos was annexed; while another expedition was necessary to drive back the murderous Ashantis. Here were the forces and factors that drove Britain inward into Africa: from the sea bases at the Cape and in Durban; from the West Coast settlements and explorations; from Livingstone's and Kirk of the Zambesi's in East Africa; from Zanzibar with the coastal trade to the Persian Gulf and India – hence the protectorate over Somaliland; finally into Egypt, which there was a genuine intention to evacuate, but which the German march to the Middle East and the two world wars of 1914–18 and 1939–45 long postponed.

It is obvious that Britain could not allow herself to be hustled by Bismarck in Africa, where her variously held positions on the coast – some of which had been hers for a long time – gave her primacy. Advance was now promoted by the formation of chartered companies, i.e. private, but with the

and doctoring the natives – he and his daughter ultimately succumbed to the fatal blackwater fever. The intrepid Richard Lander had solved the mystery of the Niger and discovered its course, contradicting the previous theories of the geographers.

In South Africa policy was muddled and inconsistent. The four states – Cape Colony, Natal, the Transvaal and Orange Free State – needed a common defence policy against the rising military power of the Zulus. The Transvaal and Orange Free State governments consented to being annexed; then, neglected, they rebelled and annihilated British forces at Majuba in 1881. Gladstone capitulated in the face of defeat, and this was deadly for the future.

After this mess he was forced to take action in Egypt, which was under atrocious misgovernment, with finances in utter disorder and which, refusing to recognize debts, was proceeding to murder many Europeans in Alexandria and train guns on the shipping. As the responsible sea power, the British bombarded the city into submission, and hence were led on to take responsibility for the government of Egypt: the security of the Suez Canal, the route to India, was at stake. A great pro-consul, Lord Cromer, operated indirectly to accomplish constructive work in putting Egypt on her feet economically, restoring order and developing her potentialities, which depended on the Nile. Neighbouring Sudan fell under the heel of the Mahdi, a Moslem Messiah who declared a holy war to drive out all unbelievers. General Gordon had been sent to hold the capital, Khartoum, and was left there

ABOVE *Englishmen on the Gold Coast, West Africa, in 1890.*
RIGHT *General Gordon of Khartoum.*

backing of government: the Niger Company, the East African, and Rhodes's in Southern Africa. These elicited the services of many remarkable men. Because of this Salisbury's government of 1886–92 was in a stronger position to negotiate a settlement with Germany. In return for recognizing Britain's position in Zanzibar and East Africa, i.e. Kenya and Uganda, a German East Africa and South-West Africa were confirmed and extended. The very recently arrived colonial power had not done so badly after all.

In South Africa the situation was transformed by the discovery of diamonds and gold in the Transvaal, which brought the remote Boer republic to the forefront of world attention. Thousands of miners poured into the country, mainly British. It was not long before they were requesting the right to vote and to have a say in the running of the country, since they were now creating its chief source of wealth and paying the taxes. 'No taxation without representation!', as the American colonies had cried. The Boers meant to keep these 'Outlanders' as second-class citizens: it was *their* country. Their leader was Paul Kruger, a wily and determined trekker, bent on keeping his country's independence.

The Outlanders' case could not but be taken up by the colonial office, which had been revivified by the aggressive spirit of Joe Chamberlain. As the head of his own party, the Liberal Unionists, he was the second man in the government and took the lead. He sent out Alfred Milner as high commissioner, an able administrator, but no diplomat. Moreover, partly German and German-educated, Milner was that rare thing in British politics, a no-compromise autocrat, a convinced Imperialist who had a vision of empire. So had a no less remarkable man, Cecil Rhodes, who had made a colossal fortune quite young, become the dominant figure in the mining industry, and entered politics at the Cape, becoming prime minister. He believed to the end in co-operation with the Dutch, as Milner did not: but to the Boers, the toughest of Teutonic stocks, this was their country.

Rhodes too was pro-German – he thought co-operation with Germany and the United States was the right course, as his visionary foundation of the Rhodes Scholarships to Oxford showed. He was the creator of Rhodesia, and had an Imperial dream of a railway route from the Cape to Cairo through British territory all the way. In Milner and Kruger two obstinate immovables met – and Kruger was arming his country with German help. When negotiations stalled, Rhodes made a fatal mistake: he allowed a raid on Johannesburg in the hope of removing the immovable Kruger. It was a fiasco; Rhodes resigned, but Britain was exposed. In this atmosphere of mistrust a negotiated settlement proved impossible. It was a tragic stalemate.

The South African War began, in 1899, with Britain totally unprepared militarily, as usual. The fighting spirit of the men was fine, though they were few to begin with; the commissariat side of the army proved itself hopelessly inefficient, so too the medical – many more died of fevers, dysentery and enteritis than were killed. The army command showed up worst of all, under generals like Buller. The Boers made intrepid fighters and superb marksmen in the field – as Kipling, the poet of empire and the South African war, celebrated them:

> *Ah there, Piet! – 'is trousies to 'is knees,*
> *'Is coat-tails lyin' level in the bullet-sprinkled breeze;*
> *'E does not lose 'is rifle an' 'e does not lose 'is seat.*
> *I've known a lot o' people ride a dam' sight worse than Piet.*

There followed a series of defeats in the field, which aroused dismay in London and delight in Germany, where the Kaiser offered Britain advice on how to conduct the war – having previously sent open encouragement to Kruger. These antics did not endear him to the British public.

The Boers invaded Natal, but now made a fatal strategic mistake: instead of rushing to the sea and keeping out British reinforcements, they locked up large forces in besieging Ladysmith, Kimberley and Mafeking. Great anxiety prevailed in London; but at the crisis it was revealed that there was a real feeling for the empire after all. Canada and Australia sent contingents to help; forces were called in from India; the enlarged army was placed under the competent command of Roberts and Generals Kitchener; the tide was turned. At the

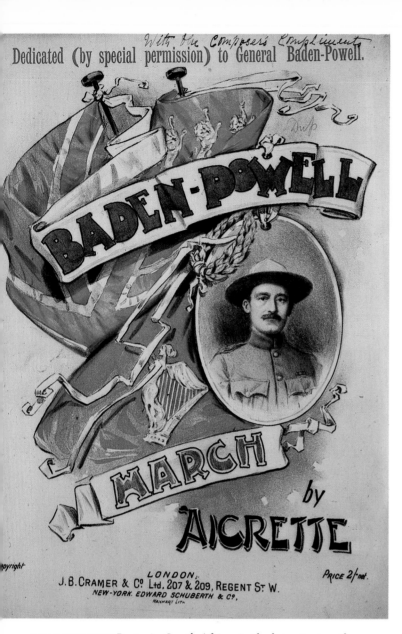

LEFT *The cover of the sheet music for a march dedicated to General Baden-Powell, defender of Mafeking and founder of the Boy Scout Movement.*
BELOW *Caricatures of Kitchener and Rudyard Kipling.*

OPPOSITE LEFT *Pretoria, South Africa, in the late nineteenth century.*
OPPOSITE RIGHT *Cecil Rhodes, creator of Rhodesia, with his secretary and his Cape 'boy' Tony.*
BELOW *Boers in camp just before the outbreak of the Boer War.*
BELOW RIGHT *The Boer fort at the siege of Mafeking.*

relief of Mafeking in 1900 the London mob went wild with delight – Mafeking Night was long remembered and contributed a word to the language, 'mafeking'. Boer resistance was worn down; Pretoria surrendered, and Kruger fled to Holland.

The worst part of the war followed. Before he died Rhodes warned that the Dutch were not beaten: nor were they – they held on to win the peace. For more than a year there was guerilla fighting all over the veld; the army was reduced to rounding up farmers and their families in camps where military conditions were primitive, and many died of fever, as British troops did. Voluntary effort proved more competent than the war office, as in the Crimea: devoted women went out to the field hospitals, as did Emily Hobhouse, to play the part of Florence Nightingale (who was still alive!).

The Dutch never forgave these later sufferings – and indeed the South African war left an appalling legacy of every kind: it was a tragedy that should never have happened. In Europe it released indignation at a big power bullying a small one, and the colossus was revealed to have feet of clay. The Germans have a word to express delight at the troubles of others – *Schadenfreude* – and undoubtedly the revelation that the empire was not invincible encouraged Germany to embark on becoming a naval power, with the construction set going by the Navy Laws of 1898 and 1900. Admirers of Victorian England and what it stood for – such as Gladstonian Liberalism, the rights of small peoples, free trade and peace – were everywhere dismayed.

Indeed a new world was coming into being; the brash and vulgar side of Imperialism displayed itself in the South African

millionaires and mining magnates, the opulence that was to be the mark of the Edwardian age, the brash patriotism of the London mob and the new journalism that catered for it. Old landmarks were disappearing: when Queen Victoria died in 1901 everyone thought that it signalled the end of an age. In the next year Lord Salisbury died, whom she had thought the ablest of all her prime ministers. The Cecil dynasty continued with his nephew, Balfour, as prime minister; but he could never control Chamberlain who, not content with all he had done at the colonial office, pushed into the sphere of foreign affairs to try to negotiate an alliance with Germany. He was rebuffed, but it created a precedent for his son Neville Chamberlain's fatal intervention, a generation later, with his appeasement of Germany, against the Foreign Office's tradition

Relief at the appearance of victory enabled the Tories to win a 'khaki' election and prolong their power for a few years. Electoral tricks of this kind were to become regular with the party in the twentieth century. For the fundamental fact was that gradually the electorate achieved full manhood (and eventually) womanhood suffrage, i.e. political democracy. The working-class vote meant that the propertied classes were in a permanent minority; the natural majority was not with the Tories – especially not in Scotland, Wales, Ireland or Cornwall, even when there was a majority for the party in England. With a mass-electorate, they depended for success on fixing the issues or on a succession of scares, as in 1924, 1931 and 1935.

The Grand Old Man of British politics, Mr Gladstone,

Prospecting for gold in South Africa, 1888.

returned to power for a brief spell. He was dependent on the Irish for a majority and introduced another Bill for Home Rule, which the Tories had hoped to 'kill with kindness'. Their administrators, particularly Balfour, had done unexpectedly well in Ireland – with the help of a huge fund of £100 millions to buy out the landlords: the end of the process was in sight. Home Rule could, however, never pass the House of Lords, and in retiring from office Gladstone foreshadowed a Radical programme which would tackle that problem with other future objectives.

The South African War divided the Liberal Party. The right wing – Rosebery, Asquith, Grey – accepted Imperial responsibilities and the necessity of fighting the war to a solution. The left wing – Sir William Harcourt, John Morley, Campbell-Bannerman – continued Gladstone's tradition; a group further to the left were active pro-Boers, prominent among whom was a Welsh MP, Lloyd George, who was to take up the cause of social Radicalism. Chamberlain was now to make a further advance along that path to campaign for a fundamental change of policy to Protectionism, allied to Imperial preferences, to keep the empire together. This did not depend upon those ties, but something deeper: common stock, traditions, language, culture and history, many

ABOVE Work – *a painting by Ford Madox Brown, expressing the Victorian cult of labour.*

RIGHT *A May Day Socialist poster, designed by Walter Crane, the famous Victorian book-illustrator.*

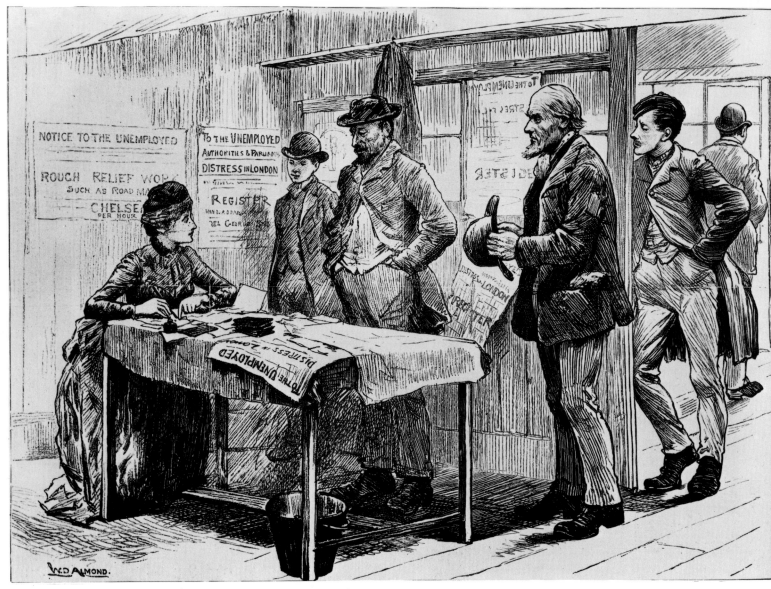

Registering the unemployed at an office in Chelsea at the turn of the century.

common experiences over the centuries. In pursuing this campaign – naturally a Birmingham manufacturer would favour protection – Chamberlain divided his new party and was a factor in their smashing defeat in 1906.

In internal affairs much good constructive work had been done. County councils came into being in 1888 to take the place of the rule of the old country gentry. In these elected bodies gentry and middle classes co-operated with proper public spirit to do good work in their localities; considerable powers came to them with the growing needs of a more democratic society – for police, highways, public health, education. Balfour's Education Act of 1902 was one of the grandest and most beneficial measures of this century. It was the culmination of years of propaganda by Matthew Arnold and his disciples for a national system of secondary grammar schools, in which Britain notoriously lagged behind Germany and France. Balfour was converted by an outstanding civil servant, Sir Robert Morant, creator of a ministry of education and later a ministry of health. The constructive work of building, staffing and administering secondary education through the county councils released a flood of enthusiasm and devotion in that generation which was almost unexampled. I was a witness, and a beneficiary, of it myself.

IN THE AFTERMATH OF THE WAR Milner's gifts were seen at their best in the reconstruction of South Africa, agriculturally and industrially, aided by generous grants from Britain. He called to his aid a group of young Oxford men, the 'Kindergarten' – Lionel Curtis as town clerk of Johannesberg created the great City Park and hospitals – who for the next generation forwarded the ideal of trusteeship for native races throughout the empire. They backed such a man as Lugard, who made of Nigeria a model to be proud of, where men could walk hundreds of miles in peace and security.

Politically, it was helpful that the election of 1906 produced a large Liberal majority, a section of them pro-Boers, including the prime minister, Campbell-Bannerman, who immediately granted self-government to the South African colonies. It took the next few years to work out the political solution, which took the form of union rather than federation. A Boer government came into being under the wise and statesman-like General Botha. Britain was to owe much to these Boer leaders, Botha and Smuts, for her safety in the two German wars – the reward for her Liberal magnanimity in entrusting them with self-government so shortly after fighting them. The hard core of Boer resentment, however, continued and ultimately won, with little benefit to South Africa.

The obvious shortcomings displayed by the war office and in the army led to a campaign for reform, in which Winston Churchill's criticisms were much resented by the Unionist Party, from which he graduated in time to enjoy the fruits of office under the Liberals. Nor was he forgiven for this. The Liberals proceeded to form the ablest government of the century, and initiated the first steps in creating the welfare state. Impetus in this direction was given by the election of fifty Labour MPs, in association with the Liberals.

This portent for the future was in itself the result of several currents making for Socialism. The most effective of these had been the Labour Representation Committee, organized by Ramsay MacDonald; and the Fabian Society (founded in 1884), inspired by Sidney and Beatrice Webb, whose research and propaganda – particularly for the re-organization of the Poor Law and integration into a national health service – influenced all parties. Other currents came from the idealist Socialism of William Morris, and the Socialist intellectuals of the Independent Labour Party. Though Karl Marx made London the centre of his work and propaganda from 1849 to 1883, his influence on the Labour Movement was marginal. The real power and push for Labour representation in Parliament came from the trade unions – much aided by a reactionary decision of the House of Lords in the Taff Vale case, which hampered trade-union action, strikes, picketing, etc. The new Liberal government at once paid its debt to Labour with a Trades Disputes Act, 1906.

Step by step the foundations of the welfare state were laid, largely by the dynamic administrative drive of Lloyd George and Churchill: old-age pensions, labour exchanges, trade boards to fix wages in sweated industries, school meals and medical inspection for school children; an eight-hour day for coalminers. With the Insurance Act of 1911 the framework of a national health service came into being – organized by Morant: a whole elaborate system of sickness and unemployment insurance, dovetailing with approved societies and trade unions. Paradoxically, it was immediately followed in 1911 and 1912 by strikes on a national scale by miners, railwaymen and dockers, which convulsed the country. All the same, 'It is one of the marvels of modern British industry', concluded Clark, 'that in the fifty-nine years from these events not a single life has been lost in the repression of industrial or political strife.' More damage was done by the remarkable Suffragette campaign unleashed by Mrs Pankhurst to gain votes for women. Today it is hard to understand why they were held up for so long.

Reforms in other spheres were no less important. Modern militarism, under the leadership of Germany – which in two wars let loose by her reached the highest level of professional accomplishment, command, techniques, and fighting quality of the soldiers – necessitated bringing the British army up to date. It was accepted that the navy was the first line of defence; the role and character of the army were determined by the profound change in the European scene brought about by the rise of Germany to dominance. The regular army, small in

BELOW *Mrs Pankhurst is carried off from outside Buckingham Palace, May 1914.*
BOTTOM *Wallpaper designed by William Morris, the Victorian artist and writer.*

itself, was brought to a high degree of efficiency, its spearhead being an expeditionary force equipped to intervene in case of necessity on the Continent – the traditional British role. Behind this a larger territorial army was given regular organization, as a reserve for service abroad if called upon. A committee of imperial defence was already the nucleus from which a general staff belatedly developed.

The navy, after a century of unchallenged supremacy at sea, was in need of a more thorough shaking-up, particularly after Germany determined to become a first-class naval power, if possible on a level with Britain, in addition to being much the strongest military power on the Continent. During the crisis of the South African war Germany announced her second Naval Law, in 1900, for a programme of thirty-four battle-ships and fifty-two cruisers over the next sixteen years. This was accompanied by an officially inspired propaganda for naval power, though Germany had no world-wide responsibilities such as Britain had with her peoples overseas; nor did she depend on imports of food for her very existence. Technical factors also announced a new era: the development of the Dreadnought battleship, more powerful in speed and gunfire than anything afloat, and the transition from coal to oil fuel. A new spirit, with a touch of genius, arose in Sir John Fisher, who was to re-create the navy: it needed all his ruthlessness to remove the barnacles. He worked in enthusiastic partnership with Churchill, who had been seconded to the Admiralty. By 1914 'the Fleet was ready': it was only just in time.

These years were no less hectic politically. Lloyd George's Budget of 1909 needed to raise unprecedented sums not only for the navy but for social insurance and welfare. He brought

Life in London, 1895, as seen in The Bayswater Omnibus, *a painting by G.W. Joy.*

forward a Radical Budget: increase of income tax and death duties, a new super tax, and a valuation of land to annex unearned increment to the state. The whole landlord interest was up in arms. The House of Lords, in which Conservatives and Unionists were entrenched, had already rejected or modified much Liberal legislation; they now made the mistake of rejecting the Budget as a whole. They had put themselves in the wrong constitutionally, since for centuries finance was the prerogative of the Commons.

All this meant a constitutional crisis and two elections – in the course of which the liberal-minded Edward VII died, and was succeeded by the more conservative George V. The elections returned practically equal numbers of Liberals and Unionists; so that the Liberal government depended on the Irish vote. This necessitated meeting the Irish demand for Home Rule, which in turn doubled the need for reducing the powers of the House of Lords, which would never pass it. The Parliament Bill which emerged was a measure marked by the moderation of Asquith, the prime minister, who had now achieved parliamentary ascendancy. It retained the House of Lords, but with the power only to delay, not prevent, legislation, and none to influence finance; it remained the supreme court of appeal at law.

Home Rule became the question of the hour; it raised party passions to fever pitch. For the Unionist Party, under the leadership of a Canadian Ulsterman, Bonar Law, committed itself irretrievably to the minority cause of Protestant Ulster;

Dublin General Post Office after the insurrection, 1914.

while the Liberal Party, committed to the Southern Irish majority, neglected Ulster's claims, and did not take sufficient account of her determination not to leave the United Kingdom or to come under any Dublin government. This was the more regrettable because this third Home Rule bill was more flexible in envisaging possible future developments in the direction of federation.

The conduct of the Unionist leaders was of the utmost irresponsibility in encouraging armed resistance; this in turn affected the army in Ireland, where a number of high officers of Unionist sentiment were disaffected. In Ulster thousands of volunteers were training; in April 1914 they landed 30,000 rifles and three million rounds of ammunition, in spite of Churchill's moving the fleet to the coast opposite Ulster. The reply to this was the landing in July of a cargo of arms for Irish volunteers in Dublin. Ireland was on the brink of civil war when the first German war broke out – and no doubt that played a part in German calculations when they caused its outbreak, by backing Austria-Hungary in its determination to eliminate Serbia and subjugate the Southern Slavs. The assassination of the Austrian Archduke Franz Ferdinand in 1914 at Serajevo in Bosnia, Yugoslavia, provided the occasion; the chancellor of the German Empire, Dr Bethmann-Hollweg, a civilian moderate, even said that there would not occur a better.

WE MUST GO BACK to the beginning of the new century, the first half of which was dominated by the German question, which few understood, nor did many appreciate the necessity of the diplomatic revolution undertaken by the foreign office – which did understand it. The South African war exposed Britain's isolation. Chamberlain's approaches for a German alliance were rebuffed. The conviction of the German foreign office, under the malign Holstein, was that Britain would be forced to come to Germany's terms. The German admiralty, under the lead of Tirpitz, was equally convinced that Britain could be forced to come to terms by Germany's building a great battle fleet. Kaiser Wilhelm II veered between peace and war, but always regarding any suggestion of naval limitation in Germany as a personal insult. He was very keen on his navy, and expressed in his exhibitionism the schizophrenic feelings of Germans about Britain, torn between admiration and envy.

It should be understood that the external policy of the German Empire reflected its internal dilemma: aggressive expansion, a German-dominated Europe, was the only alternative the militarist and industrial upper classes could offer to counteract the rise of the Socialist working classes, the largest Social-Democratic party in Europe. Behind this, consciously or unconsciously, was population pressure, for the *Drang nach Osten* (the drive to the East) or, with Hitler, *Lebensraum* (living space). It was the same thing: the policy was continous from the Kaiser to Hitler's time.

Britain was forced to re-think her policy as danger mounted: her policy of isolation was no longer possible. In 1893 the alliance between France and Russia gave them some re-assurance against the danger to themselves. In 1902 Britain

RIGHT *A Punch cartoon of Bismarck, the German Chancellor.*
CENTRE *A famous Punch cartoon of the young Kaiser, Wilhelm II, dismissing Bismarck.*
FAR RIGHT *The First World War: Kaiser Wilhelm II and his Chief of Staff, Count von Moltke.*

formed a defensive alliance with Japan to protect her interests in the Far East. The next step was to clear up the several points of conflict with France, particularly over Egypt. Lansdowne arrived at an understanding – the Anglo-French *Entente* - by which France would give diplomatic support to Britain in this area in return for support in Morocco. Germany immediately reacted in character. The Kaiser was sent to Tangier to assert German interests; a diplomatic crisis was provoked, by which Delcassé, the French foreign minister who had made the *Entente*, was forced from office. This persuaded Lansdowne to authorize military and naval agreements with France for future contingencies. At the Conference of Algeciras, in 1906, Germany found that the *entente* was consolidated and her own allies weak – Italy gave no support but looked instead to Britain.

Further pressure was applied to France in 1911, when Germany sent a cruiser to Agadir, a closed port on the Moroccan coast. Lansdowne's policy was followed consistently by the Liberal, Sir Edward Grey, who recognized Germany's grievance in being excluded: in return for recognition of the French protectorate over Morocco Germany extracted a rich slice of the Congo. She also extracted a warning from Lloyd George, the most Radical of the Liberal ministry, that Britain stood firmly with France and would not submit to bullying.

This was necessary because no progress whatever was made in the prolonged discussions of 1910 to 1913 to get an agreement with Germany to limit naval building. In 1908 an addition to her construction was laid down of four Dreadnoughts a year. No Liberal government wished to see money required for their expanding social services spent on competing with the Germans. The member of the Cabinet most sympathetic to the Germans, the German-educated Haldane, was sent on a mission to Berlin to explore the chance of ending the naval competition. What he discovered was that new building was being stepped up to provide a third fighting squadron in home waters, and that the deepening of the Kiel Canal by 1914 would allow the German battle fleet to pass freely between Baltic and North Sea. The price of ending the naval rivalry would be to agree to Germany having a free hand in Europe, i.e. to impose her domination on France in the west and in Eastern Europe: a German-dominated Europe.

What the Germans found was that Britain could not be dealt with thus. By 1914 Britain was building fifty-two per cent of all the merchant shipping in the world. She could not be out-built in naval construction; even Tirpitz recognized that his naval programme had failed to bring Britain to heel. But Germany now possessed the most powerful battle fleet in the world, after Britain's; and, secure in the Baltic, with no such dispersed demands upon it as Britain's, it could concentrate on gunnery to a superior professional degree – as was indeed found at the battle of Jutland.

It was obvious what was needed to secure not only Britain's interests, but her very survival as a power. But this was not obvious to one half of the Liberal Party, which inherited the pacifist Gladstone's ideas and hated the idea of drawing closer to tsarist Russia, which the situation demanded. Grey's freedom of action was severely restricted: the *entente* could never be converted into a formal alliance, and military conversations for probable eventualities had to be kept informal. Hence the entirely unwarranted attacks on Grey's policy, which was the best one conceived in British interests by the foreign office.

This policy necessitated clearing up points of conflict with Russia – particularly in Persia, the north of which was penetrated by Russian agents and interests. The fact was recognized in return for recognition of British interests in the Persian Gulf on the route to India. No impediment was placed in the way of Germany's projected railway to Baghdad, which eventually gave her a dominant influence over Turkey. The Russian Revolution of 1905 and the adoption there of a Duma, a representative assembly, meant that the tsarist absolutism was on its way out, Russia heading for the institutions of a

DROPPING THE PILOT.

modern state – and this eased the situation somewhat for British Liberal opinion. Russia's interest in the Southern Slavs of the Balkans conflicted with those of Austria-Hungary, which wanted to suppress them. In 1912–13 two Balkan wars resulted in strengthening Slav sentiment and the expanding young nationalities, Serbs, Roumanians, Greeks. In these crises Grey revivified something like a Concert of Europe, and presided with his complete sincerity and candour over the deliberations which headed off an explosion among the great powers and gave further liberation to these small peoples struggling for freedom. The result was to place Turkey firmly in Germany's orbit, but to worsen her situation diplomatically.

It is not generally understood in Britain that Bismarck's understanding with Russia had broken down under popular pressure – the force of nationalist feeling which has proved the dynamic impulse of this century, both for construction and destruction. In the choice between Russia and Austria, the Germans naturally chose their own people. By the same token Russia opted for her own Slav peoples. Here was the alignment, and its compulsions.

The historian Feiling concludes: 'Twenty years of blundering aggression had stripped Germany of every firm ally except Austria, while a waft of death had gone up against the Austro-Hungarian Empire.' It is no business of the historian to discuss hypotheses and to ask what line Germany should have taken, though a conclusion suggests itself that she should at all costs not have challenged Britain's existence at sea. An historian of Britain may legitimately point out, however, that since it took a world alliance, the British Empire, France, Russia, Italy, the United States, Japan, to inflict even the check Germany received in 1918, it was therefore well within her capacity, as it was her will, to dominate Europe and hold Britain alone at her mercy.

*Daddy, what did **YOU** do in the Great War?*

PUBLISHED BY THE PARLIAMENTARY RECRUITING COMMITTEE, LONDON. POSTER NO. 79.   DESIGNED AND PRINTED BY JOHNSON, RIDDLE & CO., LTD., LONDON, S.E.

Chapter 9

The Two German Wars

BY 1914 BRITAIN WAS THE PERFECT EXAMPLE of the Liberal state. Sir George Clark sums it up:

Its commercial system was almost unlimited free trade. It allowed freedom of speech, association and assembly not only to its citizens but to all who chose to enter as immigrants. The proportion of the inhabitats employed by the state was far smaller than anywhere else in industrial Europe. The parliamentary system responded to public opinion as smoothly and punctually as any that had ever been tried. The armed forces were recruited without any compulsion. Local government enjoyed considerable freedom from central control. An Englishman's home was his castle. Now, for the first time since Waterloo, this society underwent a test of strength.

By the same token, this free liberal society was quite unprepared psychologically – because it was so civilized – for the appalling holocaust that was to ensue. Germany was prepared. In many ways it was technically the most efficient country. It is considered by a military authority that, in the Second World War, the professional German army was thirty per cent more efficient than the amateur British. Naturally, in the First World War the disparity was greater: individual bravery could not make up for it.

The casualties of Britain's free society were terrible: because there was no conscription for the first two years of the war, Britain suffered the sacrifice of a whole generation of its best young men who had volunteered. The flower of that generation, who would have given leadership between the wars, was lost: that consideration must always be remembered in accounting for the feeble leadership that prevailed in the 1930s. The blood-drain the French suffered was even more terrible, with similar consequences. Germany did not suffer so badly, in proportion.

It can be considered that the two world wars were crests in the long wave of German aggression aimed at the domination of Europe: as a German historian, Fischer, writes: 'Both German public opinion and Germany's leaders were fully resolved to overthrow all their enemies and dictate peace to them.' Until defeat stared her in the face she would never accept any compromise in her war aims; these were 'a settlement of accounts not with France alone, but also with Britain and Russia'. There would be not only territorial annexations: the aim of the civilian Chancellor, Bethmann-Hollweg, was to impose 'heavy financial demands on Belgium [then in possession of the Congo], Britain and Russia, as well as France: a logical expansion of the idea of crippling the enemy powers for the long term.' What made the German chancellor think the murder at Serajevo a favourable opportunity for launching the war was his conviction that Britain would remain neutral, and that the war could be presented to the Germans as a defensive war against Russia.

Grey strove to the last minute for peace but, according to Fischer, the decision had already been taken in Berlin. 'Not only did Germany consistently reject any attempt at mediation ... but while Grey and Sazonov [the Russian foreign minister] were trying to gain time, Germany was pressing Austria to act quickly.'

Grey warned that the Germans might break the international guarantee of Belgium's neutrality as a short cut into the heart of France. Clark writes: 'They did so within hours of his warning. This was part of their previously fixed strategic plan. It made three changes in the minds of the British public. First, it was a downright breach of an international treaty [described by Bethmann-Hollweg as "merely a scrap of paper"]; secondly, it was an attack on that point in Europe which had been regarded for centuries as vitally important to Britain; thirdly, it was unprovoked attack on a small state.' The Second World War was to see far worse; but in the more civilized world of 1914 this was enough. Britain declared war on 4 August, a date from which the decline of European civilization may be dated. George V, a plain sincere man, spoke for his subjects and fellow citizens to the American ambassador: 'My God, Mr Page, what else could we do?'

The German Schlieffen Plan by which, turning the flank of

OPPOSITE *A recruiting poster in the First World War.*
ABOVE *A detail from the best known of all recruiting posters, featuring Lord Kitchener.*
OVERLEAF *'Outside Charing Cross Station, July 1916.'*

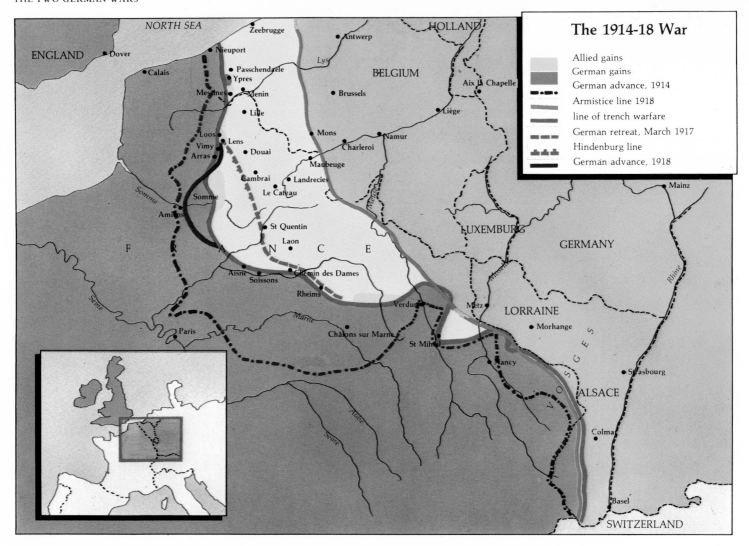

The 1914-18 War

Allied gains
German gains
German advance, 1914
Armistice line 1918
line of trench warfare
German retreat, March 1917
Hindenburg line
German advance, 1918

the French armies by the drive through Belgium, the Germans could lunge at the heart of France, Paris, and throw the British Expeditionary Force back upon the Channel ports, nearly succeeded. In 1914 this opening move was arrested at the Marne, almost by a 'miracle'. Henceforth the Western Front, from the Channel coast to Switzerland, settled down to a terrible stalemate, in which more and more men were swallowed up in mud and blood, in their hundreds of thousands.

It is impossible to tell the ghastly story in detail, of the massed battles that swung to and fro in these four years – Neuve Chapelle, Loos, Ypres, Amiens, the Menin Ridge, the Somme, Passchendaele – in which scores of thousands of lives were lost to gain a few hundred square yards of terrain. We can only pick out salient points. One was the German use of poison gas, an international crime which eventually turned to their disadvantage, for the winds were dominantly westerly. A second was the British invention of the tank; small advantage was taken of the surprise it sprang on the enemy at Cambrai. It was employed on too small a scale and was not followed up by the High Command. A chief explanation of British failures in the first two years was deficiency of armaments; this was not remedied until the dynamic Lloyd George became minister of munitions.

The appalling losses on the Western Front, with no progress registered, made keener wits like Lloyd George and Churchill look elsewhere for a decision. Turkey's entry into the war on Germany's side suggested to Churchill a break through the Dardanelles into the Black Sea, to link up with and bring aid to Russia. The combined operations were delayed in starting and muddled on the spot. Anzacs – Australian and New Zealand forces – held on to the Gallipoli peninsula bravely; but the navy encountered heavy losses from minefields in the Narrows, and opinion mounted at home against the venture. The navy – in particular, Sir John Fisher – was against it, and Churchill was made the scapegoat for its failure.

The navy was already fully stretched with its numerous tasks: protecting commerce at sea, taking part in mopping-up operations around the globe, eventuating in the surrender of German colonies; above all, in maintaining the blockade and pressing it ever closer to Germany. (There were loopholes – Holland in particular was friendly to Germany and let much material through.) All this was the navy's traditional role, providing the weapons of sea power that had helped to reduce Napoleon. A new feature was Germany's submarine warfare, which again was contrary to agreed international law. Tremendous losses were inflicted on merchant shipping; when submarine warfare was declared 'unrestricted', it was extended to passenger ships, such as the liner *Lusitania* – the sinking of which was a crime which offended the United States and ultimately helped to bring them into the war. At the height of submarine activity early in 1917, 900,000 tons of shipping

The battle of Jutland, 31 May 1916, the only great sea battle of the First World War.

were sent to the bottom, and only six weeks' food supply remained in Britain. Food rationing was already in being; not until the convoy system was adopted was the menace to Britain's survival conquered.

The one sortie of the German High Seas Fleet led to the battle of Jutland in 1916. It gave a good account of itself, inflicting heavier losses than it suffered, before it retreated from the superior forces of Jellicoe's Grand Fleet converging upon it. Luck was with it: it made a getaway, not to emerge again from its lair until the final surrender at Scapa Flow. British opinion, which expected another Trafalgar, was deeply upset. Jellicoe's caution was justified, since he was considered 'the only person who could lose the war in an afternoon' – and he did not lose it. The pressure of sea power was kept up to the end.

The long run of failures or ill-successes, the lack of progress in the war, led to the replacement of Asquith as head of the government by Lloyd George. Asquith was no war minister and he had no personal appeal in the country, but he did possess an ascendancy in Parliament hard to understand today. He had formed a coalition with the Conservatives in 1915 but kept the Liberals on top in his government. Lloyd George had the dynamism of genius, and was called upon to take over by the will of the country. He was not a strict party politician and had a divisive effect on party affiliations. In his coalition government of 1916–22, the Conservatives were uppermost, and this ultimately split the Liberals into two factions, which aided their eventual extinction as anything more than a fringe; all that was left was the remnant of the old Nonconformist vote in marginal areas. What made this inevitable was the rise of the Labour Party, with the trade unions behind it, the political expression of the organized working class.

A new spirit of resolution showed itself in the direction of the war with Lloyd George, who was in himself a sign of things to come, for he was the first prime minister of working-class origin and education. Nevertheless the year 1917 looked black for the allied cause: a series of mutinies paralysed the French armies after their grievous blood-drain; the British army, itself under strain, had to take over a portion of the French line and undertook the useless slaughter of Passchendaele to take the strain off the French. Lloyd George wept but nevertheless held on. Italy had joined the allies, but proved no match for the Austrians. The Italian front collapsed at Caporetto; once more steady British troops were called in to stave off disaster. Greece had joined the allied cause, but no progress was made from the Franco-British front at Salonika.

A decisive event of 1917 was the revolution in Russia.

ABOVE *Shooting down a Zeppelin airship.*
RIGHT *The trenches at Messines, near Ypres.*

Russia had suffered far larger losses than any other of the powers. The extreme revolutionaries under the lead of Lenin were escorted back into Russia from exile by Germany; with the October Revolution Lenin offered 'bread and peace' to the masses, and the Russian Front crumbled. The Peace of Brest-Litovsk was imposed, by which territory right up to the threshold of St Petersburg (now Leningrad) – till then the capital – was taken from Russia.

The lasting importance of Brest-Litovsk was that it alerted the United States, and instructed President Wilson, as to Germany's real aims. It should have enlightened the British as to the kind of peace the Germans would have imposed had

LEFT *Money-raising stamps, showing three eminent statesmen of the time:* left to right *Lloyd George, Asquith, Churchill.*

they won the war. For Russia, it was a trial run for what happened with Hitler's invasion and devastation in 1941–5. The aims were continuous.

Germany could not have been defeated without the help of the United States and the loyal aid of the British Dominions and India. In 1917 the United States entered the war. Before American strength could be deployed, the Germans were able to transfer their armies from the Russian Front for a last mighty onslaught in the West in the spring and summer of 1918. The allied front almost broke under the weight of it, and once more the Germans stood on the Marne threatening Paris. By now their own resources were stretched to the uttermost; the invisible strangle-hold of the blockade was having its full effect. Germany had come under the virtual military dictatorship of Hindenburg and Ludendorff. It is historically

significant that Ludendorff became the early patron and colleague of Hitler, and that Hindenburg was the last president of the Weimar Republic, who was to betray it to Hitler.

The last German onslaught exhausted its impetus and the allies were able to throw the Germans back on the defensive, American troops now taking part. Ludendorff lost his nerve, and demanded of the new Berlin government – the Kaiser having fled to Holland – that they should sue for an armistice. All the same, the German army never broke: it conducted an orderly retreat to the Rhine – to fight again another day.

For the Revolution in Germany never reached to the roots, as it had done in Russia. A political revolution installed the Weimar Republic of Social Democrats and Liberals; the balance of social forces remained unchanged, the working-class divided by the struggle unleashed by Communism against Social Democracy. Real strength remained with the unreconstructed and unrepentant military and industrial upper classes, who sabotaged the republic and, with the connivance of Soviet Russia, began the re-arming of Germany.

The peace settlement of Versailles, 1919, was never accepted by Germany. The territorial clauses were in themselves just and moderate. Alsace-Lorraine was returned to France; Poland was reconstituted, with Danzig a free city as its outlet, a corridor across East Prussia giving access. The small nationalities of the Austro-Hungarian Empire demanded and received liberation. What no one noticed, except the French, was that this belt of small nations around the east and south of Germany gave her the opening to resume her onward march of aggression, once she was re-armed.

Britain got the security of the surrender of the German battle fleet, which scuppered itself at Scapa Flow, its unrepentant commander thereupon committing suicide. The German colonies, which had no real roots, were taken over and variously provided for, under the aegis of the British Dominions or the League of Nations, which took shape at Versailles. The reparations clauses have been much disputed. Germany had occupied and devastated eleven departments of industrial North-Eastern France, besides Belgium, for four years. It was entirely just that she should make reparation. This also she never intended to fulfil.

Within Germany an intensive propaganda placed the whole responsibility for defeat – the so-called 'stab in the back' – upon the Democrats and Socialists who accepted the verdict. This was aided by the murder campaign mounted against their leaders. But it was no reason for the British to accept the propaganda against Versailles – the French were more realist and knew better; this became an important element in muddling public opinion, in Britain and the United States, throughout the inter-war period and preparing the way for Germany's second round. After all, she had so nearly brought it off in the first.

OPPOSITE *The signing of the Peace Treaty in the Hall of Mirrors at Versailles, on 28 June 1919.*

THE FALL OF THE TURKISH EMPIRE revolutionized the Middle East, and this was mainly Britain's achievement. She had suffered reverses in Gallipoli and Iraq, but from her base in Egypt she was able to roll up the Turks, with the aid of the Arabs, liberating them as she went. This campaign was accompanied by the romantic side-show of T.E. Lawrence, an Anglo-Irish-Scottish archaeologist-adventurer, who wrote it up in a classic, *Seven Pillars of Wisdom*, and became a remarkable cult figure to the next generation.

T.E. Lawrence, or 'Lawrence of Arabia', in Arab dress.

A prime objective of Britain in the war was the liberation of peoples from imperial rule – and this would have its effect upon her own empire. Her liberation of the Arabs enabled her to set up two Arab kingdoms in Iraq and Transjordan, and, for a brief period, in Syria. This last was undermined by disagreement with the French, who had prior historic interest in the area. With so much done for the Arabs, it was a matter of international justice that the Balfour Declaration of 1917, in favour of a national home for the Jews in ancient Palestine, should be honoured. This was conceived as a gradual process on a small scale, until the criminal treatment of the Jewish

The entry of the Allies into Jerusalem in December 1917, under General Allenby.

people by Nazi Germany and her satellites flooded the tiny country with immigrants. There they made the desert blossom like the rose – a constructive achievement which embittered the Arab world and led to grave difficulties for the British occupation after the war. Nor has the situation been noticeably improved by the British withdrawal, – as elsewhere.

Many Greeks were liberated from Turkish rule around the Aegean and the coasts of Asia Minor. But the Greeks bit off more than they could chew in the interior of Turkey, which underwent a revival on a national basis under Kemal, who threw them back into the sea. This was a catastrophe for Greece, and for the personal policy of Lloyd George, who – both as a Welshman and a Gladstonian Liberal – was sold on the Greek cause. At Chanak in 1922 British troops were once more confronting Turks; there was some danger of war – very unpopular in Britain, which had to withdraw. This was a prime factor in the fall of Lloyd George. The chestnuts were pulled out of the fire by Lord Curzon, the Conservative foreign secretary who knew the Middle East well, by travel and from experience earlier as viceroy of India. He brought off a reasonable settlement with Turkey by the Treaty of Lausanne, 1923, which remarkably led to firm friendship.

Another factor in Lloyd George's eclipse was his Irish settlement, never stomached by the Conservatives, upon whom he was dependent in Parliament. Asquith's Home Rule Bill was now upon the statute book, to take effect after the war by agreement with the honourable Irish leader in Parliament, John Redmond. This hopeful prospect was bedevilled by the outbreak of an armed rising of Republican extremists, Sinn Fein (Ourselves Alone), in Dublin at Easter 1916. It was wartime, and the leaders were executed. The rising had long-term consequences. Hitherto this faction had been a small fringe group; a reaction in their favour brought them to the fore, diminishing the prospects of the majority Home Rulers. For, by the same token, a reaction against armed rebellion hardened Conservative-Unionist sentiment, under their Ulster leader, Bonar Law.

This encouraged a temporary campaign of repression which, though half-hearted and sickening to liberal sentiment, brought Irish opinion over to Sinn Fein – by similar sickening reprisals. At the last moment, when repression was succeeding, Sinn Fein consented to negotiate. An Irish Free State was agreed, i.e. self-government as a dominion; Ulster was excluded, with rather too wide a boundary to the south, to form its own exclusively Unionist government at Belfast. This settlement, which had the promise of further evolution in a federal direction, was immediately sabotaged by a minority of Sinn Fein, under the leadership of the Irish-Spanish-American, De Valera. At once civil war broke out between the two factions, with executions on one side, assassinations on the other. The Free State survived; when, later, De Valera won a majority by the normal electoral process, it was not he but his opponents who made Southern Ireland a republic, carrying her out of the association of self-governing nations into which the empire had developed. Such are the paradoxes of politics.

Within Britain the war effected profound social changes. The working classes came to the fore as a prime force to be reckoned with; political, if not social, democracy was achieved with universal suffrage, women at last being given the vote. The coalition cashed in on Lloyd George's

popularity to win the 'khaki' election of 1919, which produced a House of Commons full of 'hard-faced men who had done well out of the war'. Henceforth the Conservatives were dominant, except for two short intervals, up to the Second World War. But Conservatives were increasingly at odds with Lloyd George, who cared nothing for preserving the social hierarchy. (In his Radical days he had described a duke as costing as much as a dreadnought.) After the Irish settlement and Chanak a Conservative revolt placed Bonar Law briefly in power, to be succeeded by the long-lasting Baldwin in 1923.

Described as 'the cabin boy' by the abler Tories who had held office with Lloyd George, Baldwin was the dominant figure in British politics for the next fifteen years. A kindly man of no force, he made an astute party manager; while caring for industrial peace – he was himself a Midlands industrialist – and expressing the desire to train Labour for political responsibility, he managed to keep the party in a minority most of the time. He first signalized himself by making an unfavourable settlement with the United States of the vast debt incurred to fight the war – while Britain received nothing of the equally large sums she had advanced to her allies. As a Protectionist, he precipitated an election in 1923 out of which emerged the first Labour government, under Ramsay MacDonald. In a minority, it could be safely 'groomed', and dismissed when Conservatives and Liberals agreed to dismiss it: it lasted a mere nine months.

Its only noteworthy production was the Geneva Protocol, which would commit the powers to surrender sovereignty for effective action under the League of Nations in cases of conflict. The League was a hopeful organization to have come out of the war, but was no more effective than Grey's Concert of Europe before it. It did useful work in mediating conflicts between lesser interests and powers, and supervising beneficent industrial controls, but it could not deal with the graver conflicts of great powers. Its fundamental weakness was that the United States, the greatest power in the world, repudiated it and withdrew into isolation. It was this that led to European disarray and world anarchy, for Britain and France were never strong enough to control the situation. France tried to do so by her alliances in Eastern Europe, and ultimately by a Franco-Soviet alliance. She was frustrated by Britain's liberal sentiments, aiming at Germany's recovery – the City of London was pro-German throughout the inter-war period, as was Wall Street; while Germany was secretly re-arming with the connivance of Soviet Russia. This was not dangerous until Hitler grasped power in 1933 – there was even some hope of disarmament under the auspices of the league; after that, none. In the following year Soviet Russia, appreciating the danger, joined the League – too late to make it effective.

Nor did Baldwin take any interest in the League or give much attention to foreign affairs: he would have preferred isolation, had it been possible. The 1924 election was decided by a 'red scare' over the Zinoviev letter, which purported to

ABOVE LEFT *The battle for the Four Courts, 1922, between the Irish Free State and the Republicans.*
BELOW LEFT *Lloyd George, Prime Minister from 1916 to 1922.*

A scene in London during the General Strike of 1926.

indicate Communist influence over the Labour Party. The Conservative government broke off relations with Soviet Russia. Britain's economic situation was further worsened by the disastrous return to the gold standard at the exaggerated parity of $4.88 to the pound sterling. This hit exports badly, in particular coal, in which Britain still had an export trade, and led directly to the miners' strike of 1926.

This lasted for nine months and left an ill legacy. Both coal owners and coal miners were stubborn – the latter led by the sentimental and irresponsible A.J. Cook, for whom they excluded the able Frank Hodges, who thereupon recruited himself to the management side of industry. The Trades Union Congress called, hardly intentionally, a general strike in support of the miners. This potentially dangerous pheno-menon lasted little more than a week, in an atmosphere of surprising decency and good will; it did not help the miners, who held out for months in despair and lasting resentment. The political effect was to return the Labour Party as the largest in Parliament in 1929, though still a minority dependent upon the divided Liberals, who thenceforth were reduced to a small faction exerting no consistent influence upon affairs.

The Labour government of 1929–31 was distracted by the rising tide of unemployment, and shortly engulfed by a world economic depression, unleashed by the United States, which had repercussions throughout Europe. A political crisis was set off in Britain, when the majority of the Labour government refused to balance the Budget by cuts in unemployment benefit. A 'national' government was formed, in which three Labour leaders joined with Conservatives and Liberals, to enforce the cuts and restore confidence. In the upshot they were themselves forced to devalue the pound.

THE 1930S WERE A DESPAIRING, HECTIC PERIOD dominated by the resurgence of Germany under Hitler and his enormous mass movement, which can now be seen in historical perspective as leading inevitably to Germany's resumed march to dominate Europe and to the Second World War. The only hope of arresting this was seen by the foreign office, correctly, to lie in a Grand Alliance, which had been the sheet-anchor of Britain's security over the centuries, to contain the aggressive power which threatened the safety and existence of others. Politicians of all parties refused to see this, with some notable exceptions: Churchill, Eden and, in the Labour Party, Hugh Dalton. In consequence British policy in this period was well-meaning but confused, nerveless, distracted by its fear of war and the refusal of the dominant Conservative Party to come to terms with Soviet Russia, necessary linch-pin of such an alliance. Many of them would have preferred to come to terms with Hitler, to whom every concession was made, except the last.

In 1934 Russia, alarmed, made a significant approach to the West by joining the League of Nations; a purge of leading Communists ensued, the faithful legatees of world revolution. The hint, broad enough, was not taken. In 1935 Fascist Italy, under its dictator Mussolini, attacked Abyssinia. This provided a crucial test for the League of Nations and, since British Imperial sentiment was affected, the 'national' government was willing to give a half-hearted trial to the principle of collective security (in more realist terms, the Grand Alliance) to bring Italy to heel – but without overthrowing Mussolini. The result was disaster: Mussolini won his war, Hitler drew his conclusions and embarked on his career of open aggression, beginning with the re-militarization of the Rhineland and re-armament of Germany at full speed, night and day, the creation of the Panzer tank divisions and the tactical air force which was to conquer Europe in 1940.

The 'national' government took the opportunity of the Abyssinian crisis to entrap the Labour Movement. In 1931 the Labour representation in Parliament was slashed to a mere 55 MPs, and without its leaders no Opposition was possible. In the election of 1935, caught out, Labour still could return only 155 out of a House of 615 MPs. Throughout the 1930s the 'national' government – a pseudonym for Conservative dominance – could do what it wished: so far from 'grooming' Labour for responsibility, it played into the hands of its irresponsible elements, and was an obstacle to the proper functioning of Parliament.

The years 1936–8 were dominated by the Spanish Civil War and Germany's onward march. The main Imperial problem for Britain was the growth of the Congress Movement in India under the leadership of Gandhi. Here progress was made towards self-government, without as yet envisaging handing over power at the centre. In Spain the republic was strangled by the intervention of forces from both Fascist Italy and Nazi Germany – preliminary exercises for the war to come; Russian intervention, more remote, hardly less cruel but less efficient, did not serve to turn the scale. Britain and France, whose interests were gravely damaged by these events, were reduced to a feeble posture of non-intervention; still more by Hitler's occupation of Austria in 1937, turning the flank of Czechoslovakia, the strategic key to Central Europe.

The year 1936 was occupied by the episode of the reign of Edward VIII; in the resolution of this by the king's abdication to marry Mrs Simpson Baldwin's personal touch was at its most tactful and successful. He was succeeded by Neville Chamberlain, son of Birmingham's Joe. This Chamberlain, in hostility to the judgment of the foreign office and willingly sacrificing his foreign secretary, Eden, embarked on a personal policy of 'appeasing' the dictators, really meaning to do a deal with Hitler.

In the crisis which Hitler created in 1938 over Czechoslovakia, his next 'demand', Chamberlain thrust himself forward to meet that demand. Ignoring Russia's interest in the small Slav power, opposed to any course of action in association with Soviet Russia, at Munich Chamberlain, alone with the French – enfeebled by the course of Britain's policy and distracted by her own pro-Germans – faced the dictators, Hitler and Mussolini. It was hardly surprising that Czechoslovakia was truncated, and rendered no longer defensible. On his return to a delirious London, waving a scrap of paper with its promise of peace between Germany and Britain, Chamberlain claimed that he had won 'Peace with honour'. It was, in fact, peace with dishonour, and for a short interval. When Churchill described the Munich

A newspaper front page describing the return of Neville Chamberlain from Munich in 1938.

agreement as the gravest diplomatic defeat in Britain's history he was howled down in the House of Commons.

In March 1939 Hitler occupied the remainder of Czechoslovakia, a plain breach of his pledged word to Chamberlain. Even then it took the revolt of the foreign office, in the person of Chamberlain's foreign secretary, Lord Halifax, to bring home the imminent danger – the complete overthrow of the balance of power in Europe. This was followed by a guarantee of their territory to Poland and Roumania, which Britain was in no position to fulfil – and it showed up the nonsense of the previous course of appeasement which had led to disaster. The real purpose was to serve notice on Hitler's Germany that further aggression would mean war. In the words of a foreign office official, it was 'catching the last bus'. In Germany, as in 1914, no notice was taken; the unfinished war of 1914–18 was resumed. After twenty years of Conservative dominance Britain in 1940 – quite unlike her position in 1914 – faced a Germany in control of Europe without an ally, alone.

IT WAS FORTUNATE FOR BRITAIN that in this second round she faced a Germany under a criminal régime. Its nature was obvious enough all along to persons of intelligence. Its brutalities were erected into a system: its persecution of Jews, Social Democrats, Liberals, let alone Communists, and of the

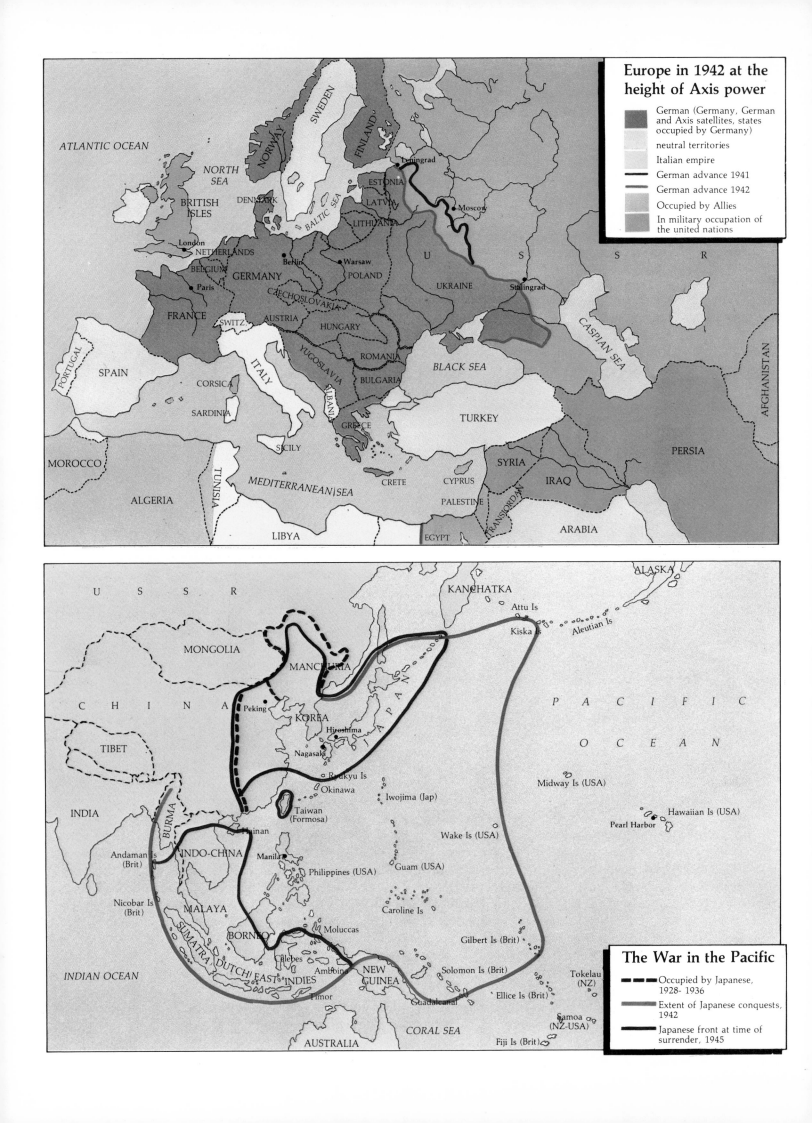

Europe in 1942 at the height of Axis power

German (Germany, German and Axis satellites, states occupied by Germany)

neutral territories

Italian empire

German advance 1941

German advance 1942

Occupied by Allies

In military occupation of the united nations

ATLANTIC OCEAN

NORTH SEA

SWEDEN

NORWAY

FINLAND

BALTIC SEA

Leningrad

ESTONIA

LATVIA

LITHUANIA

Moscow

BRITISH ISLES

DENMARK

London

NETHERLANDS

Berlin

Warsaw

BELGIUM

GERMANY

POLAND

U   S   S   R

Paris

CZECHOSLOVAKIA

UKRAINE

Stalingrad

FRANCE

SWITZ.

AUSTRIA

HUNGARY

PORTUGAL

SPAIN

CORSICA

ITALY

YUGOSLAVIA

ROMANIA

BLACK SEA

CASPIAN SEA

SARDINIA

ALBANIA

BULGARIA

AFGHANISTAN

GREECE

TURKEY

MOROCCO

SICILY

CRETE

CYPRUS

SYRIA

IRAQ

PERSIA

MEDITERRANEAN SEA

PALESTINE

TRANSJORDAN

ALGERIA

TUNISIA

LIBYA

EGYPT

ARABIA

The War in the Pacific

Occupied by Japanese, 1928-1936

Extent of Japanese conquests, 1942

Japanese front at time of surrender, 1945

ALASKA

U   S   S   R

KAMCHATKA

Attu Is

Kiska Is

Aleutian Is

MONGOLIA

MANCHURIA

PACIFIC OCEAN

C   H   I   N   A

Peking

KOREA

Hiroshima

JAPAN

TIBET

Nagasaki

Ryukyu Is

Midway Is (USA)

Okinawa

Iwojima (Jap)

Hawaiian Is (USA)

INDIA

Taiwan (Formosa)

Wake Is (USA)

Pearl Harbor

BURMA

Hainan

INDO-CHINA

Manila

Guam (USA)

Andaman Is (Brit)

Philippines (USA)

Nicobar Is (Brit)

MALAYA

Caroline Is

SUMATRA

BORNEO

Moluccas

Gilbert Is (Brit)

DUTCH EAST INDIES

Celebes

Solomon Is (Brit)

INDIAN OCEAN

Amboina

NEW GUINEA

Tokelau (NZ)

Timor

Guadalcanal

Ellice Is (Brit)

Samoa (NZ-USA)

CORAL SEA

AUSTRALIA

Fiji Is (Brit)

The evacuation of the British expeditionary force from Dunkirk in 1940.

Christian churches; its concentration camps and record of murders of opponents; and the blood-bath of July 1934, when some 1200 of its own comrades and opponents alike were murdered. Now there was no further denying the self-evident facts, and Britain's stand against this monstrous criminality in the heart of Europe elicited moral support for Britain throughout the world. Particularly after the fall of France in 1940, when it became clear that Britain would not give in, and fragments of defeated, persecuted and tortured peoples rallied to the island sanctuary of freedom. It was seen that Britain was now fighting not only for her own survival and others' but for civilization itself.

In default of a Western alliance Russia had come to an understanding with Germany by which she was to remain neutral in case of a German attack on Poland. In spite of British warnings the attack came, and once more Britain declared war on Germany. The winter following was a strange period of ominous waiting to see which way Germany would pounce next. In the spring enlightenment came: opposed ineffectively by the British, the Germans occupied Norway in a smart professional operation which demonstrated their masterly co-ordination of air and land operations. This vastly increased the length of hostile coast-line opposed to Britain and the potentialities of the submarine menace. It was followed by an unforgivable attack on Holland, announced by a sudden bombing of Rotterdam from the air. Then came the onslaught in the West, which achieved the triumph the Germans had missed in 1914, by the skilled co-ordination of tank divisions with aircraft, which broke the French resistance and drove the British army back to the Channel. Here a miracle like the battle of Marne was re-enacted: from Dunkirk the bulk of the army was saved and brought back to Britain, but with the loss of all its arms and equipment.

At this crisis Winston Churchill was catapulted into power by a coalition of dissident Conservatives and Labour, whose key figure was the trade union leader, Ernest Bevin, who proceeded to organize man-power and woman-power as never before. 'The resources of the nation were concentrated in the war effort more completely than those of any other nation on either side. Nevertheless, there was less disunion between classes and interests than in any other five years within living memory.' There was indeed a mighty resolve to resist the evil thing, Hitler's sway over the Continent, or to go down fighting if necessary. This found expression in the words of Churchill, which inspired the nation as never before.

We shall not flag or fail. We shall fight in France, we shall fight on the seas and oceans, we shall fight with growing confidence and growing strength in the air. We shall defend our island, whatever the cost may be, we shall fight on the beaches, we shall fight on the landing grounds, we shall fight in the fields and in the streets, we shall fight in the hills. We shall never surrender.

Strangely, this mood was strengthened on the fall of France, when Britain found herself alone, except for the dominions, in particular Canada, whose menfolk brought the island sustenance and strength. So too Americans, Poles, Frenchmen, Dutch, Belgians, Norwegians flocked to Britain to fight the terror occupying Europe, which sent Jews, Slavs, resisters of all kinds to concentration camps and gas chambers.

What saved Britain was what had saved her so often in the past – and at this supreme crisis her past history became a living inspiration: the fact of her being an island. The Germans were no more able to invade than Napoleon or Louis XIV or the Spanish Armada had been. Confirmation of this persuaded President Roosevelt to send urgent help, arms and supplies, in increasing amounts as the months wore on. To invade Britain, Germany would have needed to win mastery in the air, and this she was never able to achieve in spite of the numerical superiority of the *Luftwaffe*, Goering's air force. Instead, the Battle of Britain – the air warfare over Britain – constituted Germany's first defeat. She turned to bombing London and the seaports; checked here too, she turned east and south. It provided a foretaste of the unprecedented bombing Germany herself would endure, especially after the entry of the United States into the war.

A difference from the First World War was made by Fascist Italy entering the war on the German side. This made the Mediterranean almost impassable – if only France had continued the struggle from North Africa it would have shortened the war and its sufferings for everyone. Churchill's decision to send one of the only two armoured divisions left in Britain saved Egypt as a base. From Egypt Italian armies five times greater in number were easily rolled back by British troops, while the Italian navy was effectively dealt with off Cape Matapan and at Taranto. Malta was, however, continuously under attack from the air. German reinforcements, particularly armoured divisions, under Rommel reversed the situation and for a moment threatened Egypt. In consequence, in the rather absurd British way, Rommel became something of a hero to the British. The contest for North Africa waged to and fro across more than a thousand miles, until the Anglo-American invasion from the west and Montgomery's advance from El Alamein caught German and Italian armies between the two, and they were forced to surrender.

The turning-point of the war was reached in 1941 by Hitler's attack on Russia, and the Japanese attack on Pearl Harbor, which brought the United States into the war. From that moment there was no doubt of the ultimate result, because of their immense resources in man-power and equipment of all kinds. Yet such was Germany's strength, with most of Europe enslaved to her, that it took three more years to subdue her. The resources of Europe were shackled to German needs; a million or two of foreign workers were pinioned to Germany's armaments industries. At no time until near the end was the German population permitted to endure the impoverishment and want that prevailed in other countries – even in Britain the population was harshly rationed on a minimum diet, for the submarine campaign gravely endangered her once more. In this war Germany put

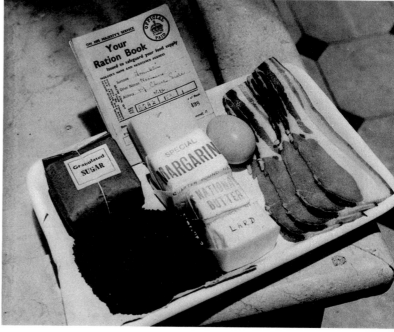

TOP *The Battle of Britain, September 1940.*
OPPOSITE *Winston Churchill visiting a bombed area in the City of London in 1941.*
ABOVE AND RIGHT, TOP TO BOTTOM
Scenes of life in Britain during the Second World War:
School-children practise using gas-masks.
St Paul's Cathedral in the Blitz.
The Home Guard.
The weekly ration.

most of her naval effort into building submarines, and now had the Atlantic and North Sea coasts of Europe from which to imperil Britain. She had no battle fleet as in the First World War, but she had built the most powerful battleship in the world, the *Bismarck*, in direct breach of the Anglo-German Naval Treaty of 1935 – a typical piece of confused thinking, which had had only the effect of dismaying and discouraging France, Britain's ally. The submarine menace was not effectively countered until 1943.

Meanwhile, the German armies nearly reached Moscow and Leningrad in 1941, such was the inefficiency of the Soviet army resulting from the appalling purges carried out from top to bottom in 1936. Russia survived through inexhaustible man-power, and because the Germans were disabled by the Russian winter. Nevertheless, the professional German military capacity enabled it to hold out against superior numbers until, over-extended, German armies were forced to surrender at Stalingrad at the same time as in North Africa. The Russian military effort was continuously aided by the Arctic convoys which conveyed supplies from Britain and America.

At last, and none too soon, the liberation of Europe was begun by the joint Anglo-American invasion of Normandy on D-day, 6 June 1944. No one who lived through those days can forget the mood of prayer, anxiety, dedication and hope that inspired the nation after such long endurance, so many sufferings, the sickness of hope deferred. Nor was it a moment too soon, for the V-bombs, rocket missiles, were beginning to fall on London. The German armies fought with their customary professional skill and tenacity. They were hampered in the rear by resistance movements among all the peoples of Europe whose hatred they had so richly earned: railway lines torn up, bridges and fuel dumps destroyed, allied air strikes directed to the right spots. Many *coups* were carried

out. In the rear of the allied landings the Continent was rising against its tormentors – though even after the surrender, the Nazi commandant of St Malo blew up the historic city.

The German military machine contested every step with professional skill, defeating the allied attempt to turn the flank by air-landings in Holland. Hitler personally inspired a last offensive in the Ardennes, which pushed back the American line; Montgomery took over to rectify the situation.

The allied invasion of Italy was as stubbornly contested; the advance up through the peninsula was unexpectedly slowed by the brilliant defence conducted by the Germans, who took over from their Italian allies, whom they treated with ruthlessness and contempt. In the east the Germans were rolled back by the weight of Russian numbers upon Berlin. Thrusts from each direction converged upon the German heartland; the Western allies held up theirs that the Russians might have the honour of entering Berlin. With the Russians in the city, Hitler committed suicide in his air-raid proof bunker beneath the imperial chancery. To the very last the German people had stood with him, fought and fell with him.

It was an end to the long duel of Teuton and Slav for dominance in Eastern Europe. For the British it was an almighty deliverance.

Allied troops about to disembark on Omaha beach on D-Day, 6 June 1944.

TOP *D-Day plus 20: the scene at Arromanches.*
ABOVE *The Conference at Yalta. From left to right: Churchill, Roosevelt and Stalin.*

IN THE FAR EAST the entry of Japan into the war as an enemy transformed the situation and produced unmitigated disaster. After her aggressions against China which had filled the 1930s with apprehension and showed up the helplessness of the League of Nations without the United States, Japan now attacked east and south, overwhelming the Dutch East Indies, Malaya, and capturing Singapore. For a time Australia lay exposed, but the Japanese made west towards India. A British army countered their thrust in prolonged jungle-fighting in Burma, developing new expertise with the aid of the native population. A pro-Japanese movement in India made no headway, but the spectacle of defeat of Western powers at the hand of an Eastern had detonating effects throughout the East, and signalled the end of Western colonialism in that area, Dutch, French, British or American. And it speeded up the withdrawal of the British from India. Henceforth, the liberation of the peoples was the watchword – with what results we see all round the world today.

The dropping of nuclear bombs on Hiroshima and Nagasaki resulted in the immediate surrender of Japan, and the saving of hundreds of thousands of lives in any further prolonged struggle. It also announced a new and terrible world.

Epilogue

THE RESULT OF THE SECOND WORLD WAR, with its resort to brute force, was to speed up the processes of history in every direction, political, social, technological. It settled some historic issues, and opened up others of which no one can tell the outcome.

In the first place it ended the German bid to dominate Europe. The history of this century has shown that other peoples in Europe could not live with a unified Germany; or that they might have been able to live with a federal pacific Germany that was not concentrated on 'Blood and Iron', military power and aggressive expansion at the expense of others. So the war ended with Germany divided from top to bottom. Even so, she has emerged as the strongest power in Western Europe. That shows how unwise Britain was to depart from her age-long policy of the Grand Alliance to maintain a proper balance, to weaken France and make the concessions to a criminal régime which renewed the danger to Europe in a more monstrous form.

This civil war within Europe – because the German governing classes did not know how to take their proper place in it or play a decent rôle – has ended European ascendancy in the world. Its place has been taken by an unstable relationship between the super-powers, the United States and Russia, in conflict over emergent Africa. Whether that is any improvement over the historic British ascendancy at sea, with trusteeship for backward peoples until they matured to self-government, may be doubted. In any case China – the country with the longest historic record of civilization continuously over the largest area, the most numerous human family in the world – is bound to have a large say in it.

The British Empire was already evolving, in accordance with the inner logic of British history, towards self-government of its constituent parts. That process also has been speeded up: the acceleration has not always been to the benefit of the peoples concerned – the evidence is to be seen all over Africa. Even in India, where the eventual hand-over of power to the Indians was always in mind, it can hardly be thought that it has been beneficial in all respects to the peoples concerned. It is probable historically that people prefer to be governed less well by themselves – one sees that internally in societies with the advent of social democracy.

A characteristic of English history has been an inner flexibility while retaining useful external forms. It has been of great use, and more than mere use, to retain the monarchy, which goes continuously back to the ancient royal house of the West Saxons, with its ancestor of Celtic name, Cerdic. The monarchy is more than a symbol, it is also more than a link in the chain. But the reality behind empire is the fact of people of British stock inhabiting self-governing dominions across the oceans – the result of our history and the natural expansion of a maritime, trading, colonizing people. These bonds do not depend upon formal links.

Britain's blissful good fortune in history depended upon her insular security; this also has come to an end, though it saved us as recently as 1940. It enabled Britain to impose a pause upon revolutionary movements and ideas from abroad and to work out her own moderate, and moderating, solutions. Hence the development of political self-government within the island, with its accompanying free institutions, wide liberties and growth of tolerance. This has been enormously influential, and taken as a model, in the outside world in the past two centuries. It was entirely consistent with this tradition that Britain should have handed over power, with notable good will, for example in India.

Modern civilization, for good and ill, is an industrial one – also speeded up as the result of the war. Nuclear power, for example, might not otherwise have been released, let alone have proliferated, for some decades. The basis of industrial civilization was first worked out in this fortunate island, rich in minerals, water power and seaways – now extended with further resources in the oil and gas around its shores.

At the same time the war accelerated the transition from political to social democracy. It remains to be seen how the people, in common with other peoples in Europe and beyond, work out their own fate; and whether in this lucky island it will be worthy of so remarkable a history.

Queen Elizabeth II pauses on the steps of St Paul's Cathedral during her Silver Jubilee celebrations.

Acknowledgments

The pictures in this book are reproduced by kind permission of the following (numbers are page numbers, numbers in italics indicate black and white pictures):

The Admiral President, Royal Naval College Greenwich 91
John Bethell 50 top
Bibliothèque Nationale, Paris 30–1
Bodleian Library 34 bottom left and right, 35
British Museum 13 (John Freeman), 16, 17 bottom, 23 bottom, 24, 25, 26, 32–3 top, 32 bottom, 34 top left, 37 top, 41 top, 51 bottom, 51 top, 57 top right, 60–1, 61 bottom, 64 top, 65, 71 *bottom left*, 71 *bottom right*, 73 *left*, 104, 108 *top left*, 116 bottom, 125, 129 *bottom*, 132–3, 134 bottom, 135
British Tourist Authority 48
Duke of Buccleuch and Queensberry, K.T. 38, 39
City of Birmingham Art Gallery 129 top
Cooper-Bridgeman Library 1 (Bodleian Library), 15, 22, 27, 34 top right (Corpus Christi College, Cambridge), 37 bottom (Duke of Northumberland), 40, 41 bottom, 43 bottom (Collection Thyssen-Bornemiszo), 52–3, 55, 64 bottom (Lady Lever Art Gallery), 67, 68–9, 74 top (House of Lords), 76, 79, 80–1 (Guildhall, London), 89 (by kind permission of his Grace the Duke of Marlborough and Marquis of Brandford), 92 top, 92 bottom, 93 bottom, 93 top, 97, 98, 100, 101 top, 101 bottom, 102 left, 103, 108 bottom (Science Museum), 110–1, 114, 115, 118–9, 120–1, 128, 130 top left 130–1, 136–7, 141 top, 142–3, 151 top (Manchester City Art Gallery), 153 bottom, 154 (London Museum), 158
Crown copyright, the Controller of Her Majesty's Stationery Office 47
The Directors of Warwick Castle 71 top
C.M. Dixon 36, 72 right top and bottom, 123 top
Mary Evans Picture Library 63, 72 left, 75, 78, 82 *left*, 90 bottom, 99, 106, 124 *bottom*, 130 bottom, 131 bottom, 141 bottom, 143 top, 146, 149 *bottom left*, 151 bottom, 153 top, 169 top, 175 *bottom right*
Folger Shakespeare Library 58
Werner Forman 95, 105 top (Victoria and Albert Museum), 131
Fox Photos 169 *bottom*, 170, 175 *top right*
John Frost 171
The Governing Body, Christ Church 143 bottom

Sonia Halliday 42–3
Robert Harding Associates 46 top
By gracious permission of Her Majesty the Queen 62, 69 bottom, 84–5
Michael Holford 6, 7 top, 9 bottom, 10 top, 10 bottom, 12, 18–9, 20, 45 top, 57 top left, 57 bottom, 59 (National Maritime Museum), 108 top right, 116 top
Illustrated London News 124 *top*, 152
Imperial War Museum 149 *bottom right*, 159, 160–1, 163, 164 top, 164 bottom left, 164–5, 166, 167, 168, 173, 174–5, 176–7
Mansell Collection 73 *right*, 84, 112, 156, 157 *right*
Lord Mountbatten 139
National Army Museum 94 bottom, 96, 134 top, 138 *top*, 149 top left
National Gallery of Scotland 54
National Maritime Museum endpapers, 2–3, 56 top, 113
National Museum, Stockholm 21
National Portrait Gallery 42 bottom, 44 right, 46 bottom, 49, 50 bottom, 56 bottom, 66, 77 bottom, 83, 86, 88, 94 top, 102–3, 147 bottom
Peter Newark's Western Americana 82 *right*
Popperfoto 174 *bottom*, 175 *middle right*, 176 *bottom*
Press Association 179
Public Record Office 23 top (Domesday Book ref: E31)
Radio Times Hulton Picture Library 70, 123 *bottom*
Rhodes Museum 148 *right*
Rijksmuseum, Amsterdam 77 *top*, 87
Royal Commonwealth Society 149 top right, 150
Royal Society 81
Scottish National Portrait Gallery 74 bottom
Ronald Sheridan 7 bottom
Spectrum 11 bottom, 45 bottom, 109
J.W. Thomas 105 bottom
Victoria and Albert Museum 17 top, 122
Weidenfeld and Nicolson Archive 69 top, 85, 124, 127 *bottom*, 129 *top*, 138 *bottom*, 140, 142 *left*, 147 *top*, 148 *left*, 155, 157 *left*, 175 *bottom left*
Zefa 9 top (W.F. Davidson), 11 top (W.F. Davidson), 29 (R. Everts), 117 (Clive Sawyer)

Bibliography

Becker, Carl *The Declaration of Independence* Random House 1958
Clarke, Sir George *English History – a Survey* OUP 1971
Feiling, Sir Keith *A History of England* Macmillan 1950
Fischer, Fritz *Germany's Aims in the First World War* Chatto & Windus 1967
Rowse, A.L. *The Cornish in America* Macmillan 1969
   The Expansion of Elizabethan England Macmillan 1955

Heritage of Britain Artus 1977
Homosexuals in History Weidenfeld and Nicolson 1977
Matthew Arnold: Poet and Prophet Thames & Hudson 1976
Windsor Castle in the History of the Nation Weidenfeld and Nicolson 1974
Trevelyan, G.M. *History of England* Longman 1973

Index

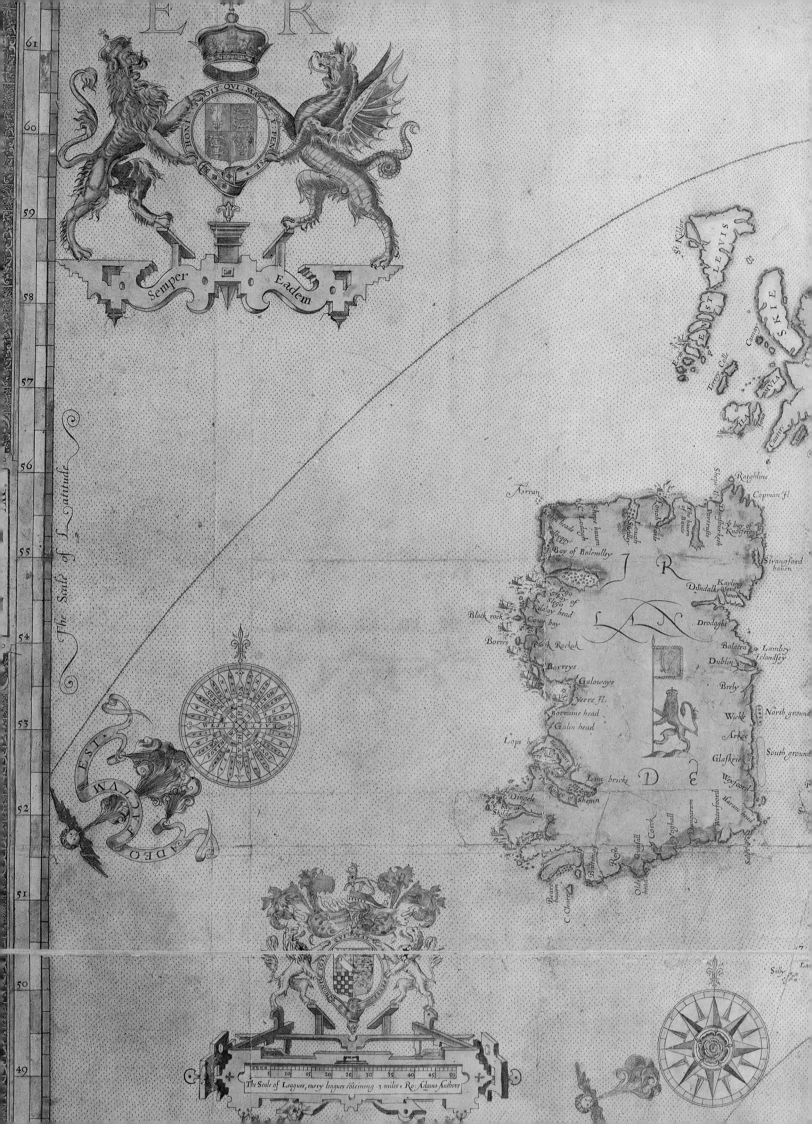